ANTEBELLUM POSTHUMAN

Antebellum Posthuman

Race and Materiality in the Mid–Nineteenth Century

Cristin Ellis

FORDHAM UNIVERSITY PRESS

New York 2018

Fordham University Press has no responsibility for the persistence or accuracy of URLs for external or third-party Internet websites referred to in this publication and does not guarantee that any content on such websites is, or will remain, accurate or appropriate.

Fordham University Press also publishes its books in a variety of electronic formats. Some content that appears in print may not be available in electronic books.

Visit us online at www.fordhampress.com.

Library of Congress Cataloging-in-Publication Data available online at https://catalog.loc.gov.

Printed in the United States of America
20 19 18   54 3 2
First edition

CONTENTS

Antebellum Posthuman

Beyond Recognition: The Problem of Antebellum Embodiment

"Am I not a man and a brother?" the eighteenth-century abolitionist motto demands. This question is meant to be rhetorical—to indict a blindness to one's fellow human so obscene that today, as Hortense Spillers notes, it "might be denied, point blank, as a possibility for *anyone*, except that we know it happened."[1] Indeed, Anglo-American abolitionists regularly diagnosed slavery as the product of a monumental failure—or deliberate refusal—to recognize the humanity of enslaved persons, and their rhetoric survives today in the commonplace assertion that slavery and racism are practices that operate by dehumanization. But while, as the famous abolitionist motto suggests, the "question" of Black humanity was undeniably on the line in the debate over slavery, this focus on recognition overlooks the full scope of the struggle that was pitched on the battleground of the Black body in the antebellum United States.[2]

In this book, I argue that the ideological struggle over slavery in antebellum America was one that contested not just the constituency of humanity (who qualifies?) but also the meaning of "the human" as such. That is, I suggest that to understand the true stakes of the fight for recognition—and of the ferocity with which that recognition was denied—we must be alert to the fact that the antebellum debate over Black humanity unfolded at a time when the definition of "human" being was in flux, destabilized by the rise of a newly empirical episteme. At the dawn of the nineteenth century, Western culture had, for centuries, defined human being by contrast to its material body, identifying the mark of humanity in mankind's supposedly transcendent freedom from material causality—a moral autonomy guaranteed by the uniquely ensouled or rational nature of the human. Indeed, in the late eighteenth century, this faith in humanity's inherent autonomy from nature fueled democratic revolutions in the United States, France, and Haiti by underwriting popular appeals to mankind's universal right to freedom. As Michel Foucault argues, however, in this same late eighteenth-century moment a very different conception of human being was also beginning to take shape and transform this Western episteme of "Man."[3] As Foucault explains, thanks to a host of newly emerging fields of knowledge dedicated to the empirical study of human life (fields such as natural history, biology, ethnology, demography, political economy, public health, and statistics), "Western man was gradually learning what it meant to be a living species in a living world, to have a body, conditions of existence, probabilities of life, and individual and collective welfare."[4] In contrast to the humanisms that preceded it, then, this new empirical episteme proposed to define human being by physical traits—identifying human thought and action *with* embodied processes rather than by freedom from such material forces. In the wake of this epistemic shift, Foucault writes, "the human being begins to exist within his organism, inside the shell of his head."[5] The late eighteenth century thus marks the onset of a new volatility in the Western conception of the human. Just as democratic revolutions began to enshrine the principles of liberal humanism, promising to extend rational subjecthood to all man- (and possibly woman-) kind, the burgeoning of empirical discourse was proliferating a new episteme that threw humanity's rational freedom into question.

Of course, the rough timeline I have just sketched indicates that this epistemic upheaval would have been already well under way by the mid–nineteenth century, the period on which this book focuses. Indeed, as studies by Jonathan Kramnick, Alan Richardson, and Justine Murison demonstrate, materialist discourses of mind circulated widely across a range of philosophical, literary, and popular outlets in eighteenth- and early nineteenth-century Anglo-American culture.[6] But although the queasy coexistence of liberal and biological epistemes was therefore no longer news in the antebellum era, this study proposes that the antebellum moment in America nonetheless marks an important point of inflection in the ongoing rearticulation of "the human." In these years, the intensifying debate over U.S. slavery triggered a popularization of racial science that charged biological accounts of the human with newly explosive political significance. As Americans increasingly turned to the body for ostensibly objective empirical proof of the slave's inherent equality or inferiority, the problem of human materiality was thrust to the center of midcentury political—and, as we shall see, literary—concern.

The advent of immediatist abolitionism in the 1830s and the ensuing intensification of antislavery sentiment in the North put mounting pressure on proslavery apologists to justify their support for the embattled institution, and in their efforts to do so slavery's advocates increasingly looked to what we now know as modern, biological racism. By the 1850s, the center of gravity in the debate over U.S. slavery had noticeably shifted from the question of whether it is morally acceptable to enslave a human being toward the question of whether Black bodies should be considered fully human in the first place. Whereas the former question—is slavery *humane?*—is a moral one referred to the consciences of voting Americans, the latter question—are Black humans really *human?*—was increasingly understood to be an empirical question "upon which science alone has the right to pronounce."[7] On the face of things, this appeal to empirical analysis merely redirects the central question of Black recognition (*"Am I not a man and a brother?"*) from voters' consciences to scientific analysis. But in fact, as this study contends, this redirection fundamentally alters the stakes of the question at hand. For to refer the question of the Black body's humanity to science is to presume that "humanness" is a quality best determined by the sort of features that science is equipped to investigate—it is, in other words, to assume that human being is ultimately defined by corporeal (material or empirically demonstrable) as opposed to moral features. Thus the embodied episteme of human being implicit in the latter version of the question (is the Black body *human?*) can be understood to index a broader cultural transformation. If the spike in racial science's popular authority in antebellum discourse suggests an intensification of racist antipathies, it moreover also signals the ascent of a new, materialist conception of the human that brought with it the promise—or the threat—of newly materialist, nonhumanistic ethical imaginaries.

This study therefore suggests that by the 1850s, the problem of recognition had subtly but profoundly changed. In this decade, the struggle for the recognition of Black humanity opened onto an even more elemental disagreement about the meaning or stakes of that recognition, as liberal and biological epistemes competed to define the nature of human being as such. In light of this epistemic revision, we can begin to see how racism functioned, in the antebellum context, not simply to "dehumanize" Black Americans but moreover to justify *indifference* to the fact of Black humanity. For under its empirical redescription, (biological) humanness strictly vouches for a basic *physiological* commonality across the human species that makes no definite claim about the moral equality of all members.[8] To recognize a Black body's speciological humanity, then, need not entail acknowledging her moral equivalence to other humans (her "full" humanity). And thus we underestimate biological racism when we treat it as strictly an exclusionary logic—a rationale for refusing to recognize the humanity of one's fellow human. More radically, the spread of biological racism indexed the advent of an empirical reconceptualization of the human which, as the chapters to follow will investigate, posed a variety of acute challenges to the moral significance of human belonging and to the conception of human being enshrined, at least in theory, in American liberal democracy. Our analyses of the debate over slavery therefore cannot afford to stop at the politics of recognition: the fight for recognition presumes the integrity of a liberal humanist conception of the human that was increasingly destabilized by the rise of biological discourse in the late eighteenth and nineteenth centuries, and by the new forms of racism that surged out of this empirical turn.

Accordingly, *Antebellum Posthuman* endeavors to think beyond the politics of recognition in an effort to explore the shifting sands upon which recognition's liberal politics stood in the antebellum era. More specifically, this study will endeavor to restore a sense of biologism's remarkable political lability at midcentury—its ideological open-endedness. Against a common critical tendency to treat antebellum biologism as synonymous with biological racism, this study highlights alternative discourses of embodiment that disputed racist ideology, charting the emergence of a materialist strain of antislavery thought in the 1850s.[9] In chapters on Frederick Douglass, Henry David Thoreau, and Walt Whitman, I show how these authors appropriate the materialist ontology, but not the racist politics, of antebellum racial science, producing an antislavery materialism that rebuts biological racism in its own empirical terms.

This strain of antislavery materialism did not amount to an explicit philosophical program or political platform; rather, it surfaced as a leaning or tendency within these authors' writings in the 1850s as they began to explore new perspectives on human identity and community that were opened up by embodied discourse. We must, then, keep an ear to the ground for this incipient refrain. But when we do, the effect is often quite striking because the antislavery materialism these authors develop takes them far afield of some of the most basic liberal principles (commitments to human equality, moral freedom, and individualism) for which Douglass, Thoreau, and Whitman are widely remembered as spokespersons, and by the light of which we continue to read their work. This departure from the liberal principles these authors espouse elsewhere in their writings signals the divergence of antislavery materialism from the larger antislavery movement: despite the congruity of its antiracist aims with abolitionism, this tentative new strain remains something philosophically distinct. I will be suggesting, then, that "the human" was fracturing along at least two different fault lines in the mid–nineteenth century. The contest to define the meaning of the human played out not only in the clash between liberal humanist and biological discourses of the human, but also between pro- and antislavery strains of biological thought that vied to define the political ethics of this new empirical episteme.

Excavating this twofold volatility of the human in antebellum discourse does two important things for our understanding of the politics of embodiment in this fraught historical moment. First, by demonstrating that biological essentialisms like racism and sexism were not the only ideologies of embodiment circulating in the nineteenth century, antislavery materialism reminds us that biologism does not inherently fund discrimination. On the contrary, as these antislavery materialisms demonstrate, biological racism is as much a conservatively *humanistic* reaction against biologism as it is an expression of biologism's challenge to humanist principles. Biological racism attempts to limit embodiment to subjugated populations, casting Black Americans, Native Americans, and women as (in Saidiya Hartman's phrase) "the ultimate bearers of the bodily."[10] Quite apart from its empirical falsehoods, then, (i.e., quackeries like the suggestion that skull size varies by race), midcentury biological racism departs from strict biologism insofar as the former treats materiality as if it were unevenly distributed among humans—as if some peoples are inherently more and others less embodied, as if we are a species unevenly evolving from apes to angels.[11] Seen from this angle, biological racism begins to appear antibiological—an attempt to quarantine privileged populations from the illiberal taint of their own materiality. The antislavery materialisms outlined in my chapters contest this differential attribution of embodiment, and in doing so help us to disarticulate biologism's materialist ontology from ideological encrustations like racism that cling to it. In this sense, recognizing the diversity of antebellum embodied thought can help to interrupt the reductive circuit according to which biologism is presumed to condemn us to fleshy prisons that justify discrimination against us.

As it happens, the idea that biological materialism is not inherently essentializing and therefore politically regressive informs some of the most exciting new work in critical theory today. Across a range of fields, scholars have begun to scout the possibilities for a progressive materialism as they recoil from what have come to seem like the excesses of the linguistic turn—a turn whose emphasis on interpellation and performativity fostered what Stacy Alaimo and Susan Hekman describe as a "flight from the material" and a foreclosing of "attention to lived, material bodies and corporeal practices."[12] Recent critical theory has therefore sought to navigate a corrective "turn to the body" by exploring new ontologies that highlight the agency of matter without collapsing into the essentialism, determinism, and teleological evolutionism that drove critical theory away from discourses of nature and embodiment in the first place.

At the radical end of this present groundswell are revisionary materialist ontologies that insist upon the constitutive entanglement of mind and body, human and nonhuman being, material and cultural forces. For the purposes of this study, I will use the term "posthumanism" to refer to this admittedly heterogeneous set of material ontologies because, although not all of the critics I will refer to under the sign of posthumanism have embraced this term, it allows me to foreground both the epistemic stakes (the *not*-humanism) and the historical position (the *after*- humanism) implied in the ontological shift that they frame.[13] Challenging the immateriality of both poststructuralism's discursively constituted subject and liberal humanism's transcendently autonomous subject, posthumanist materialism presents us with an embodied subject whose subjectivity processually emerges from her neural networks and flows of subconscious affect, from relations with nonhuman beings and agencies, and from unpredictable interactions between her physiological, material, and cultural environments. Posthumanist theory thus suggests that a truly materialist conception of the human obliges us to relinquish—or at least steeply qualify—Western humanism's conception of the human as an autonomous subject free from physical causality. In doing so, posthumanism erodes the grounds upon which Western humanism has traditionally upheld the innate superiority of the human to all other forms of being.

A second advantage, then, of excavating antislavery materialism now is that this antebellum discourse can offer insight into the prehistory of the posthumanist critical turn we are now witnessing. By keeping one eye on the present (as the deliberate anachronism of my title, *Antebellum Posthuman*, invites us to do), we may begin to discern the philosophical commonalities that link antislavery and contemporary posthumanist materialisms. As Marjorie Levinson points out, the anachronism involved in such a trans-temporal mode of reading need not be thought of as the enemy of historicism—a license to overwrite the past with the present. On the contrary, Levinson argues, reading "conjuncturally" across time can help us to recover dimensions of the past that have grown closed to us. By using "the knowledges and imaginaries of our own time to summon up particular pasts," Levinson proposes, we can make those forgotten histories "flash upon us in ways that neither they nor we could have anticipated."[14] Thus, as I hope to show, reading for the resonances that contemporary posthumanist theory elicits from these antislavery writings allows the conceptual lability of the human in antebellum literature to become visible to us in ways it has not been heretofore.

But while my chapters on Douglass, Thoreau, and Whitman will suggest commonalities their materialism shares with contemporary posthumanism, I am ultimately even more interested in the ways in which these antebellum writers can help open up new vistas onto our present theoretical moment. In particular, I find that reading contemporary theory through the lens of its antebellum precursor helps to focalize one of the most imperative critical challenges contemporary posthumanist theory currently faces: namely, the conspicuous absence of race as a critical term in posthumanist discourse. An increasing number of scholars have begun to voice concern at what Zakiyyah Jackson calls the "resounding silence in the posthumanist, object-oriented, and new materialist literatures with respect to race."[15] This occlusion of race subtends what Alexander Weheliye has diagnosed as a more fundamental epistemological exclusion in posthumanist theory: its minimization of the centrality of racism to the Western humanist tradition that it proposes to move beyond, and its failure to engage with counterdiscourses of the human articulated in nonwhite and non-Western cultural traditions.[16] But if race remains largely undertheorized in contemporary posthumanist thought, race and racism are unmistakably at the center of its antebellum precedent. Attending to posthumanism's prehistory in antislavery materialism can therefore serve as a provocation to reexamine the racial politics and racist political legacies involved in the contemporary posthumanist turn. Examining recent critiques of posthumanism by theorists of race and social justice, my final chapters will assess the considerable strengths as well as the limitations of posthumanism's materialist politics. These chapters will outline opportunities for posthumanism's more rigorous collaboration with theories of race and social justice going forward, as well as highlight philosophical obstacles to this closer alliance with which both posthumanism and materially minded social justice criticism have yet to fully reckon.

Thus in addition to highlighting the volatile and contested status of embodiment's politics in antebellum discourse, this study will suggest that reading across the archives of antislavery and posthumanist materialism can help us to sharpen our sense of both, not only by highlighting their commonalities but also by clarifying their angles of divergence. Below, I will offer a very brief overview of the rise of materialist politics in the post-Enlightenment era, charting the contours of the biological turn from the late eighteenth century to the birth of biopolitics, and offering a fuller account of the posthumanist turn in critical theory today. With a clearer sense of what posthumanism is, and of the ideological formations to which it responds, we can better recognize its historical and conceptual continuities with the nineteenth-century materialisms of Douglass, Thoreau, and Whitman.

Embodiment from Biopolitical Racism to Posthumanism

When Edmund Burke published his conservative *Reflections on the Revolution in France* in 1790, his pamphlet triggered a deluge of liberal responses including, most famously, Thomas Paine's *Rights of Man* (1791) and Mary Wollstonecraft's *A Vindication of the Rights of Woman* (1792). Rather less notably, in 1792 Thomas Taylor published his parodic manifesto, *A Vindication of the Rights of Brutes*. Citing "those wonderful productions of Mr. PAINE and Mrs. WOLLSTONECRAFT," Taylor glibly proposes that their "sublime theory" of human equality ultimately points to an even larger moral truth poised to "give perfection to our researches into the rights of things." This larger truth: *"the equality of all things, as to their intrinsic dignity and worth."* Taylor thus proceeds to facetiously argue that universal equality is indeed universal, and ought therefore to include everything from nonhuman "brutes" to "vegetables, minerals, and even the most apparently contemptible clods of earth."[17]

For the most part, Taylor's satire of liberal egalitarianism operates by the fallacy of the slippery slope—commoners equal to kings? Women equal to men? *What next?* But his pamphlet finds its teeth when it subtly conflates two distinct logics closely associated with the French Revolution: the liberal discourse of human rights and the ontology of radical materialism. This conflation appears in the pamphlet's opening gambit, where Taylor defines the disagreement between monarchist conservatives and liberal revolutionaries as a conflict of ontologies—as, in fact, a dispute over dualism. Adapting Aristotle, he explains that conservatives believe there is a naturally "slavish part of mankind" comprised of those "born with strong bodily and weak mental powers," and that this slavish class "ought to be governed by the independent [class], in the same manner as the soul governs the body, that is, like a despot or a tyrant." By contrast, he observes, "this is a conclusion which will surely be ridiculed by every genuine modern, as it wholly proceeds on a supposition, that mind and body are two distinct things, and that the former is more excellent than the latter, though almost every one is now convinced, that soul and body are only nominally distinguished from each other, and are essentially the same."[18] Taylor thus asserts that the new materialism abolishes not only hierarchies of the human but also hierarchies of being. For if what was traditionally called the human "soul" or "mind" is now taken to be embodied—simply an effect of physiological processes—then this mind's "mental powers" are not, in fact, "independent" of matter but rather enchained to physical causality in the same way as the physical body.[19] This means that so-called rational men are not intrinsically more free than the "slavish" men and women—those (ostensibly) subrational persons defined by their machinic muscles, animal instincts, and organic appetites—over whom they presume to govern. Extending this logic, Taylor insists that, once divested of its transcendental "soul" or autonomous "mind," humanity ceases to be ontologically exceptional and therefore can no longer claim to be morally superior to nonhuman beings. Hence Taylor's conclusion that "genuine modern" (i.e., materialist) philosophy leads to the conclusion "that there is no such thing in the universe as superiority of nature."[20] By his reasoning, there is no such thing as superiority of nature because there is no such thing as superiority *to* nature. Once we acknowledge that humans do not enjoy a special exemption from the laws of matter, then we will be in a position to recognize our ontological equality not only with "brutes," but with "vegetables, minerals, and . . . clods of earth."[21]

Ultimately, then, Taylor suggests that "genuine modern" philosophy is self-defeating, that in fact it abolishes the equality its exponents purport to defend. For Taylor, there can be no ontological freedom in the absence of a corollary category of unfree being called "property" (embodied in wives, slaves, horses, or houses, and finally, most fundamentally, in one's own body).[22] Hence, at its grandest and most unsettling, *Rights of Brutes* maintains that a thoroughgoing materialism is logically incompatible with a rights-based version of the political: the latter, Taylor proposes, ultimately depends upon an exceptionalist model of the human that the former fatally undermines. Of course, as a critique of Wollstonecraft and Paine, Taylor's satire misses the mark, for to arrive at his parodic egalitarianism he must first rewrite their liberal position as a materialist one. Nonetheless, the argument of *Rights of Brutes* remains compelling for the way it highlights the tension implicit in the Enlightenment's dual (although not always simultaneously held) commitments to liberal and materialist philosophies.

At the turn of the nineteenth century, then, Western culture sponsored what Taylor suggests are incommensurable epistemes of the human: liberal Man defined (in Foucault's words) "by his freedom, or by the opposition of soul and body," on the one hand, and empirical Man defined by his body and the economy of his biological interests, on the other.[23] But although the liberal and empirical figures of Man appear to be incommensurable in the abstract, in practice, as Foucault argues, their joint appearance at the end of the eighteenth century produced a reorganization of Western politics—the birth of biopolitics—that oversaw their unstable imbrication. Briefly described, biopolitics refers to a subtle but profound reconceptualization of state power according to which Western states came to conceive of their citizenry not (or not only) as rights-bearing liberal subjects but as an aggregate biological population—a "multiple body" that "cannot . . . be counted" because its life is not proper (not the property of individuals) but rather processual, unfolding across its fluctuating collective mass.[24] Accordingly, although long dedicated to maintaining law and order, in the early nineteenth century Western states began to take a new interest in managing the biological processes of populational life, and to this end they began to develop policies aimed not at disciplining individual bodies—punishing criminals, for instance—but at controlling the collective body—regulating rates of health, mortality, reproduction, labor productivity, and the like. In other words, under biopolitics Western states began to conceive of the populace as so many liberal citizens *and* as biocapital, a statistical mass life whose biological economies and embodied interests can, like any other material resource, be mined and administered for maximum productivity.[25]

As Foucault details, biopolitics erodes the freedoms of liberal subjecthood by turning the state's attention from the individual to the population, even as it insinuates state power ever more comprehensively into the material conditions of individual life. Underscoring this shift, Wendy Brown objects that biopolitics gave rise to a "subject so profoundly integrated and hence subordinated to the supervening goal of macroeconomic growth that its own well-being is easily sacrificed to these larger purposes."[26] Hartman's sobering study of the "amazing continuity" between slavery and freedom in the experience of nineteenth-century Black Americans amplifies this assessment by illustrating how the freedom of liberal personhood accorded to Black Americans by the Fourteenth Amendment proved a vastly diminished prize in the wake of biopolitics' ascendance.[27]

But as Hartman's analysis further demonstrates, if the birth of biopolitics threatened the freedoms of the liberal citizen, it moreover also made biological racism insidiously structural to the logic of modern governance. Racism, Foucault explains, is fundamentally "a mechanism that allows biopower to work."[28] It does so by inscribing "caesuras within the biological continuum of life," dividing what would otherwise be an undifferentiated mass of interrelated material processes (the immanent "biological continuum" of life encompassing all being) into life that has been selected to live ("the population") and life that has been "dysselected"—deemed biologically inferior, degenerate, a risk to the "true" population's health and purity.[29] Biological racism thus distinguishes between types of life that are deemed "fully" human and types of life (sub- or nonhuman) that are deemed biologically inferior and even potentially deleterious or infectious—populations that may, or even *must* be sacrificed in order for the designated population to thrive.[30]

Far from leveling all distinctions, then (as Taylor perhaps only half-jokingly feared), the ascendance of empirical Man instead funded a powerful new hierarchy of human being. In the eighteenth and nineteenth centuries, empiricism did not immediately displace prior Western epistemes of Man but rather fused with and rearticulated them. Thus Sylvia Wynter shows how the advent of the biological discourse of man did not supplant but rather wove itself around preexisting hierarchies of human being that had been organized first by Western Christianity and later by Western humanism. Reinflecting those earlier hierarchies of the human (faithful/pagan, rational/nonrational), biopolitical racism recast human inequality according to an ostensibly empirical distinction between the biologically "full" human (those endowed with moral autonomy and value) and the biologically less-than-human, those anatomical humans still enthralled to their animalistic embodiment.[31] In this way, biopolitics brokered a toxic truce between Christian, humanist, and empirical epistemes of the human, all of which would continue to tenuously coexist in the modern era.

In contrast to empiricism's history of collaboration with these hierarchical epistemes, contemporary posthumanist theorists now suggest that, properly understood, biological man *is* in fact (as Taylor facetiously suggested) incompatible with any system of thought premised upon the

notion of humanity's uniquely transcendental being. Whereas the Western tradition that Wynter outlines presumes that humans—or at least that
subset of *Homo sapiens* deemed "full" humans—enjoy autonomy from matter,
posthumanists insists that "human life is embedded in a material world of
great complexity, one on which we depend for our continued survival."[32]
From this embodied perspective, an organism is never sovereign nor exceptional to nature but rather exists as and through a vast ecology of
interdependencies—a "biological continuum" of material flows within
the multitude that is the organism, among organic and nonorganic entities,
and between the organism and its natural, social, and technological environments. But if posthumanism thus limits human freedom by highlighting
human beings' dependence upon nonhuman beings and forces, unlike
biological racism it denies that embodiment is strictly deterministic. Posthumanism's processual ontology is materialist yet irreducibly unpredictable, premised (as Nigel Thrift economically puts it) "on the leitmotif of
movement in its many forms."[33]

Contemporary posthumanist materialism therefore undermines the
humanist tradition in two ways. On the one hand, its embodied subject
erodes the moral distinction between human and nonhuman life. As we
have seen, whereas humanism divides life into "the human" (beings understood to be free from material causation, and hence moral actors) and
"the nonhuman" (beings, including "subhuman" *Homo sapiens*, who are understood to be simply embodied), posthumanism rejects this division by
maintaining that a human being is like all beings insofar as it, too, is strictly
(albeit nondeterministically) constituted through physiological processes,
and insofar as its actions are, likewise, "nested in [material] forces beyond
its control."[34] In other words, although posthumanism does not deny that
there are substantial differences between forms of life (between, say,
humans, octopi, and mushrooms), its materialism does highlight the impossibility of empirically justifying the categorical moral superiority of
any one form of life over others. Indeed, posthumanism makes categorical
distinctions difficult by exploding the ontological closure that is characteristic of liberal humanism's transcendental subject. Emphasizing the
"transcorporeal" and "intra-active" interpenetration of human with nonhuman bodies, posthumanism overwrites the image of the bounded, autonomous, and sovereign human self with the image of a heterogeneous
yet continuous plenum that Roberto Esposito (borrowing from Merleau-
Ponty, not Hortense Spillers) terms "the flesh."[35] Thus, as Jasbir Puar observes, posthumanist theory works to "deprivilege the human body as a
discrete organic thing" by underscoring the fluidity, multiplicity, and

porosity of the embodied self.[36] The posthumanist subject is at once embodied and yet nonsingular, imbricated by virtue of her embodiment with bodies and environments beyond the border of her skin. In this way, posthumanism not only breaks down the categorical moral difference between human and nonhuman being but moreover denies their physical separateness, highlighting the "vibrant" throng of unexpectedly "animate" nonhuman bodies and forces that subtend and infuse what we call human bodies and agencies.[37]

This revisionary, nondeterministic materialism has spread across several areas of critical theory in the late twentieth and early twenty-first century, becoming a defining feature of the current theoretical moment. It is, for instance, particularly salient in work downstream of Deleuze and Guattari, who coined many of the key terms and topoi that organize contemporary posthumanist discourse. But although the prevalence of materialist ontologies may seem distinctive of the critical landscape today, materialism is, of course, on the contrary, an ancient philosophical tradition with a long history in both Western and non-Western thought.[38] Moreover, as Foucault's and Wynter's genealogies emphasize, the epochal rise of empiricism in the late eighteenth century proliferated materialist discourses of human being that predate contemporary posthumanism by two centuries, and which proceeded to crucially shape nineteenth-century politics.

We therefore need not be surprised to find precursors to posthumanist materialism haunting the antebellum literary imagination. Whether figured as the transpersonal continuum of "the flesh" or as Whitman's great, peristaltic "ocean of life," posthumanism's vision of being as embodied and entangled may perhaps best be understood as a conceptual tendency nested within the epochal turn to empiricism—"a latency," as Mark McGurl argues, "within the discourse of the 'modern.'"[39] Although posthumanism has only crystallized as a theoretical movement in the last twenty-odd years, and despite its frequent association with distinctly postmodern developments like poststructuralist philosophy and cyborg technologies, its materialism bears no necessary relation to the present day. And if this is so, then the fluid, inclusive, and dispossessive ontology articulated by posthumanists today has a prehistory we have yet to fully explore.

Antebellum Posthumanism

Toward this historicizing effort, *Antebellum Posthuman* offers three case studies in antislavery materialisms of the last century, highlighting the emergence of a proto-posthumanist imaginary within American literature.

Acknowledging these dissenting antebellum materialisms can help us to recognize that the debate over U.S. slavery was not simply a debate over the borders of the human, with liberal universalists vying against racist materialists to define who gets included. Instead, this debate also housed an epistemic disagreement over the relation of the human to its embodiment, and this study hones in on a struggle between biologically minded thinkers to define the shape of embodiment's politics going forward. In its simplest terms, my claim is that although racism was by far the most prevalent and consequential form of embodied thought circulating in the antebellum era, it was not the only one: the authors I examine testify to the emergence of an alternative, antislavery discourse of human materiality and biological collectivism. This is to suggest that the politics of human embodiment did not go without saying in this decade, and that while many antislavery activists worked to combat the rise of biologism, others were working in these years to rewrite its politics from within.

My first three chapters profile the antislavery materialisms that Douglass, Thoreau, and Whitman began to develop in the 1850s, when racial science had succeeded in making the biology of Black humanity a central feature of the debate over slavery. In each case I examine how these authors responded to this epistemic shift by adopting their own version of embodied discourse, condemning slavery in the same empirical idiom that proslavery racial discourse was then so powerfully wielding. As I shall demonstrate, however, if this reversal allowed Douglass, Thoreau, and Whitman to answer racist science in its own terms, their antislavery materialism was also unsettling to the liberal democratic principles and transcendental liberal subjectivity that these authors are otherwise known for having championed. In this sense, as I shall argue, their forays into materialist thought led them to frame arguments against slavery that do not neatly align with the liberal political commitments they express elsewhere, producing a minor refrain within their writings that speculatively resigns the doctrine of human equality, queries the autonomy of human agency, and explodes the singularity of human identity. Although pitched against slavery, the antislavery materialism these authors develop cannot properly be called liberal. Tentatively, experimentally, and repeatedly, these authors' late antebellum works move in strange new directions, framing an alternative to both liberal universalism and racist essentialism that resonates unevenly, in ways I shall explore, with posthumanist materialism today.

Chapter 1 examines how the rise of racial science spurred Douglass to supplement his moral appeals to human brotherhood with a new antislavery argument that bracketed the question of his race's humanity. As

Douglass perceived, by recasting "the human" as a biological category, racial science was able to suggest that humanity's embodied diversity indicates a basic moral diversity among humans, making it possible to imagine that not all humans are equally entitled to the same "human" rights. In the wake of racial science's rise, then, abolitionism's insistence on the slave's shared humanity did not carry the same moral weight. Frustrated with the ineffectiveness of abolitionism's moral rhetoric at answering biological charges of Black inferiority, and disillusioned by the pervasiveness of racism on both sides of the Mason-Dixon, Douglass began to develop his own alternative ethnological discourse in the 1850s. Reading across several of Douglass's major and minor writings of this decade (including "The Claims of the Negro Ethnologically Considered," "What to the Slave Is the Fourth of July?," and his sole novella, *The Heroic Slave*), this chapter details how, rather than simply denounce scientific racism, Douglass responded to its growing influence by strategically appropriating its discourse of Black animality. Douglass argues brilliantly and perilously that *even if* Black Americans were proven to be less rational and more animalistic than white Americans, abolition would remain a *pragmatic*, if no longer a moral, necessity because even irrational animals inevitably become violent when their instinct for self-preservation is aroused. Thus, ironically embracing the bestialization of Black humans by scientific racism, Douglass redeploys this as the basis for a new kind of naturalistic justification of revolutionary violence. Deliberately evoking and recasting the founders' appeals to natural law, Douglass argues that resistance to violent oppression is not simply a human right but an instinct embodied in all biological life. Therefore, he concludes, slavery is not just morally but practically untenable: on the wrong side of physical law, it is, he writes, "dangerous as well as wrong."[40] In these late antebellum writings, Douglass explores ways to bypass the stalemate over human equality by strategically reappropriating racial science's speciological discourse of the human.

Chapter 2 traces an analogously materialist reconceptualization of the human in Thoreau's writings of the 1850s. In this decade, Thoreau became immersed in empirical studies of ecological succession and speciological development, which spoke directly to the ongoing debate between monogenist and polygenist racial scientists. Working in the shadow of Harvard's celebrity naturalist, Louis Agassiz, who was one of the most influential voices in midcentury American science and polygenism's most erudite ally, Thoreau's late antebellum naturalism set out to disprove Agassiz's polygenist theory of "special creation" and to substantiate the "developmental theory" of nature (a pre-Darwinian theory of evolution). As I show, however, while Thoreau engaged with this midcentury discourse of species, he understood its political significance quite differently from most. Instead of weighing in on the question of racial difference and equality, Thoreau's late antislavery essays translate his studies of ecological and evolutionary change into a vastly revised theory of political reform. Rethinking his faith in individual moral conscience, Thoreau began to conceive of conscience as a physiological trait ("a matter of constitution and temperament, after all") that may be more highly developed in some persons than others.[41] Individual agency thus begins to recede in Thoreau's late political essays as he comes to understand moral judgment as a capacity that is unequally distributed, and unevenly developing, across the human population. Accordingly, his late antislavery writings suggest that Thoreau had begun to map the politics of abolition onto the inhuman expanses of evolutionary time, imagining that anomalously advanced moral "specimens," as he calls John Brown, create "the possibility, in the course of ages, of a revolution" in America's political conscience.[42] Against racist biopolitical arguments for segregation and fears of miscegenation, Thoreau's evolutionary politics stress the inverse: not the necessity of deploying politics to prevent white America's biological (and moral) "degradation," but the inevitability of America's biological (and moral) development by the unelected forces of material history.

This inversion—this emphasis on the constitutive priority of sub- or suprahuman biological processes over and against humanity's power to control them—also haunts the popular Spiritualist discourse of bioelectricity which inspired Walt Whitman's poetry of "the body electric." Turning to the 1855 *Leaves of Grass* in Chapter 3, I argue that although Whitman is often credited with inventing a radically new democratic aesthetic, his early poetry in fact conjures a nation comprised of porous subjects who bear little resemblance to liberal persons, and who are constituted by material attachments that have no place in the voluntaristic landscape of democratic contractualism nor the imagined community of white nationalism. Highlighting Whitman's fascination with the theory of electrical embodiment that he encountered in the mid-nineteenth-century Spiritualist press, I show how the bioelectrical subject inspired Whitman to reinvent the lyric subject—that is, both the persona and the propositional subject of the lyric poem—in the first edition of *Leaves of Grass* (1855). On the bioelectric model of mind, perception is an embodied event: as Whitman puts it, in the moment of perception "things enter with electric swiftness," inscribing themselves on the body's nervous system and thereby "quivering [it] to a new identity." In this chapter, I argue that the permeability of the nervous body led Whitman to conceive of poetry as an embodied medium—a site for the communication not of meanings but of physical contact, a means of orchestrating the bioelectrical inscription of the reader. Thus I suggest that Whitman's perplexingly embodied poetics (his insistence, for instance, that we should not read but kiss his poems, or his promise that reading will turn our very flesh into a "great poem") makes strict sense within his materialist theory of mind. Moreover, just as Whitman's antirepresentationalist poetics empties poetry of its meaning, so too it lights up the fictitiousness of bodily identity, exposing the porosity, impressionability, and historicity of the nervous self. In place of the bounded and legible liberal subject, then, *Leaves of Grass* represents the embodied subject as a dynamic and open-ended process, a site—like the lyric poem—of sensuous exchange in which the boundary between the sentient self and its environment cannot be confidently drawn. Whitman's bioelectrical ontology is thus materialist and yet anti-essentialist—his permeable and networked subjects escape the biological determinism that characterizes so much antebellum racial science. And yet by the same token, as I discuss, liberalism's basic grammar of political actors, identities, and interests breaks down in the face of Whitman's unbounded processual selves.

These first chapters endeavor to highlight the proliferation of biological accounts of the human and to examine how these three authors responded to the racist tendencies within midcentury science by constructing discourses of human materiality that do not support slavery. But if their antislavery materialisms are often ingenious, they are also costly to the liberal ideals these authors espouse elsewhere in their writings: leading Douglass, for instance, to bracket his insistence upon human equality, Thoreau to qualify his faith in conscientious action, and Whitman to unwittingly—or perhaps blithely—detonate the lyric/liberal subject into an unfolding process inimical to representation, including representational democracy. All three of these authors therefore speculatively invite us to conceive of the nation as a material collectivity fused as biological continuums are—not by the formal similarity of their constituents, the shared sentiment of imagined community, nor even the abrogable social contract of the Constitution, but instead by the dense weave of material mutuality.

Thus I suggest that, in their more radical passages of thought, these authors draft an image of material community that differs in subtle but consequential ways from some of the richly productive accounts of affective nationalism that have appeared in recent critical literature. From Christopher Castiglia's study of "the federalization of affect" in the early republic to Peter Coviello's account of race as a language for inciting feelings of "inborn connectedness" among strangers in the antebellum era, recent critical analyses of the problem of nation-building in the nineteenth century have highlighted the importance of affective attachments as a vital supplement to the power of legal instruments to bind the nation together.[43] Against this vision of sympathetic or imagined community, the authors I examine describe a nation bound, first and foremost, by material attachments: by physical dependencies and mutual vulnerabilities that conjoin the population *regardless* of how its members feel about one another, which is to say, despite the ideological or affective rifts that might otherwise divide the population by differences of belief or (race, sex, class, or even species) identity. In shifting our attentions from intentional and sentimental attachments to involuntary material intimacies, these three antebellum authors anticipate contemporary posthumanism's emphasis upon the ways in which human life and politics are complexly entangled with diverse "publics" of nonhuman beings and agencies.

My purpose in identifying commonalities across nineteenth- and twenty-first-century materialisms is, however, not simply to discover posthumanism *avant la lettre*. More urgently, I think that the materialist politics that Douglass, Thoreau, and Whitman experimentally develop can help us to confront deep and still unanswered questions about the desirability or even viability of a posthumanist politics. Today, posthumanist theorists often suggest that their materialist ontology helps us to envision a more radically inclusive and egalitarian liberal politics. Posthumanism lights up the way to a "parliament of things" or "democracy of objects," preparing us for a future in which "the scope of democratization can be broadened to acknowledge more nonhumans in more ways, in something like the ways in which we have come to hear the political voices of other humans formerly on the outs."[44] The proto-posthumanism we encounter in Douglass, Thoreau, and Whitman likewise appears to be progressive and politically inclusive, at least within the context of their slaveholding era. And yet, as my readings will underscore, these authors' materialism is also *illiberal*, so thoroughly corrosive to the fiction of autonomous individuality that it obliges us to rethink the tenets of liberalism (including individual rights, freedom, and equality) at very basic levels. Both then and today, posthumanism's materialist ontology challenges us to envision a world without discrete persons, "a world populated not by active subjects and passive objects but by lively and essentially interactive materials."[45] But what would a politics without persons even look like? And how could a politics premised on such a liquefying ontology address, let alone redress, demands for racial, gender, sexual, or speciological equality?

My fourth chapter examines the tension between posthumanism's illiberal ontology and its avowedly liberal politics by highlighting an absence that has, I suspect, particularly enabled this tension to go unaddressed: namely, the occlusion of race as a critical term in posthumanist theory. Indeed, in this respect, contemporary posthumanism arguably still has much to learn from its antislavery precursors insofar as racism and the discourse of social justice were defining features of the historical conditions of the latter's emergence. On this cue, Chapter 4 seeks to recenter the question of racial identity and human difference for posthumanist materialism by reading contemporary posthumanist theory through the lens of contemporary discourses of social justice. Here I survey some of the most trenchant current critiques of posthumanism's blind spot for race and for the critical tradition of thinking about the politics of embodiment in postcolonial, indigenous, critical race, and social justice theories. In addition to examining the correctives these studies offer to posthumanist theory, I am particularly interested in highlighting possibilities for collaboration between posthumanist and social justice criticism going forward. To this end, this chapter stages a conversation between contemporary posthumanism and Wynter's postcolonialist critique of Western humanism, which anticipates key features of posthumanist thought while also insisting upon racism's centrality to humanism's construction of the human. Exploring these two theories' congruencies, I argue that posthumanism's project is clarified and refined by a closer engagement with Wynter's theory of social justice, and that both discourses are strengthened through collaboration. At the same time, as my Coda takes up, this comparative work also raises difficult questions about the political and ethical limitations of a rigorously (i.e., philosophically self-consistent) posthumanist materialism.

It is thus my wager that reading antebellum and contemporary materialist politics through one another can teach us something new about both. On the one hand, our current fascination with the ontology of embodiment can help to make us more attentive to the ontological speculations of antebellum authors. In this regard, this project's contribution to the field of antebellum literary study does not have to do with canon expansion (clearly, my authors are squarely canonical) but, rather, involves rereading known authors in ways that may be estranging to our assumptions about them. Moreover, by emphasizing the epistemic volatility that nineteenth-century biologism introduced, this project seeks to unsettle the humanistic assumptions according to which this canon has been assembled and read up to now. We have been too ready, I think, to read Douglass, Thoreau, and Whitman as mouthpieces for the humanistic principles of liberal democracy and expositors of "the age of the first person singular" that Emerson so confidently pronounced.[46] In neglecting the materialist turn of their late antislavery thought, we risk oversimplifying the epistemic stakes at play in the debate over slavery, and hence underestimating the scope of slavery's legacy in the postbellum world. At the same time, the urgency of catching up to these antebellum authors' sense of the dense imbrications of political and material systems only continues to grow more distinct for us today amid the gathering threat of ecological change.

Indeed, politics after the biological turn may well challenge us to rethink our assumptions about the correlation between freedom and existential well-being. Although the Declaration of Independence insists that liberation is a matter of disentanglement—stating that we must "dissolve the political bands which have connected [us] to another" in order to assume a truly "separate and equal station"—it may be that, going forward, we will find ourselves tasked to embrace our relationality, which is in any case inescapable. Instead of championing freedom as a blanket principle, then, the pursuit of happiness today may oblige us to reimagine emancipation as something that does not follow from breaking bonds so much as from rearranging them, finding ways to be immersed and intertwined differently, with an eye toward the contingency, fragility, and irreducible collectivity of embodied life.

In that spirit of interdependence, I want to acknowledge that this project's exploration of antislavery materialism is indebted to the work of a number of critics whose projects have enabled my own. For instance, this book aims to affirm and extend recent efforts to document the proliferation of embodied discourse across nineteenth-century literature. In particular, Justine Murison's elaboration of the "open, vulnerable, and fraught" embodied self codified in early nervous physiology (in *The Politics of Anxiety in Nineteenth-Century American Literature*), and Jane Thrailkill's account of the "interanimation of the human mind and body" in postbellum scientific and literary works (in *Affecting Fictions*), both richly illuminate the challenges that embodied accounts of the human posed to liberal conceptions of subjectivity.[47] Building upon these studies, I aim to spotlight the centrality and volatility of embodied discourse in the U.S. debate over slavery and racial equality which, I submit, served as a kind of cultural lightning rod to focus literary attention on discourses of human embodiment while at the same throwing their political consequences into sharper relief. In this sense, I hope to contribute to recent efforts to trace the historical emergence of biopolitics through its reflection and contestation in nineteenth-century literary imaginations. Like Kyla Tompkins and Colleen Glenney Boggs, I situate the antebellum discourse of embodiment within the history of biopolitics in order to explore the antebellum body's political ambivalence—the way in which it was simultaneously used to construct and, elsewhere, to deconstruct the distinctions (white/ Black, human/nonhuman, self/other) that nineteenth-century biopolitics sought to police.[48] And in highlighting the ways in which this deconstructive tendency seems to prefigure contemporary posthumanist theory, I am preceded and inspired by Matt Taylor's and Mark Noble's investigations of proto-posthumanist materialisms that crop up across literatures of the nineteenth and early twentieth centuries.[49] Toward those efforts, I hope that *Antebellum Posthuman*'s historical focus on literatures of the 1850s can add to our growing appreciation of posthumanism's prehistory by reframing the crisis of slavery and the question of racial difference as a catalyst for materialist discourse in the United States. If the ascent of the embodied subject at midcentury gave rise to new racist and biopolitical regimes, it also, I submit, precipitated the emergence of a new, proto-posthumanist materialism that indelibly transformed literary imaginaries in its wake.

Douglass's Animals: Racial Science and the Problem of Human Equality

"We hold these truths to be self-evident, that all men are created equal, that they are endowed by their Creator with certain unalienable Rights, that among these are Life, Liberty and the pursuit of Happiness." It is no secret that the liberal revolution these words seem to promise—affirming the basic political equality of all humans—was not, and arguably still has not been realized in the nation these words helped to envision. The truths the Declaration of Independence finds so glaringly "self-evident" are, in fact, far harder to make out in the text of the U.S. Constitution, which creates some humans only three-fifths equal, and in the voting laws of the early republic, which rendered most Americans something less than equal by imposing sex and property requirements on the franchise.

Today we tend to describe this inconsistency as the product of hypocrisy: despite professing egalitarian principles, the founders in fact held racist and sexist prejudices that allowed them to justify disenfranchising so many Americans. The legal history of U.S. voting rights, however, suggests a slightly more complicated story, for the initial justification for limiting the franchise in the early republic in fact did not depend upon a notion of biological inferiority. It was, instead, not until the wave of democratizing

reforms in the early to mid–nineteenth century that the doctrine of natural inequality became necessary to the justification of voter exclusion. Thus
ironically—or something worse—it was an upsurge in the egalitarian
sentiment that "all men" really ought to mean all *biological humans* that
helped to crystallize the dehumanizing discourse of modern biological racism that this chapter will explore.

Despite the revolutionary liberal rhetoric of the Declaration, the laws
of suffrage in the early United States remained largely unchanged from
the colonial period and thus reflected the more conservative political ethos
of British republicanism.[1] On this theory, voting is not a natural human
right because rationality—the precondition for political suffrage—is not
an inalienable trait of all humans. Instead, republicanism holds that rationality is a faculty that may be enabled or disabled by one's financial condition. Owning property gives one a rational stake in the nation—"a
permanent common interest with, and attachment to, the community," as
George Mason puts it in the Virginia Declaration of Rights (1776). By contrast to the landed man's rational interest, John Adams suggests, "Men
who are wholly destitute of property" are as "dependent upon others . . .
as women upon their husbands or children on their parents" and thus are
not in a position to exercise the "good judgment" of "independent minds."[2]
The property restrictions on voting in the early republic thus implied that,
whether or not all humans have a *capacity* for reason, the power to exercise
that rationality is contingent upon the ideological freedom conferred by
economic independence. On this eighteenth-century view, then, limiting
the franchise to propertied men did not specifically entail denying the *humanity* of nonvoters; instead, the prevailing republican logic presumed
that humanity, alone, is not a sufficient qualification for full political
personhood.

All this began to change in the first half of the nineteenth century, when
a wave of democratic reforms across the states reduced or overturned the
property requirements for suffrage. "Stated simply," Alexandar Keyssar reflects in his comprehensive history of U.S. voting rights, "more and more
Americans came to believe that the people (or at least the male people—'every
full-grown featherless biped who wears a hat instead of a bonnet') were
and ought to be sovereign."[3] The extension of the franchise to nonproper-
tied white men in the early nineteenth century thus not only expanded
voting rights; crucially, it rearticulated their justification. The new laws
rejected the notion that rationality is a power contingent upon freehold
property: as one Virginian scoffed, the old arrangement was "ludicrous"
in that it effectively proposed "to ascribe to a landed possession, moral or

intellectual endowments."[4] Instead, those endowments were presented as a speciological endowment characteristic of humanity (hence the tongue-in-cheek taxonomic reference to "featherless biped[s]"). The new democratic doctrine unequivocally held *"that every man has a right to vote, simply because he is a man."*[5]

In the wake of this reconceptualization of the justification for suffrage, remaining restrictions on the vote posed a conspicuous philosophical problem. For if the right to vote derives from a rationality that is inborn in all speciological humans, then to deny a class of persons the right to vote is tantamount to denying their humanity. It is therefore, of course, no mere coincidence that the U.S. abolitionist and feminist movements were both born at this moment in the early nineteenth century. In 1829, at the crest of this wave of democratizing reforms, David Walker penned the opening salvo of what would become the radical abolitionist movement, citing the democratic promise of the Declaration and challenging white Americans to "tell me if their declaration is true—viz., if the United States of America is a Republican Government?"[6] Two years later, inspired by Walker's example, William Lloyd Garrison likewise invoked the Declaration to call for "the immediate enfranchisement of our slave population."[7]

In making their appeals, Walker and Garrison exposed a contradiction in the democratizing spirit of the age that slavery's defenders found themselves suddenly pressed to justify. Over the ensuing three decades, a wide variety of proslavery arguments would circulate, but none were more effectively calculated to deny Black equality while preserving the democratizing impulse of the era than those that asserted the innate, biological inferiority of Black humanity. If the expansion of the franchise had affirmed the political equality of all biological men, these new proslavery arguments set out to prove that not all biological men are biologically equal. Accordingly, in the 1840s and 1850s the political exclusion of slaves—like that of women and Native Americans—increasingly came to be justified biologically. The proliferation and popularization of racial science in these decades thus marks an important shift in the debate over slavery: what had begun as a debate over whether the enslavement of humans is morally acceptable increasingly became a debate over whether Black humans were, biologically speaking, fully human to begin with.

To be sure, racist and misogynist prejudices were hardly new in the 1830s. The biological arguments that circulated in this era did not invent the idea of innate inferiority, but they did reinvent it by transposing it into empirical language and legitimating it with the stamp of scientific authority. Thus, as the historian Mia Bay argues, although racism may have been old, *scientific* racism—"a rationalized ideology of Black inferiority"—was a relatively recent invention which gave racial discrimination an unprecedented air of objectivity and cultural authority in the antebellum era.[8] Scientific racism was an outgrowth of racial science, which emerged in the eighteenth century as a field of inquiry that proposed to apply the methods of natural history to the study of the human species. As we shall see, racial science housed a number of competing theories over the years, not all of which were overtly racist—or, more accurately, all of which were racist to different degrees and in different ways. But underneath this internal diversity, racial science was unified in its assumption that human identity is conferred biologically, and that our moral and cognitive characters are essentially embodied traits. From its earliest beginnings, racial science propounded the notion that "the intellectual man is inseparable from the physical man; and the nature of the one cannot be altered without a corresponding change in the other."[9]

The increasing centrality of race as a justification for slavery—and thus the increasing centrality of racial scientific discourse to both pro- and antislavery argumentation in the late antebellum era—is a significant historical development. In this chapter, however, I will argue that to understand the full impact that racial science had on the American political imaginary, we must also look beyond the role it played in racist defenses of slavery. For even more profoundly, as I shall argue, the biologism implicit in racial scientific discourse (whether pro- or antislavery) presented a potentially fatal challenge to the then still novel liberal ideals of universal human rights and equality. In place of the abstract and uniform figure of Man typically invoked in liberal democratic discourse, biologism draws attention to our embodied diversity: empirically speaking, no two persons are the same. Seizing upon the fact of diversity, racial science concluded that humanity, or *Homo sapiens*, is in fact fractured into a variety of distinct taxonomic subtypes. Regardless of whether it was being used to bolster or to dismantle racist prejudice, then, racial science forwarded a newly biological conception of the human that erodes the universalizing imaginary enshrined in liberal politics. From this new embodied perspective, belonging to the human race no longer ensures one's basic similarity nor, therefore, one's basic equality with other members of the species.

This chapter investigates this crisis in the meaning of "the human" by tracing its effects on the remarkable transformation of Frederick Douglass's antislavery thought during the decade or so of racial science's ascendancy in antebellum discourse. In the late 1840s and 1850s, Douglass reinvented his stance on slavery. Parting ways with the Garrisonian abolitionists and abandoning their platform of disunionism and pacifism, he made new alliances in New York, throwing his weight into electoral politics and his money into his newspaper and John Brown's armed resistance. Among the myriad factors that contributed to his transformation, I highlight Douglass's growing sense that the battle for freedom must not only be a campaign against slavery but against racism and the pernicious ideology of Black inferiority that midcentury ethnology was then fortifying. As an example of how the growing influence of racial discourse altered antislavery argumentation, Douglass is a fascinating case not because his response to racial science was typical, but because it was not. Douglass's writings of the 1850s show him to not only have sensed the importance of being able to frame his antislavery argument "ethnologically" (as a number of contemporary Black writers had begun to do), but to have *also* been keenly alert to the steep costs associated with doing so. In his response to racist science, Douglass refutes Black inferiority on ethnological grounds but seems to recognize that simply by acknowledging racial difference—even if just to deny its political significance—he is weakening his case for human equality. "Let it once be granted that the human race are . . . naturally different in their moral, physical, and intellectual capacities," he ruefully observes, "and a chance is left for slavery."[10]

As I shall argue, Douglass solves this problem by developing a new strain of argument against slavery that is materialist yet not racialist—an argument that, speculatively and at great political hazard, brackets the question of Black humanity and embraces the materiality and animality of the human. This difficult argument emerges intermittently across Douglass's writings of the 1850s and sits uneasily alongside his continued affirmation of Black humanity and racial equality. It becomes particularly loud in his prophecies of an imminent racial conflict, whose violence, as I shall demonstrate, he proleptically justifies by portraying this as the natural and ineluctable expression of a universal biological instinct for self-preservation. In these moments, Douglass invokes a rhetoric of assertive Black "manhood" that is paradoxically animalistic, proposing that Black Americans can best demonstrate their humanity through acts of physical resistance that Douglass consistently compares to the violent resistance of animals. Indeed, as I will demonstrate, the comparison to animals allows Douglass to present racial uprising as not only natural but, because natural, *inevitable*—if the intolerable conditions of Black life in America do not change.

Thus just when it would seem to have been most urgent to disavow all comparison to nonhuman animals, Douglass begins to think more consistently through them, and it is my contention that he does this not in spite of but because of the rise of racial science and the dehumanizing discourse of Black animality it fostered. Recognizing the ways in which racial science's materialism erodes the epistemic assumptions underlying appeals to human rights and equality, Douglass develops a rearguard defense against this new onslaught, framing an antislavery argument that is strategically agnostic toward the "question" of his race's humanity. As it diffusely takes shape in his late antebellum writings, this new strain of antislavery thinking depicts the systematic oppression of Black Americans as a moral crime that is, moreover, a mounting national liability: a practice that is "dangerous as well as wrong."[11] Although he by no means abandons his moral opposition to slavery, Douglass's late antislavery writings supplement that moral critique with a new strain of thinking that works from a logic of risk rather than wrong. Tactically engaging racial science's biological reconceptualization of the human, Douglass experiments with a new, materialist antislavery argument that is indifferent to the question of the slave's—or anyone else's—humanity.

Racial Science's Challenge to Human Equality

By 1850, racial scientific accounts of Black inferiority had become deeply woven into the fabric of the proslavery position, providing a seemingly authoritative rationale, coolly removed from the subjective chaos of moral sentiment, for the wisdom and justice of slavery.[12] Proslavery ethnologies suggested that Black Americans were, at best, innately dependent humans (like women and children), and perhaps even not quite human: "A man must be blind not to be struck by similitudes between some of the lower races of mankind . . . [and] the Orang-Outan," write the authors of *Types of Mankind*.[13] This racist science was answered by antislavery ethnologies, many written by prominent Black thinkers, that decried this bestialization and fought to establish the full humanity of the Black race. To appreciate the true scope of the impact that racial scientific discourse had on the slavery debates, however, we must look beyond this antebellum struggle between pro- and antislavery ethnologies. As crucial as it was to empirically discredit racist science's attempts to dehumanize and bestialize Black Americans, the very fact that this was a debate *between* racial sciences— that, in other words, racial science had become a vital new battleground in the debate over slavery—was itself consequential. For, as I shall elaborate below, quite apart from its political usages, the materialist logic of racial science fundamentally challenges basic assumptions of humanistic ethics and liberal democracy. To understand the political significance of racial

scientific discourse, then, we must learn to recognize how, from the beginning—in its basic conceptual premises, which became more explicit
over the course of its historical development—racial science undermined
Enlightenment notions of universal human rights and equality.

The field of racial science was born when eighteenth-century natural
historians began to apply their empirical and taxonomizing procedures to
the study of humans. Racial science was, in this sense, an attempt at reflexivity: much as the word "race" had originated as a term of art in sixteenth-
century animal husbandry before migrating to its usage in humans, the
discipline of racial science originated out of a taxonomizing science originally developed to systematize and instrumentalize the nonhuman world.
Racial scientists proposed to study humankind as a species like any other
animal, endeavoring to enumerate, describe, and account for the causes of
embodied diversity.

By its very premise, then, racial science undermined the categorical
distinction between humans and animals. Humanism differentiates the
human from the animal by positing that humans are uniquely in possession of a moral quality (reason or soul) that marks humanity's exceptionality to nature—its independence from its animal body and freedom from
the chains of physical causality. By contrast, natural history restricts its
inquiries to physical phenomena, and from this strictly empirical perspective, as the eighteenth-century godfather of taxonomy, Carl Linnaeus,
observed, there is hardly "a distinguishing mark which separates man from
the apes, save for the fact that the latter have an empty space between their
canines and their other teeth."[14] Linnaeus proposed to sidestep the incommensurability of humanism's doctrine of human exceptionalism and natural history's commitment to empirical evidence by suggesting that the
question of humanity's moral nature "belongs to another forum" than
natural history, a deferral he signals in his landmark volume, *Systema na-
turae* (1775), by suspending his taxonomic system at the human, refusing
to identify this species by any distinguishing physiological marks. Instead,
he designates humankind by the curious epithet, *Homo nascem te ipsum*
("Man know thyself")—a singularly recursive construction that Giorgio
Agamben reads as a nod to the aporetic logic at the heart of Western humanism, the circularity by which humans do not prove but simply assert
their moral and ontological exceptionality to animal life. But if Linnaeus
thus foresaw and sought to deflect a confrontation between empirical and
humanistic discourses of humankind by suspending the former, eighteenth-
century racial scientists were not so cautious and forged ahead with their
speciological rearticulation of humanity.

In doing so, they were developing a discourse that not only undermined the doctrine of human exceptionalism and natural rights but moreover remade the logic of human equality. In natural history, as Linnaeus reminds us, facts are determined by observation: what makes this five-pointed body human and that five-pointed body starfish is a matter of distinguishing physical marks, anatomical forms, and other measurable traits. In order to qualify as true by the standards of scientific authority, propositions like the doctrine of human equality therefore had to be empirically verifiable: the equality of one person to another had to be a demonstrable, measurable "fact." Accordingly, as Winthrop Jordan observes, "From the facts of natural history, [racial science] spoke for an equality among men which derived from their corporeal sameness. . . . Men had been created equal by the Creator, yes, but the evidence for this creation now lay in man's physical being."[15] In other words, natural history's empirical episteme demanded that human equality be manifest: equality could not inhere in a strictly inward and disembodied human trait—an unobservable soul or rational freedom—and still count as *true*. Thus instead of arguing for a universal moral equality or shared human nature, racial scientists sought to ground the doctrine of human equality in demonstrable physical likeness. Seeing is believing.

As equality migrated from an inward to an outward trait, the corporeal diversity of human bodies consequently became freighted with unprecedented significance. As Irene Tucker argues, empiricism's "demand that universalism be not simply a political aspiration but something that might be *experienced*" caused the visible attributes of persons—and most especially skin color—to take on political import as a sign of a person's categorical likeness (or not) to others in the political body.[16] That racialist ideology was on the rise in the West in the same historical moment when democratic and antislavery sentiment was spreading can seem like a glaring hypocrisy, or at least evidence of a conservative retrenchment against the Enlightenment's liberal ideals.[17] But Tucker's point is that, however antithetical they may seem, abolitionism and racialism are equally logical outcomes of the Enlightenment, expressing its commitments to liberal universalism and the empirical method, respectively.[18] The necessity of empirically confirming human equality made physical diversity fraught with political meaning to a degree it had not been before. And thus, previously negligible to the question of human likeness, material embodiment—and more particularly, the infinite diversity of bodies—now posed a powerful obstacle to liberal universalism.

This impasse, however, was not fully apparent before Douglass's day. In the eighteenth and early nineteenth centuries, the reigning paradigm in racial science, termed "environmentalism," worked to reconcile physical diversity with human equality by asserting the latent empirical likeness of all humans. This theory held that all humans descend from a single ancestral stock (an idea called monogenism), and that this original human race diverged as humans dispersed across the globe and came under the influence of different climatological and social circumstances. "The pliant nature of man is susceptible of many changes from the action of the minutest causes," Samuel Stanhope Smith explains in his *Essay on the Causes of the Variety of the Complexion and Figure in the Human Species*, "and these causes habitually repeated through a sufficient period of time, can create at length, the most conspicuous differences."[19] Environmentalism was not antiracist: its expositors generally described racial diversification as a process of degeneration from the original and ideal racial standard embodied in Europeans.[20] However, the same scientists also proposed that the process of racial degeneration could be reversed—that nonwhite races were capable of reverting to the original, ideal form of humanity (could quite literally turn *white*) through changes in climate and education.[21] By treating racial differences as secondary acquisitions superimposed over an original and inalienable (if only virtual) empirical sameness, eighteenth- and early nineteenth-century environmentalism finessed the tension between embodied diversity and human equality.

This uneasy détente fell apart in the nineteenth century, when environmentalism increasingly lost ground to more rigidly essentialist theories of race. The first wave of the new ideology arose in conjunction with romantic philosophy, at one step removed from the discipline of natural history, which celebrated the distinctiveness of different races and national *volk*. Like environmentalism, romantic racialism believed racial differences to be the product of adaptations to local climate and culture; however, it tended to view these differences as irreversible once acquired, and deeply determinative of personal identity. The fixity of race in romantic racial theory thus revoked environmentalism's notion of a latent human uniformity; however, romantic racialists generally did not use the permanence of racial difference as an excuse for erecting a divinely ordained hierarchy of human races. "There was in fact some tendency to celebrate diversity, as showing the richness and plenitude of the human spirit," George Frederickson notes.[22] The result was a discourse that was not aggressively racist, although it was essentializing and often patronizing—as, for instance, when

George Catlin enthuses over "the proud yet dignified deportment of Nature's man" in his *Letters and Notes on . . . the North American Indians* (1841), or when Moncure Daniel Conway praises Black Americans for bringing "an infusion of this fervid African element, so child-like, exuberant, and hopeful."[23] As these stereotypes attest, even absent overtly racist intentions, romantic racialism codified a new view of race that was much more difficult to reconcile with a universalizing discourse of "the human." Transforming race from a reversible acquisition to a permanent identity determined by deep biology, romantic racialism ushered in a new era of racialist thinking in which, as Frederickson describes it, conversation increasingly tended "to start from a common assumption that the races differed fundamentally."[24]

This new aesthetic of difference paved the way for a much more aggressively racist strain of racial science known (because its leading expositors published in America) as the "American school" of ethnology. In 1839, at the tail end of a decade of increasing racial conflict in the United States (with the passage of the Indian Removal Act in 1830 and its brutal implementation thereafter; Nat Turner's Rebellion in 1831, Black Hawk's war in 1832, the Amistad mutiny in 1839, the organization of the immediatist abolitionist movement and underground railroad, and the galvanization of their proslavery opposition), Philadelphia physician and naturalist Samuel George Morton published *Crania Americana*, a craniometrical study of the indigenous peoples of North and South America. Morton's work inaugurated the American school of racial science by reviving a lesser eighteenth-century racial theory known as polygenism. Unlike monogenism, polygenism holds that the human races were created separately, constituting originally distinct and unrelated populations. "Each Race was adapted from the beginning to its peculiar local destination," Morton asserts in *Crania Americana*; "In other words . . . the physical characteristics which distinguish the different Races are independent of external causes."[25] The American school's case for polygenism relied heavily on Morton's craniometrical research as well as the work of the renowned Swiss-born Harvard naturalist, Louis Agassiz (on whom more in Chapter 2), and American Egyptologist George Gliddon. More unusually, American school ethnology was aggressively promoted to lay audiences by nonscientists, including the savvy propagandist Josiah Nott, as well as John Van Evrie, George Sawyer, and Samuel Cartwright.

The American school's polygenist brand of racial science gradually gained ground through the 1840s, but it was with the publication of Nott and Gliddon's *Types of Mankind* in 1854—a monumental compendium of polygenist ethnology—that its thesis reached a new apogee of popularity. Despite *Types'* cumbersome eight hundred pages and even heftier $7.50 price tag, this lavishly illustrated volume sold out in four months and went through ten editions by 1870.[26] Drawing from a smorgasbord of anatomical, zoological, archaeological, and philological research, and liberally quoting from the work of other prominent ethnologists (both polygenist and not), *Types* gathered evidence that "mankind is divisible into *distinct species*" and that "the differences existing between the races of men are of the same kind as the differences observed between the different families, genera, and species of monkey or other animals."[27] Nott and Gliddon thus explicitly denied that the slave is "a man and a brother"; instead, they argued that "the human race" is a misnomer, obscuring a much more attenuated taxonomic reality. By 1860, this polygenist thesis had won important converts among the shapers of Southern opinion, including editors of *DeBow's Review* and *Southern Quarterly Review*, John C. Calhoun, James Henry Hammond, and Jefferson Davis.

At midcentury, racial scientific discourse in the United States was thus a heterogeneous yet consequential free-for-all. Scientifically, polygenists and monogenists disagreed over the nature of human origins. Among themselves, environmental and romantic monogenists further disputed the nature of racial difference, debating whether racial characteristics were fixed or mutable, and whether interracial mixing was physiologically possible and, if so, whether it was sociologically desirable. Theologically, all sides laid claim to biblical authority. (Although monogenists had an easier time of this, given the congruence of their vision of humanity's single origin with the doctrine of Adamic descent, many polygenists also worked hard to prove that the theory of separate human creations accorded with Scripture.)[28]

But what is most perplexing, these competing biological and bio-theological arguments were attached to a strikingly fungible range of political ideologies. To be sure, polygenism had very strong ties to proslavery politics (Douglass estimated that "Ninety-nine out of every hundred of the advocates of a diverse origin of the human family" were proslavery apologists).[29] Polygenists certainly came the closest to claiming that Black and Native American peoples constituted distinct and inferior species of humanity taxonomically closer to the animal life over which the biblical God granted Adam's descendants dominion.[30] For this very reason, however, many proslavery advocates decried polygenist science. To men like George Fitzhugh, whose defense of slavery turned on its being a benevolently patriarchal system more humane than Northern capitalism's brutally

impersonal "wage slavery" (Southern "slavery protects the weaker members of society, just as do the relations of parent, guardian, and husband,"
he insisted), polygenism's literally dehumanizing thesis was anathema. "It
encourages and incites brutal masters to treat negroes, not as weak, ignorant, and dependent brethren, but as wicked beasts without the pale of
humanity," Fitzhugh objected.[31]

Meanwhile, that polygenists were likely to be proslavery does not mean
that monogenists were not. As nineteenth-century racial science had increasingly come to perceive race as a deep and permanent feature of identity, monogenism became increasingly consistent with patriarchal proslavery
ideologies like Fitzhugh's (think, for instance, of Moncure Conway's praise
for the "child-like" exuberance of the African race). Proslavery racial science thus also encompassed monogenist theories like that of the Reverend
John Bachman, whose treatise on *The Doctrine of the Unity of the Human
Race* insists "that nature has stamped on the African race the permanent
marks of inferiority," rendering this race inherently dependent beings, like
women and children.[32] As tracts like Bachman's prove, monogenist "unity"
presents no necessary impediment to proslavery politics, affirming Nott and
Gliddon's claim that "the doctrine of unity gives no essential guarantee of
universal liberty and equality."[33]

Indeed, what Nott and Gliddon seem to recognize is that racial science's
challenge to the doctrine of human rights does not turn on the question
of human origins (shared or separate) but rather inheres in racial science's
antagonism to the idea of a shared human nature. Increasingly and across
the board, nineteenth-century racial discourse moved away from eighteenth-
century environmentalism to portray race as a fixed and determining feature of moral identity—indeed, as Bay has shown, even Black ethnologists
in this era (whom I will discuss below) assigned transhistorical characters
to the races, reifying race as a meaningful marker of moral difference.
This emphasis on human diversity emptied the category of "the human" of
moral significance: instead of indicating a fundamentally shared moral essence, humanity now functioned as a speciological designation that guaranteed a baseline morphological, but not moral, similarity. From this
perspective, the differences between polygenist and monogenist racial sciences recede: whether human races represent different species of humans
or simply different varieties of a single species starts to look like a taxonomic squabble of minor political importance. For, either way, midcentury
racial science seemed to reveal that there simply is no universal "human
nature," nor any "great fundamental laws of humanity to which all human
passions and human thoughts must ultimately be subject."[34] Thus if poly-

genism seemed to suggest that the slave was not, in fact, "a man and a brother" to white Americans, monogenism suggested that the fact of the slave's humanity might, after all, be moot, since to be recognized as a human in the new empirical dispensation now only specified a nominal biological likeness that made no claims about your moral endowments. To be speciologically human did not guarantee your equality with other humans and thus did not vouchsafe your entitlement to the same human rights.

But though it is fair to conclude that antebellum racial science was more overtly racist than eighteenth-century racial science, in another sense what we are seeing is not simply the rationalization of racial prejudice but the belated unfolding of the incommensurability of empirical and liberal democratic discourses of the human. As I have argued, racial science's empirical epistemology precludes it from asserting an essential moral equality that is not also materially measurable. Given that, from a strictly materialist perspective, measurable equality is impossible (no two bodies could ever be empirically identical), the materialist outlook of racial science (of any stripe) necessarily throws the liberal assertion of human equality into doubt. In this sense, racial discourse reverted to the hierarchical view of "the human" enshrined in the republican doctrine and voting laws of the early republic, which likewise represented the human race as unevenly capable and hence unequally qualified for political rights.

Over and above the debate between monogenists and polygenists, then, the underlying shift to an empirical discourse of "the human" enshrined in all strains of racial science undermined democratic arguments for universal equality and human rights by disabling the logic according to which those arguments operate. Across the spectrum of its political affiliations, racial science's biological conception of the human was transforming what it meant to recognize someone as human. Transposing "the human" from a moral to a taxonomic designation, racial science's empirical epistemology destabilized the liberal democratic conception of humanity, exploding the latter's abstract uniformity into an embodied diversity and placing humans in an ontological continuum with nonhuman life. The rationale for equality and human rights—the idea that "all men are created equal"—once again rested on ideologically shifting sands.

Antislavery Ethnology: Douglass Responds

Given the difficulty of aligning racial science with liberal humanistic doctrine, it makes sense that many antislavery advocates simply refused to engage with it. Leading abolitionists like Garrison, Theodore Weld, and

Wendell Phillips remained staunch humanists through the 1850s, rejecting the invidious distinctions of race. "Convince me that liberty is not the
inalienable birthright of every human being, of whatever complexion or
clime, and I will give [the Declaration of Independence] to the consuming
fire," Garrison pronounced in 1854, the year *Types of Mankind* was published.[35] For these abolitionists, human equality is a right endowed by the
exceptional yet unobservable moral value that is inherent in all humans
irrespective of race, gender, or other features of human embodiment.

And yet, for all its ideological purity, this principled indifference to
racial distinctions became a liability to the antislavery cause. Like it or not,
racial science was increasingly central to the debate over slavery in the years
leading up to the Civil War. Surveying the landscape of proslavery argument in 1861, one Southerner wryly observed that the case for slavery was
now being made "theologically, geologically, oryctologically, paleontologi-
cally, archaeologically, chronologically, genealogically, orismologically,
philologically, etymologically, zoologically, osteologically, myologically,
ethnologically, psychologically, [and] sociologically."[36] Here was an arsenal
of empirical and quasi-empirical discourses to which abolitionism's moral
platform had no way to directly respond. When men such as Josiah Nott
demanded evidence of human equality, asserting that "numerous attempts
have been made to establish the intellectual equality of the dark races with
the white; and the history of the past has been ransacked for examples, but
they are nowhere to be found," abolitionists like Garrison could not provide
proof without abandoning their moralistic high ground.[37] This abstention
cost them, Frederickson argues: "The inability of the abolitionists to ground
their case for the Black man on a forthright and intellectually convincing
argument for the basic identity in the moral and intellectual aptitudes of all
races weakened their 'struggle for equality' and helps explain the persistence
of racist doctrines after emancipation."[38]

But of course, that invoking humanity's "inalienable birthright" or innate moral essence no longer constituted an "intellectually convincing argument" for human equality was precisely the problem. If equality must
be empirically demonstrated to be compelling, then liberal humanism has
already lost crucial ideological ground. In this sense, racial science's influence worked to disable Garrisonian-style abolitionism's primary rhetorical strategy, moral suasion. For once moral standing is understood to inhere
in a being's embodied attributes or capacities, testing and measurement
become the only sure ways to decide how a being ought to be treated. Hence,
as the philosopher Cora Diamond argues, the idea "that what is involved
in moral thought is knowledge of empirical similarities and differences"

deflects us from the work of examining our consciences and the prompt-ings of moral sentiments such as sympathy, compassion, pity, and love.[39] Instead of consulting our hearts, we are tasked with analyzing the marks and features of the other—an empirical project in which, as Dana Nelson and Kyla Schuller point out, sentiment is banished as irrelevant if not mis-leading, replaced by a "male sensibility" that is embodied in the disciplined sensuality of empirical methods, privileging purity, professionalism, and self-control.[40] As racial science's cultural authority grew, it threatened to moot moral suasion by suggesting that the question of whom or what de-serves our full sympathy is a topic "upon which science alone has the right to pronounce."[41]

The rapid ascendency of racial scientific discourse in the late 1840s and 1850s may thus help us to account for Frederick Douglass's dwindling faith in moral suasion in these years. As we know, his ideological and political stance underwent a transformation between 1847 and 1851, during which time he moved to Rochester, founded a newspaper, the *North Star*, began to associate with James McCune Smith and Gerritt Smith of the Liberty Party, and finally broke with the Garrisonians by publicly proclaiming the U.S. Constitution to be an antislavery document. From this point forward, he renounced the Garrisonian platform of disunionism to throw his weight into electoral politics, and he abandoned their pacifistic commitment to moral suasion to embrace an increasingly fiery rhetoric of racial uprising— words he backed up with deeds by providing material support to John Brown. To many observers both then and today, Douglass's foray into po-litical and even militant antislavery circles has seemed like a concession to expediency—a calculated betrayal of his lofty humanistic ideals.[42] In his 1899 biography of Douglass, Charles Chestnutt somewhat apologetically accounts for this decade by explaining that Douglass was not above "sub-ordinating the means to the end."[43]

But if it is the case that the Garrisonians retained the moral high ground, as we have just seen there is also evidence to suggest that lofty arguments were losing traction against racist prejudices that were, with the help of midcentury racial scientific discourse, luxuriating in the light of newfound cultural authority. By 1850, after two decades of abolitionist appeal, the number of slaves in America had doubled, and the passage of the Fugitive Slave Law made the likelihood of emancipation seem to be, if anything, on the wane. Moreover, by this time Douglass's personal experience of freedom had also been soured by the racism he encountered in the North— prejudice he experienced even among his Anti-Slavery Society colleagues, and which became all the more evident to him after his sojourn in Ireland

and Great Britain, where he noticed that, for the first time in his experience, "no delicate nose grows deformed in my presence."[44] Thus though Douglass certainly did not cease to believe that slavery is morally abominable, he does seem to have concluded, as Marianne Noble suggests, "that moral sense was evidently so overwritten by racist ideology that it was not useful in the fight for justice."[45] As Douglass became convinced that America would not be free until racism was defeated, he repositioned himself to fight not only for emancipation but also for racial equality, and in doing so he seems to have realized that moral suasion alone would not defeat the ideology he was up against.

Indeed, Douglass watched the rise of racial scientific discourse closely and with growing alarm. After the publication of *Types of Mankind* in 1854, he was sufficiently convinced that "Messrs. Nott, Gliddon, Morton, Smith, and Agassiz" were now being "duly consulted by our slavery propagating statesmen" that he felt compelled to respond to their science directly.[46] He did this in the form of an address entitled "The Claims of the Negro Ethnologically Considered," delivered at Western Reserve University in August of that year (in what was also the first U.S. commencement address given by a Black American speaker).[47] The public demand for a transcript of this speech was apparently clamorous enough that Douglass ventured to republish his text as a pamphlet—a move that also indicates how central biological discourse had become to the discussion of slavery, and how urgent it now seemed that slavery's opponents be able to frame their case "ethnologically." Indeed, in his opening remarks, Douglass justifies his topic by remarking that science was now established as a crucial arbiter of racial politics. "The relation subsisting between the white and Black people of this country is the vital question of the age," he writes, and "in the solution of that question, the scholars of America will have to take an important and controlling part."[48]

In writing "Claims," Douglass was contributing to a tradition of Black American ethnographic writing that stretched back to the late 1820s.[49] Well before racial science had become a lynchpin of proslavery discourse, Black activists, editors, ministers, and men of science had become aware and alarmed by racial science and "felt compelled to disprove, rather than dismiss, even the earliest, tentative arguments for Black inferiority made by white Americans."[50] Thus, for instance, two decades prior to the formation of the American school of ethnography, John Russwurm, an editor of *Freedom's Journal*, decried craniological speculations that the Black race was endowed "with faculties little superior to the tribe of the Ourang Outangs," and forms "something between man and brute creation."[51] Responding to similar accusations in 1837, Hosea Easton ruefully observed, "What could better accord with the objects of this nation with reference to Blacks than to teach their little ones that a negro is part monkey?"[52] Against such bestializing racial theories, Black ethnological writers constructed counterarguments that blended aspects of eighteenth-century environmentalism with romantic racialism. Men such as Russwurm, Easton, Henry Highland Garnet, and James Pennington argued that Black Americans suffered "an intellectual and physical disability or inferiority" that was directly caused by the "damning influence of slavery."[53] However, once emancipated, they argued, Black Americans would be free to develop the unique characteristics that are truly endemic to their race. These "true" characteristics were typically understood to include intellectual gifts, as demonstrated by the genius of ancient Egyptians and Ethiopians, who "astonished the world with their arts and sciences."[54] "The world now would be in a heathenish darkness, for the want of that information which their better disposition has been capable of producing," Easton writes.[55] The race was also understood to be naturally endowed with a particularly Christ-like moral temperament, a capacity for long-suffering endurance that contrasted sharply with "the love of gain and the love of power," which were understood to be "the besetting sins of the Anglo-Saxon race."[56] "Nothing but liberal, generous principles, can call the energies of an African mind into action," writes Easton, who looks forward to an age, after the "continual scene of bloodshed and robbery" that has characterized the era of white dominance, in which Africa's sons will naturally "take the lead in the field of virtuous enterprise, filling the front ranks of the church, when she marches into the millennial era."[57] Whereas the extant character of the Black race in America was understood to be the product of social conditioning, these latter intellectual and moral endowments were understood to be expressions of the race's natural and permanent character; this blend of environmentalist and romantic racialist rationalization typifies the Black ethnological tradition that Douglass inherited.

In taking up ethnological discourse, these men sought to do what the Garrisonians would not: refute racist science on its own empirical terms. But if their adoption of ethnological discourse helped to challenge the cultural authority of proslavery science, their strategy did not come without price. On the one hand, as Bay notes in her masterful study of Black ethnography, the effort to combine environmentalism with romantic racialism produced an inherently contradictory theory of racial difference. "By assigning transhistorical characteristics to the races, African-American thinkers seemingly undercut their own environmentalist explanations of human differences," Bay explains.[58] This ambivalence might itself be seen as a symptom of a more basic problem: simply engaging in racialist discourse required Black writers to concede to the notion of racial identity, reifying the idea that racial differences fragment human likeness, making the principle of human equality more difficult to uphold. Hence Bay suggests that Black ethnologists were, "to some degree, ensnared by the idea of race even as they sought to refute racism's insult to their humanity;" as she argues, Black ethnology's "arguments for difference and equality were beset by some of the same difficulties contained in the late nineteenth-century white segregationist doctrine of 'separate but equal.'"[59]

Given this logical difficulty, it is not surprising that some Black activists called for racial separatism, invoking the romantic idea that nations had to be racially homogeneous. In the same year Douglass wrote "Claims," Martin Delany published his manifesto of Black nationalism, "The Political Destiny of the Colored Race on the American Continent," announcing that "we are not identical with the Anglo-Saxon," and arguing that Black Americans must therefore emigrate elsewhere: "A people, to be free, must necessarily be their own rulers."[60] For Delany, however, racial segregation is only a temporary solution to the problem of human difference; ultimately, he anticipates an apocalyptic future showdown between the world's races, "upon which must be disputed the world's destiny," and in which "every individual will be called upon for his identity with one or the other" race.[61] Controversial though it was, Delany's antagonistic separatism offered a solution to the logical tension between difference and equality by doing away with the latter.

The larger context of Black ethnological writing and the problems it faced prepares us to recognize just how nuanced Douglass's self-positioning is in "Claims." If Douglass was determined to answer racist science on its own terms, he nonetheless seems to have been acutely aware that doing so meant conceding vital ground in the struggle for human equality. At the same time, he was also determined to stave off Black separatism (a policy he did not endorse), which meant that he would have to navigate an alternative route through the internal contradictions of the Black ethnological tradition. Juggling his ambivalence toward racialist discourse and his commitment to a multiracial America, Douglass constructs an argument in "Claims" that is curiously double-voiced. The bulk of the essay sets out to refute the dehumanizing theory of polygenism by putting forward a fairly conventional environmentalist defense of racial unity. In these principal sections of "Claims," Douglass marshals archaeological and physiological evidence to support the thesis that the world's existing racial lineages converge in ancient Egypt and that their subsequent divergence reflects "the effect of circumstances upon the physical man."[62] And yet, at the outset of the essay, Douglass signals his wariness of the ideological concessions that this kind of ethnological argumentation wrings from him. Indeed, if the main body of the essay offers an environmentalist defense of human unity (along with occasional assertions of racial distinctiveness), its opening and closing remarks introduce a countervailing, speculative strain of thinking that trenchantly queries the assumptions that underpin the racialist discourse the main body takes up. In other words, "Claims" manages to simultaneously deploy and detonate racial science. Bracketing—even preempting— the essay's central argument, Douglass's framing remarks embrace racial science's embodied conception of the human only to challenge the notion that embodiment has anything to teach American politics.

In his opening remarks, Douglass invites us to ask what the assignation "human" means in the first place. As he points out, the question at hand is really two: before approaching the question of humanity's multiple or "common ancestry," he must first address the question of "the manhood of the Negro." In the effort to prove that he is "a man," Douglass admits he finds himself immediately at an impasse: "I cannot . . . argue; I must assert."[63] This impulse to assert his humanity by fiat rather than empirical demonstration echoes Linnaeus's designation of the human as the being who must recognize itself as such (*Homo nascem te ipsum*). Linnaeus arrives at this aporetic self-reference because he recognizes that what we mean by the human when we invoke it in humanistic discourse is ultimately a matter of moral rather than empirical judgment and thus belongs "to another forum" than natural history. But if man is therefore the animal that recognizes itself as not-animal—if human life is that which deems itself morally exceptional to animal life—Douglass is also aware that self-nomination is a privilege that has been revoked for members of his race. His own assertion of his humanity is thus rendered inadmissible by the racism that presumes him to be subhuman until proven otherwise, obliging him to first "establish the manhood of anyone making the claim."[64]

This catch-22 forces Douglass to seek other means of demonstration besides assertion, and so he gamely proceeds to review the criteria according to which humanists have historically distinguished human from animal kind. "Man is distinguished from all other animals, by the possession of certain definite faculties and powers," he reminds us, including the power of self-recognition: "Men instinctively distinguish between men and brutes." But here Douglass's argument again threatens to collapse, for having named the ability to instinctively distinguish between human and animal as a characteristic mark of the human, he proceeds to point out that "The horse bears [the Negro] on his back. . . . The barnyard fowl know his step. . . . The dog dances when he comes home, and whines piteously when he is absent. All these know that the Negro is a MAN." Douglass offers this animal testimony as proof of his humanity, "presuming that what is evident to beast and to bird, cannot need elaborate argument to be made plain to men." But the irony of this evidence is as rich as it is paralyzing. For, on the one hand, one cannot help but notice that it is "brutes" *rather than* "humans" that here demonstrate the capacity to "instinctively distinguish between men and brutes." By the classical criteria Douglass has just re-hearsed, these animals are therefore more reasonable—more *human*—than racist Americans, who have come to rely on specialized sciences to tell them what every barnyard animal already intuitively knows. But in a further irony, these animals' testimony to Douglass's humanity is inad-missible for the same reason that he has already recognized his own is—because of its presumed animality. Douglass's effort to distinguish himself from an animal thus manages to reify the categorical moral difference between men and animals even as it simultaneously demonstrates the log-ical indefensibility of this distinction's aporetic center. Emphasizing the obviousness of the moral boundary between humans and nonhumans ("a distinction as eternal as it is palpable," he insists), Douglass's now twice-failed efforts to invoke it highlight the insusceptibility of this boundary to rational argumentation. If only human speech is admissible testimony to one's humanity, then one must first be acknowledged to be human before one can testify to one's humanity. In "Claims," however, Douglass does not linger to press this point. Instead he merely gestures to this circular logic by concluding his opening discussion where it began: "I assume . . . that the Negro is a man," he reiterates, and without further comment, shifts tack.[65]

Douglass now reframes the question before him: assuming his race is human, he proposes to consider whether the races are genealogically re-lated. Still he delays his ethnological argument here, prefacing the case for monogenetic descent that he is about to deliver with reflections on science's susceptibility to bias and distortion. "Science is favorable to distinction," he notes, cautioning that it tends, by disciplinary habit, to proliferate types regardless of whether those distinctions *matter*. Indeed, Douglass here presents science as a kind of aesthetic—"a demand for classes, grades, and intellectual capacities," a *taste* not just a technique for discriminating be-tween things. Building upon this insight, he observes that "fashion is not confined to dress" since science, too, has its vogues: "Scientific writers, not less than others, write to please, as well as to instruct," and hence they may "unconsciously . . . sacrifice what is true to what is popular."[66] Moreover when the case is race, the room for bias—unconscious or otherwise—is irremediably broad, for as Douglass observes, "viewed apart from the authority of the Bible, neither the unity, nor diversity of origin of the human family, can be demonstrated."[67] It is, in other words, "impossible to get far enough back" to definitively determine humanity's origins, leaving ethnologists to weigh the evidence on both sides—a task in which "the temptation . . . to read the Negro out of the human family" does battle with the desire to uphold "the credit of the Bible" and to honor "the instinctive consciousness of the common brotherhood of man."[68] By way of preface to the ethnological argument he is about to launch, then, Douglass gives us a discourse on the myriad ways in which science, too, is subject to unempirical bias.

Douglass's prefatory remarks in "Claims" thus cast doubt both on racial science (with its disciplinary and extradisciplinary biases) *and* on humanistic discourse (with its groundless self-assertions), leaving us to cast about for an authority that could help us to definitively answer "the vital question of the age." In this way, the essay's opening provocatively creates what Jared Hickman describes as "a situation in which the rhetoricity of all knowledge-claims is somewhat uncomfortably exposed."[69] Indeed, the vacuum of authority extends even to Douglass, who has by this point preempted the force of the ethnological argument he is about to deliver. Had Douglass concluded his essay by resting his case for monogenism, we would have been left with an essay that is perversely self-defeating. Instead, at the end of "Claims" Douglass expressly lets his case for monogenism unravel in order to reframe the question of his humanity once again. In his final paragraphs, Douglass abruptly turns aside from his exposition of human unity to acknowledge the possibility that science will ultimately side against him. "What if all this reasoning be unsound?" he speculates; "What if ingenious men are able to find plausible objections to all arguments maintaining the oneness of the human race?"[70] In a climactic final pivot, Douglass sets aside his defense of monogenism to make one last pitch for "the claims of the Negro" from a slightly different materialist perspective. Here Douglass invokes a new authority to fill the vacuum his essay has exposed; unlike the essay's earlier candidates, this authority is immune to "the rhetoricity of all knowledge-claims" because it makes no claims to truth, only power.

Working in an entirely new vein, the conclusion of "Claims" frames an alternative theory of human rights that does not depend upon establishing that all races share a common identity. In other words, as Douglass shows us, the genealogical debates that absorb racial science may not, in fact, be decisive. "I sincerely believe, that the weight of the argument is in favor of the unity of origin of the human race, or species," he assures us, but

> What, if we grant that the case, on our part, is not made out? Does it follow, that the Negro should be held in contempt? Does it follow, that to enslave and imbrute him is either just or wise? I think not. Human rights stand upon a common basis; and by all the reasons that they are supported, maintained and defended, for one variety of the human family, they are supported, maintained and defended for *all* the human family; because all mankind have the same wants, arising out of a common nature. A diverse origin does not disprove a common nature, nor does it disprove a united destiny.[71]

The major claim Douglass makes here is that even two races of "diverse origin" may nonetheless, serendipitously, share a "common nature" and therefore be entitled to the same rights. But this discussion also introduces a rather different line of argument. Alongside his image of a biologically unrelated "human family" conjoined by a "common nature," Douglass describes a biracial nation related by mutual interests ("wants") and bound together by a "united destiny." In pointing to this "united destiny," Douglass reminds us that genealogical kinship is not the only form of relation there is. Geographical proximity—the shared nature that is one single American landscape—produces its own kind of relations, as neighbors cannot help but impinge on each other in going about the business of seeing to their "wants" in a shared physical economy. And the thing about these kinds of relations is that they bind populations together through interdependence and mutual vulnerability regardless of whether those populations are homogeneous or diverse.

In this sense, Douglass's appeal to an American future bound to a biracially "united destiny" sets up a new kind of argument on behalf of the claims of his race. As Foucault observes, "the subject of right and the subject of interest are not governed by the same logic," and in his closing remarks, Douglass underscores this difference by suggesting that denying his race's demand for freedom is not only not "just" but also not "wise."[72] Against the conclusions of white segregationists and Black emigrationists, he insists that "the Negro and white man are likely ever to remain the principal inhabitants of this country." Ironically repurposing proslavery arguments about how the African race is uniquely designed to withstand hard labor in harsh climates, he notes that "the history of the Negro race proves them to be wonderfully adapted to all countries, all climates, and all conditions," thus proving that, barring genocidal "extermination" ("not probable") or mass exodus ("out of the question . . . [the Negro's] attachment to the place of his birth is stronger than iron"), "all the facts in his history mark out for [the Negro] a destiny, united to America and Americans."[73] Whatever racial differences might divide them, Black and white Americans, Douglass suggests, will inevitably remain united by *another* "common nature" in the national landscape to which their "common destiny" is bound. And in this shared physical environment, interdependence is unavoidable even if other forms of relation (familial, ideological, or sympathetic) are not.

Having established the inevitability of ongoing proximity, Douglass closes with the clear and ominous warning that acknowledging his race's right to freedom, life, liberty, and knowledge is therefore not just right but *prudent*.

> Whether this population shall . . . be made a blessing to the country and the world, or whether their multiplied wrongs shall kindle the vengeance of an offended God, will depend upon the conduct of no class of men so much as upon the Scholars of this country. . . . There is but one safe road for nations as for individuals. . . . The flaming sword of offended justice falls as certainly upon the nation as upon the man. God has no children whose rights may be safely trampled upon. The sparrow may not fall to the ground without the notice of His eye, and men are more than sparrows.[74]

With these portentous words, Douglass suggests that to refuse to accommodate the interests of Black Americans is to put the interests of white Americans in peril. Couched in the language of divine vengeance, Douglass summons the specter of an imminent Black uprising against the "multiplied wrongs" of slavery and racial oppression, presenting the ethnological "Scholars of this country" with the prospect of their own violent death as a different kind of rationale for granting that Black Americans are entitled to freedom. Moreover, in this shift from identity to interests, the significance of the ethnological question with which Douglass started (is the Negro human and related to the white race?) falls away. For the problem of proximity—which necessarily presents a choice between peacefully accommodating one's neighbors' needs or else denying their interests with violence—remains the same regardless of who (or what) the players are. Indeed, as Douglass's citation of Matthew 10:29 above suggests (and as passages discussed in the next section of this chapter will underscore), the same truth holds for men as for sparrows: "God has no children whose rights may be safely trampled upon."

Thus without relinquishing his claim to humanity, Douglass concludes "Claims" by bracketing the relevance of that claim's controversy. Instead, he points to the problem of interdependence—of the mutual vulnerability to which we, of all species, are exposed by virtue of our proximity in a terrestrial "common nature," the resources of which we all rely on to supply our needs and wants. What is so fascinating, then, about this final pivot in Douglass's response to ethnology is the way that the prospect of our physically "united destiny" takes him beyond the question of "the human"—beyond, that is, both liberal humanist and racialist logics that make moral consideration contingent upon speciological belonging. In the next section, I will explore how Douglass develops this nonhumanistic reasoning across his other writings of the 1850s. As we shall see, animals, animal instincts, and the physical laws of nature loom large in this work, supplementing his moral critiques of slavery and appeals to human sympathy with a new logic of material risk and existential necessity.

Abolitionist Animals

The rising cachet of scientific racism in American political discourse in the 1850s made it increasingly urgent for abolitionists like Douglass to disavow any similarity between slaves and animals, and yet his writings of this decade are in fact strewn with animals, deliberately courting animal comparisons in ways his earlier writings do not. In the very historical moment in which he might have had the most at stake in distancing himself from animals he starts to think more regularly through them about the moral claims—and perhaps more important, as I shall suggest, the amoral claims—that the nonhuman world holds on the human. For through the animals he represents—animals that stampede, rear, kick, and bite— Douglass highlights the speciologically universal instinct to violently resist any threat to one's life and liberty, marking these things as basic, more-than-human rights. I will thus argue that Douglass's identifications with animals in the 1850s are part of his systematic effort to frame an abolitionist argument that is strategically agnostic toward the question of his race's humanity—an argument that operates outside of the liberal discourse of human equality and moral right by tactically embracing, instead, the specter of human animality and the threat of physical violence. In other words, I suggest that Douglass embraces animals in the 1850s not in spite of but because of scientific racism and the doctrine of Black bestiality it codified.

Around the same time Douglass published "Claims," he was also at work on a revised and expanded version of his autobiography, titled *My Bondage and My Freedom*, which he published the following year in 1855. The re-written text includes a striking alteration in his account of the pivotal year he spent hired out to Mr. Covey, a man known locally for "breaking" slaves. As Douglass had recounted in *The Narrative*, on his first day at Covey's he was whipped for losing control of a team of "unbroken oxen" who twice make a break for freedom, overturning their cart and destroying a gate in their stampede. In his retelling of this scene in the 1855 autobiography, Douglass inserts a curious moment of reflection, set off on its own in an uncharacteristically short paragraph in the text. Now, in the midst of this harrowing experience, the young Douglass stops to take note of his like-ness to the oxen causing him so much trouble. "I now saw, in my situation, several points of similarity with that of the oxen," he writes. "They were property, so was I; they were to be broken, so was I. Covey was to break me, I was to break them; break and be broken—such is life."[75]

In 1855, Douglass was well aware of the compelling reasons to disavow any "points of similarity" between himself and these beasts of burden—reasons that had, if anything, grown more acute in the interim since his first autobiography. *The Narrative of the Life of Frederick Douglass* betrays no such inclination to sympathy: where comparisons between slaves and animals appear in this text, it is to critique the glaring injustice of a sys-tem in which "horses and men, cattle and women, pigs and children, all [hold] the same rank in the scale of being."[76] Yet despite the intervening ascent of ethnological discourse and the seemingly authoritative support racist science lent to the idea that the African race comprises, as Russwurm encapsulates it, "something between man and brute creation," *My Bondage and My Freedom* underscores two basic commonalities: both oxen and slaves are subjected to an overwhelming physical power and, when pressed, both may also assert a violent force of their own.

This lesson is even more explicit in the opening scene of Douglass's 1854 novella, *The Heroic Slave*. During a quiet moment in the forest, the story's hero, Madison Washington, observes the bold behaviors of the wild ani-mals around him and ruefully contemplates his own acquiescence to slav-ery. "Those birds, perched on yon swinging boughs . . . though liable to the sportsman's fowling piece, are still my superiors," he chides himself. "They *live free*, though they may die slaves." Noting that even a nearby "miserable" snake, "when he saw my uplifted arm ... turned to give me battle," Washington confesses, "I dare not do as much as that. I neither run nor fight, but do meanly stand," answering the lash with "piteous cries."[77] The example of these forest animals leads Washington to conclude that he, too, has a natural right to self-determination, and the scene ends with his resolution to resist: "Liberty I will have, or die in the attempt to gain it," he proclaims. Thus echoing Patrick Henry's iconic revolutionary ultimatum, the rousing conclusion of Washington's forest soliloquy (which carries on for several more climactically declamatory lines), rings with an eloquence that Ivy Wilson glosses as "an exercise in liberation through literacy"—a performance of both Washington's and, by extension, Douglass's rational intelligence.[78] However, the irony of Douglass's callback to Patrick Henry here is that, in this case, Washington's willingness to martyr himself for his liberty is explicitly modeled on the defiant freedom of birds and snakes. The humanism implicit in Washington's insistence that liberty is "the inalienable birth-right of every man" is thus preemptively undercut by the fact that this is a lesson he has learned by observing the inalienable instinct of animals to live free or die. Rather than exemplifying Washington's uniquely *human* rationality, then, his principled insistence upon self-determination here appears as a belated obedience to a much more basic and universal instinct for self-defense. The right to freedom does not depend on one's species designation—in fact, we might say that, on this view, freedom is not a "right" or moral entitlement at all so much as it is a reflexive urge that is built into the nature of organic life.

Douglass seems to have begun developing this line of thought as early as 1851—before he had weighed in on racial science, but when he was deeply embroiled in rethinking his relation to the U.S. Constitution. In that year, Douglass wrote an editorial on the "Christiana Riot," an armed skirmish that erupted in a border town of Pennsylvania when a Maryland farmer arrived to reclaim four fugitive slaves and was rebuffed by a local party of primarily free Black men who assembled to defend the fugitives. By the end of the fighting the Maryland farmer was dead and the four fugitives, as well as the freeman who had housed them, were en route to Canada (aided in a leg of their escape by Douglass himself). What inspired Douglass's editorial on this first real test of the 1850 Fugitive Slave Law was a rumor that the federal government intended to indict the four fugitive slaves for treason, a proposition Douglass found outrageous. As he argues in his paper, it makes no sense to try a man for treason against the government that enslaves him:

The only law which the alleged slave has a right to know anything about, is the law of nature. This is his only law. The enactments of this government do not recognize him as a citizen, but as a thing. In light of the law, a slave can no more commit treason than a horse or an ox can commit treason. A horse kicks out the brains of his master. Do you try the horse for treason? Then why the slave who does the same thing? You answer, because the slave is a man, and he is therefore responsible for his acts. The answer is sound. The slave is a man and ought not to be treated like a horse, but like a man, and his manhood is his justification for shooting down any creature who shall attempt to reduce him to the condition of a brute.[79]

Douglass's diatribe here is deceptively simple. On a first reading, he seems to call back to humanism's founding assertion of the "natural law" that distinguishes between animals (who are slaves to their nature) and men (whose rationality renders them autonomous from biological compulsion, and hence morally accountable beings). Thus Douglass points out the hypocrisy of legally denying the slave's humanity while proposing to hold him morally responsible for his actions. However, Douglass's reasoning here also moves outside the lines of this very rationale that he invokes. For even as he suggests that the slave who shoots his master is a moral agent, while the horse that brains his master is not, the argument he ultimately advances is that *neither* horse nor slave could rightfully be hauled into court. As he explains, the slave's act of violence can only be judged by natural, not national law, and according to natural law the act is innocent, since by nature a man has a perfect right to "[shoot] down any creature who shall attempt to reduce him to the condition of a brute." Under this description, the slave's resistance becomes morally identical, not antithetical, to the resistance of the horse, who likewise kicks his master when his master attempts to "reduce him to the condition of a brute." Thus though Douglass attributes the slave's right to self-defense to his "manhood," the analogy he draws to the instinct for self-preservation in a horse testifies to the trans-specific universalism of this natural law—"manhood," in other words, shades here into something more like "self-assertion."[80] Neither men nor horses will tolerate being treated like beasts, and in violently resisting their oppression they exercise an instinctive and naturally ordained right to self-defense. This passage therefore courts a very different reading than the one I began with. Instead of simply locating the slave's right to freedom in his humanness, the passage ultimately suggests that this right is universal— that freedom is synonymous with the instinct for self-preservation common to all autopoetic life.

Douglass's rebellious animals thus conjure a rather different conception of freedom than the one that has typically circulated in discussions of Douglass's growing militancy in the 1850s. Readers ranging from Martin Luther King and Malcom X to Eric Sundquist and Russ Castronovo have noted how passages like these strategically invoke the founders' appeals to natural law in justifying the violence of the American Revolution in order to preemptively justify the armed uprising against slavery that Douglass now anticipates.[81] These citational echoes have prompted heated debate about whether deploying the founders' idiom signals Douglass's cooptation by America's patriarchal and white supremacist national legacy, or whether this is instead an example of subversive appropriation, an act of what Castronovo terms "discursive passing."[82] While I'm sensitive to these concerns, I think this debate fails to account for Douglass's revolutionary animals. Through these nonhuman figures, Douglass conjures scenes of violent resistance in which the question of that violence's justifiability is superseded by its naturalness, or biological inevitability. For Madison Washington to learn of his natural right to liberty from a snake, or for the young Douglass to recognize the necessity of violently resisting Covey from the oxen who resist his own whip, suggests that Douglass might not, after all, have much at stake in whether Black revolutionary violence will be deemed rational rather than animalistic. In place of the higher moral law that documents such as the Declaration assert, Douglass's rearing snake, stampeding oxen, and kicking horse refer to a different kind of natural law—a material force that is prior to moral calculation, an embodied imperative for self-preservation in the face of which questions of justice and legal precedent wither away.

Put differently, Douglass's writings in the 1850s endeavor to *naturalize* natural law, locating moral rights not in humankind's transcendental reason or immortal soul, but in the instincts and energetic economy of the material body (human or nonhuman). Thus, although he invokes the American Revolution as his precedent, in Douglass's hands natural law is not simply a paralegalistic justification for violent resistance (as America's founders and Garrisonian abolitionists deployed it), but moreover functions as a mechanistic explanation of that violence's material necessity. This conflation of moral law with physical laws makes freedom curiously hard to distinguish from automaticity—hence the tortured ambivalence of the Christiana Riot editorial, which cannot decide whether self-defense is a moral action or an instinctive reflex. This ambivalence is even more apparent in another of Douglass's editorials on the aftermath of the fugitive slave law, provocatively entitled, "Is It Right and Wise to Kill a Kidnapper?" (1854). Here Douglass defends the killing of U.S. Marshal James Batchelder at the Boston courthouse during the failed attempt to rescue Anthony Burns by arguing that Burns's right to freedom was upheld by a moral law that is as inexorable as the physical law of gravity. As Douglass asserts, by defying this moral law Batchelder therefore forfeited his right to life in the same way that a man who "flings himself from the top of some lofty monument, against a granite pavement . . . forfeits his right to live [and] dies according to law." In other words, Douglass reasons, "As human life is not superior to the laws for the preservation of the physical universe, so, too, it is not superior to the eternal law of justice."[83] Here again we can see how Douglass's conflation of moral and physical law throws the concepts of justice and freedom, as we know them, into turmoil. For if the "eternal law of justice" is understood to operate as mechanically as the physical law of gravity—if, that is, the act of shooting Batchelder is no more voluntary than the pavement's "act" of crushing a suicidal jumper—then undertaking to justify Batchelder's murder seems as irrelevant, in the first place, as attempting to defend the moral legitimacy of falling downward. If justice and gravity act upon us as natural necessities, their moral virtue is superfluous.

This is, again, an ideologically risky move for Douglass to make at this moment. For although his materialized account of rights allows him to frame his case for racial equality and justified violence within the empirical idiom of "the human" that racial science makes authoritative, it also breaks down the moral distinctions (between humanity and animality, and between moral and amoral actions) that might otherwise seem to form the crux of that case. But herein, I think, lies the force of his naturalization of natural rights, for it suggests that however the "question" of Black humanity is decided, a violent racial uprising against slavery is nevertheless not only possible but in time *guaranteed* by the mechanisms of physical law. That even the simplest nonhuman organisms resist harm by fight or flight—that nature itself hates oppression in the same lawful way that it abhors a vacuum—means that slavery is materially unsustainable in time, attempting as it does to pervert and repress the liberty-loving physics of the natural world.[84] Thus Douglass concludes, in an 1857 editorial announcing that "Peaceful Annihilation of Slavery Is Hopeless," that "the recoil, when it comes, will be in exact proportion to the wrongs inflicted."[85] If the equitable proportionality of this projected racial violence (in "exact proportion to the wrongs inflicted") would seem to be an argument for its justice (echoing Robert Levine's sense of the self-restraint implicit in what he dubs Douglass's "temperate revolutionism"), that word "recoil"—drawn as it is from the mechanical physics of springs stretched too far and guns that go off—simultaneously works to move the violence it conjures into the amoral realm of automatic and compulsory action.[86] As such, antislavery violence comes to look as unstoppable as it is unavoidable.

As we saw at the end of "Claims," in the face of the persistent denial of his race's humanity, Douglass begins to supplement his critique of slavery's injustice with warnings about its risk: slavery, he argues, is "dangerous as well as wrong."[87] As he suggests, even those listeners who refute his humanity and deny that his race is endowed with inalienable rights will nonetheless soon find themselves obliged by sheer necessity to accommodate his claims or else brace for a kick to the head. Thus he proposes that "whatever character or capacity you ascribe to" his race, and however the questions of slavery's moral, legal, and theological justifiability are popularly decided, slavery is structurally unsustainable. It has, he writes, "no means within itself of perpetuation or permanence," and must therefore either be abolished or implode.[88] There is no appeal to humanity or morality in this new argument's reasoning; instead, in line with the biological dispensation that racial science augurs, Douglass attributes antislavery violence to an instinctive demand for self-determination that is inherent in all organic being, and in so doing appeals to the no less compulsory and unreflective instinct for self-preservation among his white audiences.

But if this new strain of argumentation sidelines appeals to white sympathies, it does not dismiss the political importance of sentiment. On the contrary, it doubles down on it by suggesting that a knowledge of rights manifests in embodied instincts, affects, appetites, and desires, rather than through the transcendental operation of reason. Thus, for instance, in the same scene of *The Heroic Slave* in which Madison Washington learns to imitate the instinctive self-assertion of wild animals, George Listwell, a white man eavesdropping on Madison's soliloquy, is instantaneously converted to abolitionism, finding that Washington's speech "rung through the chambers of his soul, and vibrated through his entire frame."[89] As a number of critics have noted, the sonic imagery here emphasizes the embodied and even erotic nature of Listwell's reaction, underscoring the corporeality of this moral conviction.[90] Conversely, Douglass represents moral oppression as an experience that is as much an affront to the body as it is to reason. In *My Bondage and My Freedom*, he amends his memorable description of slave songs by noting that he once "heard the same *wailing notes*, and was much affected by them. . . . during the famine of 1845–6" in Ireland.[91] Of course, Douglass's comparison here works on many fronts at once: there is political strategy in linking slavery to injustices in Europe so as to align American abolitionism with a transnational revolutionary movement, and there may also be financial interest in it, since Douglass raised significant funds for his newspaper abroad.[92] However, this comparison between the slaves' "melancholy" songs and the sounds of people literally starving also lends the slave's "grief and sorrow" all the existential urgency—all the physiological desperation—of the Irishman's dying complaint. On this view, moral wrongs register as corporealized burdens in the body—forming what Douglass elsewhere describes as "pent up energies of human rights and sympathies."[93] Like any other compiled physical stress, these pent-up energies may be absorbed by the body only up to a point.

In this regard, my analysis of Douglass's abolitionist animality diverges from recent critical readings of Douglass's response to the problem of human difference in the racial scientific 1850s. In her astute reading of animality and biopolitics in Douglass's work, Colleen Glenney Boggs also argues that Douglass does not outright denounce but rather recodes the bestialization of Blackness in racial science in ways that show him to have been willing to abandon the discourse of rationality (a move that, as Boggs points out, "flies in the face of roughly thirty years of commentary on African American writing that has emphasized the acquisition of language and literacy as a key liberatory tool").[94] On Boggs's reading, Douglass turns away from the language of rationality (as the distinguishing mark of the human) in order to make the body (human or nonhuman) "the basis for a relational subjectivity" premised upon the shared language of suffering. Thus she argues that Douglass "treats the pained body as the locus of an embodied language that bespeaks the cruelty endemic to slavery's symbolic order," challenging audiences to reimagine subjectivity as something that extends to all beings who are subject to suffering, regardless of racial or speciological difference (including the capacity to cognize a "symbolic order").[95] Along related lines, Brigitte Fielder demonstrates how frequently abolitionist texts deploy "domesticated animals to mediate their readers' sympathy for enslaved people," a substitution that allows them to frame an "alternative model of sympathy that deprioritizes notions of sameness, acknowledging that even humanist sympathy can function across relations of alterity."[96]

Like Boggs and Fielder, I find that Douglass's animals respond to the problem that racial (or, as polygenism codifies it, speciological) difference seems to pose to interracial sympathy and recognition. But if, like Boggs, I find that Douglass's defiant animals draw our attention to the shared vulnerability of all embodied beings, unlike Boggs I am particularly interested in how Douglass invokes that vulnerability not in order to engender a sympathetic connection across speciological differences but to convey a timely reminder of the violence that suffering unleashes, lighting up the precariousness of proximity and the necessity of mutual accommodation with or without intersubjective sympathy or recognition. Whether or not Madison Washington feels an affinity with "that accursed and crawling snake," he acknowledges the force of its bodily threat to him and therefore accedes to its demand to be left alone. In this way, proximity constitutes a community around the material interrelations of diverse bodies that is not contingent upon kinship or affects of solidarity. In keeping with Lloyd Pratt's reading of "strangerhood" in Douglass's late antebellum writings, then, I suggest that Douglass's animals identify "an ineluctable barrier to mutual intelligibility that also functions as a kind of hinge point for mutuality."[97] In his turn to the animal body, Douglass develops a new strain of antislavery rhetoric in which relations of sympathy and intersubjective recognition take a backseat to material relations of proximity, embodied necessity, and mutual exposure.

But this new argument also creates difficulties for Douglass since, unlike his appeals to sympathy and moral conversion, his invocations of slavery's systemic risk can seem to leave audiences with very little to do. By the lights of his new, materialist antislavery logic, slavery not only *ought* to be abolished, but it inevitably *will* be, with or without white America's consent, lending this argument a fatalistic providentialism uncharacteristic of Douglass's earlier work. Thus, for instance, in his powerful Fourth of July address, Douglass boldly asserts that "the doom of slavery is certain"—vouchsafed not by a preponderance of antislavery votes or by the sure vengeance of an angry god, but by the much more diffuse and not-quite-human agency of what he describes as "the obvious tendencies of the age" toward globalization and (which turns out to be the same thing) freedom.[98] As he tells us, "No nation can now shut itself up from the surrounding world and trot round in the same old path of its fathers without interference," for "intelligence is penetrating the darkest corners of the globe. It makes its pathway over and under the sea, as well as on the earth. Wind, steam, and lightning are its chartered agents. Oceans no longer divide, but link nations together."[99] Although the nation-dissolving "intelligence" Douglass alludes to here is clearly communicated by human technologies—"wind, steam, and lightning" metonymically referencing oceanic navigation, railroads, and telegraphs—his heavily allegorized prose distances these circulations and the "intelligence" they spread from human action and intentions. Instead, the globalizing "tendencies of the age" he describes here take on the impersonal dimensions of a world spirit or hidden hand—an emergent systemic rather than strictly human force whose fugitive and deterritorializing freedom of circulation Douglass most directly identifies with "agents" of matter itself.

Thus this essay's famously fiery denunciation of American hypocrisy ends on a paradoxically quietist note. Bracketing the issue of racial difference ("Must I undertake to prove that the slave is a man?," Douglass sighs; "The time for such argument is passed") and likewise waiving its earlier call for a recommitment to American Revolutionary ideals, Douglass's jeremiad concludes by heralding emancipation's inescapability: in this essay, abolition is both the means of national repentance and the globally wrought apocalypse that awaits an unregenerate nation.[100] And thus instead of reaffirming American self-determination, Douglass's natural law rhetoric ends by challenging the very notion of individual and national sovereignty that the founders had originally used that rhetoric to defend. In Douglass's empiricized version, the nation's naturalness indicates its inability to "shut itself up from the surrounding world," highlighting its exposure to and imbrication within a global community of human and nonhuman beings interrelated through biological, geophysical, ideological, and economic systems whose multiplied complexity no individual nor nation could hope to finally control. It is, consequently, unclear what role is left in this climatological drama for Douglass's audiences to play. As Carrie Hyde argues in her brilliant reading of weather in *The Heroic Slave*, by "depicting nature as the principle agent" of antislavery resistance, "Douglass is able to suggest that opposition to slavery is more fundamental than the actions of any one individual or group."[101] Indeed, he suggests that opposition to slavery may originate in forces that are not human at all.

In this respect, Douglass's Fourth of July prophecy is not only antiracist and transnationalist but also posthumanist. Resurrecting the discourse of natural rights as a self-executing modality of natural *laws*, Douglass turns the founders' liberal humanistic logic on its ear by making freedom an involuntary instinct of the body and an inexorable tendency of matter itself. Far from marking a uniquely human autonomy from natural laws, this empirical freedom is all but indistinguishable from physical necessity. Moreover, it conjures an empirical public that likewise breaks from the founders' nationalistic vision. For whereas America's liberal institutions convoke a public constituted by formally equal and enfranchised individuals conjoined by contract and brought together by rational, deliberative debate, Douglass's revolutionary animals and abolitionist oceans point to a public that comprises all earthly beings whatsoever, conjoined by material interrelations and brought together by the ongoing struggle to satisfy their basic "wants"—including, most basically, the freedom to pursue those interests. Access to this embodied public is not restricted by qualifications—one need not be accredited as "rational," or "human," or "morally free" to participate in it. On the contrary, the polemical force of this embodied public is that participation in it—and thus exposure to it—is strictly unavoidable, a condition of being. In his invocations of an empiricized natural law, then, Douglass makes an end run around the efforts of some racial scholars to definitively exclude his race from the ranks of the human by dismantling the humanistic logic that makes humanity a criteria for political participation in the first place. As Bruno Latour might describe this, Douglass renounces the arbitrary distinction between "natural" (passive, animalistic) and "political" (free, human) action, challenging us "to redefine politics as *the entire set of tasks* that allow the progressive composition of a common world."[102] If racial science should succeed in disproving our "common nature," it cannot deny this common world: with this insight, voiced in "Claims" and developed across Douglass's images of natural violence in the 1850s, Douglass twists racial science's empiricism to his advantage, demonstrating how its embodied and hierarchical account of the human might in fact sponsor a more capacious and inclusive postnationalist and nonhumanist vision of worldly community.

From our contemporary standpoint, this may seem like a powerful (or at least fashionable) move. Douglass's insistence upon the way in which proximate bodies impinge on each other regardless of their political status boldly renounces what Mel Chen describes as humanism's "animacy hierarchy"—the systematic denial of nonhuman agency by which humanism licenses the political exclusion of, and moral indifference to, racialized, animalized, and objectified bodies.[103] However, this liberatory renunciation also comes with steep costs to Douglass's politics, for, as we have just seen, it erodes the liberal politics he is otherwise inclined to champion. Thus if Douglass's antislavery materialism defuses the force of denials of Black humanity, it does so by giving up on the unique moral and political value of human belonging and mooting the question of racial equality—both of which (unique moral value and racial equality) he was understandably keen to claim for Black humanity. While his insurgent bodies clearly resist objectification, their agency cannot serve Douglass as proof of their liberal personhood. Instead, his embodied public is full of unowned agency, agency that (like freedom, on his redescription) is not a property of persons but rather percolates up from materiality itself. Although antislavery, this materialist riposte to racial science leads Douglass a long way off from the liberalism he might like to inhabit.

To be sure, Douglass never explicitly formulates the challenges his materialism poses to the liberal principles he champions. However, his sense of their contradiction may be registered in the reluctance with which he turns to this argument. As it appears in his late antebellum writings, this antislavery materialism functions (like the antislavery violence that he usually summons it to justify) as a kind of position of last resort. Indeed, in "Claims" his appeal to our materially "united destiny" explicitly appears as the essay's last line of defense against polygenist racial theory, and in his Fourth of July address it again emerges only after his appeal to America's liberal principles is exhausted. Such reluctance suggests, as I have already speculated, that Douglass was a liberal driven to develop a materialist argument against slavery by the popular ascendance of racial science and empiricism's cultural authority, more broadly. But if, on this view, Douglass's embrace of embodiment is a local strategy and not the political endgame, the same cannot be said of posthumanist materialisms today, raising the question of whether the illiberalism of materialism's politics is fully registered in these theories. I will return to this in Chapter 4, where I will suggest that the question of the contradictions between materialism and liberalism is one whose absence has shaped posthumanism's failure to rigorously theorize its relation to racial and social justice traditions.

By way of conclusion, I would like to look at one final example of Douglass's antislavery materialism that lights up its illiberal and nonhumanistic tendencies. I have argued elsewhere for the burgeoning materialism and "amoral abolitionism" of *My Bondage and My Freedom*; rather than recapitulate that argument here I would like to return to *The Heroic Slave* which, as Douglass's only foray into fiction, allowed him to distill his ideas with vivid concision.[104] We have already seen how the novella's opening scene naturalizes natural law by identifying Madison Washington's natural right to freedom with the instinctive self-assertion of animals in the forest. At the end of the novella, in the climactic scene of Washington's successful mutiny aboard the *Creole*, Douglass again rewrites the rational violence of American Revolutionary liberalism as natural, inhuman, and involuntary violence—a demand for freedom that is systemic to the material order of being.

Like the prior three episodes of the story, which are narrated by Mr. Listwell, this pivotal episode is also narrated by a white character, Tom Grant. Grant survived the mutiny aboard the *Creole* and now, two months later, relates the story to an audience of dubious fellow sailors at a Richmond coffeehouse. He is goaded into the retelling by a sailor named Williams who blames the affair on mismanagement: "All that is needed in dealing

with a set of rebellious darkies, is to show that ye're not afraid of 'em,"
Williams scoffs. "A drop of blood from one on 'em will skeer a hundred."[105]
Routing the narrative of the mutiny through Grant's defense of his defeat
thus allows Douglass to specify precisely what, in the eyes of this unsympa-
thetic white Southerner, overmastered him. And as Grant tells it, the lesson
of the mutiny is a curiously blended one. For on the one hand, contrary to
Williams, Grant insists that Washington is proof that "there are exceptions
to this general rule" that "[Negroes] are ignorant," and Grant leaves the
Creole affair convinced that "this whole slave-trading business is a disgrace
and scandal to Old Virginia."[106] However, when pressed, Grant does not
ascribe the mutiny's success to Washington's exceptional intelligence and
bravery. Instead, he compares the mutiny to a hurricane or maelstrom, a
natural disaster in the face of which "we lose our indignation and disgust in
lamentation of the disaster, and in awe of the Power which controls the
elements."[107]

   In Grant's eyes, then, Washington's agency disappears into the impersonal forces of nature, and this eclipse is borne out by the account he gives
of the role of the weather in the mutiny's events. Grant was knocked unconscious early in the fighting and, upon waking, attempts to rally the crew,
who have retreated to the ship's rigging. But Washington interrupts Grant's
efforts with an eloquent defense of the justice of his cause, invoking his
namesake's example: "God is my witness that LIBERTY, not malice, is the
motive for this night's work. . . . We have done that which you applaud your
fathers for doing, and if we are murderers, so were they."[108] If *The Heroic
Slave* were a conventionally liberal story, this speech should have been the
end of it. But in fact it makes little impression on Grant. For although he
"forgot [Washington's] blackness in the dignity of his manner, and the eloquence of his speech," these evidences of Washington's equal humanity
are nevertheless not enough to overcome Grant's racial prejudice: "It was
not that his principles were wrong in the abstract; for they are the principles of 1776," Grant confesses. "But I could not bring myself to recognize
their application to one whom I deemed my inferior."[109] Thus rational discourse and appeals to shared principle fail to end Grant's standoff with
Washington; instead, it is finished by force. First, there is the sheer force
of Washington's desire for freedom: Washington tells Grant that if they
come near "a slave-cursed shore" he will set fire to the ship's magazine and
blow them all "into a thousand fragments," an oath that convinces Grant
"that resistance was out of the question." Next, as if to underscore Washington's threat of fragmentation by fire, a storm suddenly blows up, howl-
ing with sublime fury and threatening to splinter the ship. If Washington's

threat convinced Grant to defer his resistance, the ocean's threat momentarily convinces him to forget his objection altogether: "For awhile we had dearer interests to look after than slave property." It is thus not Washington's idealistic rhetoric but the storm's existential threat that ultimately engenders cross-racial cooperation here, activating everyone's "dearer interests" in survival than in preserving "slave property." Looking grimly out upon the spectacle of "the dreadful hurricane," Washington calmly proclaims, "Mr. Mate, you cannot write the bloody laws of slavery on those restless billows. The ocean, if not the land, is free." With this, his last reported line in the novella, Washington identifies his freedom with the exigencies of a "restless" nature that has compelled Grant to acquiesce to Washington's demand for freedom despite his continued denial of Washington's equal humanity. *The Heroic Slave* thus frames emancipation as a matter of self-preservation, as Grant finds his imminent death far more persuasive than any of Washington's rhetorical appeals on behalf of his own human rights.

But the point here is not simply that Douglass allows Washington's rational agency—his heroic resistance and the humanness it evinces—to be eclipsed by the ocean's sublime and irrational power. Rather, the point is that by the naturalistic logic with which the story begins—the logic that identifies the right to freedom in "animal" instincts—Washington's violence *is of the same order as* the ocean's: both are construed as elemental forces impersonally inscribed in the "restless" or freedom-loving order of matter. One measure of the radicalism of this conceptual move is that, in modeling Washington's uprising on the unruly ocean, Douglass in fact embraces the argument that Daniel Webster had advanced in 1842 in an attempt to re-enslave the people of the actual *Creole*, who had been officially liberated when the mutineers landed at Nassau. As Carrie Hyde reminds us, on the day of the historical mutiny there had been no storm; instead, Douglass's invented storm seems to derive from Daniel Webster's subsequent effort to establish that the British lacked jurisdiction when they freed the *Creole* by arguing that the mutineer's "unlawful force" ought to be regarded like the "stresses of weather" (according to maritime law, when foul weather drives a vessel into port, it is exempted from becoming subject to the laws of that country).[110] Hyde suggests that Douglass's squall "strategically reappropriates natural metaphors as a figure for natural rights," converting Webster's conflation of violent mutinies and violent weather into a "universalizing rhetoric of natural law as a model for political reform in the United States."[111] I concur with Hyde's analysis but wish to add that the natural law Douglass hereby invokes is conceptually alien to the one to which Madison Washington's forebears appealed, and that the mechanisms of political change this naturalized natural law envisions likewise exceed the deliberative rationality and national self-constitution the founders' liberal institutions enshrined. This is what Douglass means by taking seriously Webster's de-animating conflation of slave uprisings with bad weather: his naturalization of natural rights drains the rational agency out of Washington's revolutionary action, transforming freedom from a human prerogative into an ontological imperative. As Douglass's 1850s writings suggest, far from distinguishing the free (human beings) from the materially determined (nonhuman beings), this natural freedom percolates throughout the world, finding expression in snakes and birds no less than in transatlantic commerce and violent weather. And where this irrepressible urge breaks out—in stampedes, uprisings, and cyclones—it confronts those in its way with their own freedom: fight, fly, accommodate, or die.

Douglass's depictions of freedom's empirical imperative in the 1850s thus bracket the question of racial difference and human equality that both liberal and racialist discourses had made to seem paramount to the question of slavery and the prospect of a multiracial national community. And yet by making freedom an instinct of matter, his antislavery materialism creates problems for the notion of rational agency and human autonomy that ground liberal humanist doctrine. My next chapter will further explore this erosion of agency in antislavery materialism by turning to the late work of Henry David Thoreau. Like Douglass, Thoreau also followed the rise of racial science closely, adopting and adapting its empiricism in ways that indelibly reshaped his antislavery politics in the 1850s.

CHAPTER 2

Thoreau's Seeds: Evolution and the Problem of Human Agency

> Henry often reminded me of an animal in human form. He had the
> eye of a bird, the scent of a dog, the most acute, delicate
> intelligence—but no soul. No . . . Henry could not have
> had a human soul.
>
> —RALPH WALDO EMERSON[1]

> I am not responsible for the successful working of the machinery of
> society. I am not the son of the engineer. I perceive that, when an
> acorn and a chestnut fall side by side, the one does not remain inert
> to make way for the other, but both obey their own laws, and spring
> and grow and flourish as best they can, till one, perchance,
> overshadows and destroys the other. If a plant cannot live according
> to its nature, it dies; and so a man.
>
> —HENRY DAVID THOREAU, "Resistance to Civil Government" (1849)

What does it mean for Thoreau to compare society's workings to the op-
erations of "machinery"? According to what logic could he suggest that
debate in a deliberative democracy obeys something like the dynamics of
resource competition that govern forest succession? What does it do to our
conception of belief to say that moral convictions are inscribed in our "natures" in the way that different habits of growth are inscribed in the natures of oaks and chestnuts? What prompted Emerson to suspect Thoreau
had an animal body but no "human soul"?

As we have seen, the idea that moral and biological identity are ineluc-
tably linked—that the human mind is not autonomous of the body—is central to biologism's challenge to the humanist episteme, and a key premise
of antebellum racial discourse. "The intellectual man is inseparable from
the physical man," write the authors of *Types of Mankind*, "and the nature
of the one cannot be altered without a corresponding change in the other."[2]
In the previous chapter we saw how this embodied episteme created a crisis for the ideal of liberal equality at midcentury. The present chapter will
examine a different aspect of the crisis that biologism's embodied account
of the human created for liberal doctrine, a problem symptomatized in

Thoreau's comparison of moral to speciological succession, above. As Thoreau suggests, since he is simply obeying the law of his embodied "nature" when he stands up against slavery, he cannot be held responsible for the actions he takes or their effect on "the machinery of society." If moral character is indeed inseparable from physical character, then human agency is merely an expression of biological forces that are beyond our design or control. Already in Douglass's appeal to instinctive violence we can discern the horizon of this reconceptualization of conscientious action: the biologization of belief transforms rational debate into a scene of existential struggle, in which men (like oxen, horses, snakes, and, Thoreau adds, trees and plants) must "live according to [their] nature" or die.

In this chapter, I examine the ways in which Thoreau's increasingly empirical understanding of nature in the 1850s reshaped his late antislavery thought. Reexamining the shift in Thoreau's style in the 1850s, a shift often described as lurching from the lyricism of his early *Journal* to the ostensibly "dry" objectivity of his late naturalistic writings, I highlight the continuousness of Thoreau's commitment to an embodied conception of the human across this decade, and examine the difficulties this commitment created for his faith in the freedom of moral conscience, the founding principle of his natural law doctrine. The line I will be charting from the early to late *Journal*, and culminating in his essays for John Brown and unfinished manuscripts on seeds and fruits at the end of the decade, tells the story of Thoreau's sustained investigation of the phenomenon of environmental influence—of the plastic responsivity of the human body and mind to their physical surroundings. As I will argue, if Thoreau's conception of nature's moral influence is at first nearly indistinguishable from Emerson's depiction of nature as a moral text written in physical ciphers, it nonetheless progressively evolved into something markedly different: an idiosyncratic theory of environmental adaptation and speciological development that put Thoreau in conversation with the most controversial debate within antebellum racial science in his final years.

At its broadest, then, my claim is that we have not yet fully reckoned with Thoreau's embodied conception of the human and the effects that his late ecologism had on the liberal antislavery politics we habitually ascribe to him. Critical interest in Thoreau's empiricism has blossomed in the last three decades in the wake of groundbreaking studies by Sharon Cameron, Lawrence Buell, and Laura Dassow Walls, who taught us to recognize the philosophical import of Thoreau's long-disregarded late naturalistic writings.[3] Dispelling the notion that Thoreau's "dry" empiricism signaled his declining artistic powers and withdrawal from social activism, these critics, and those who have followed them, celebrate the late work as evidence of Thoreau's intellectual maturation from Transcendental idealist to ecological materialist.[4] Lawrence Buell memorably charts this as a progression "from homocentrism to biocentrism," arguing that Thoreau gradually learned to prioritize "nature's interest over the human interest" in his study of natural phenomena.[5] On this revised view, the increasing facticity of Thoreau's writing in the late 1850s no longer appears as a renunciation of social activism but instead indicates the redirection of his concerns from the "homocentrism" of self-culture and antislavery reform to the "biocentrism" of environmentalist advocacy.[6]

Below I retrace Thoreau's intellectual development in the 1850s in order to highlight an aspect of his thought overlooked in this account of his environmentalist politics: the consanguinity, in antebellum science, of ecological and racial theory. As Richard Schneider observes, in the mid–nineteenth century the study of what we now call ecology was synonymous with the study of human ecology—of human origins, racial difference, and what was then widely assumed to be the teleological progress of civilization.[7] Indeed, readers of the last chapter will recall that in eighteenth- and nineteenth-century natural history, "environmentalism" refers to the idea, central to monogenist racial theory, that human and other species change in response to physical and cultural agents in their environments—a key premise of monogenist racial theory. In this first heyday of racial scientific controversy, even the driest ecological research—a study, for instance, on the varying girth of Galapagos finch beaks or on the mechanisms of seed dispersal—was rife with consequences for the racial politics by proxy unfolding in the pages of midcentury science.

The close affiliation of ecological and racial theory suggests that our accounts of Thoreau's late politics may need to be readjusted. For not only does it indicate that we may be overlooking the racialist implications of Thoreau's ecological vision, but moreover it suggests that our representations of ecologism as a correction to homocentrism may be misleading. The conjunction of ecology and racial science renders the epistemological distinction between nature's interest and human interest untenable: it collapses what Dipesh Chakrabarty has dubbed the "age-old humanist distinction between human history and natural history."[8] And therefore when we describe Thoreau's late naturalism as an implicit renunciation of his earlier anthropological concerns—expressing "a passion for nature divorced from social meaning" or illustrating his mature interest in "much vaster cycles of time than those generated by the American political system"—we risk reasserting a distinction between natural and political life that Thoreau's ecological outlook, as I shall be reading it, energetically works to dismantle.[9]

In addition to providing a more complete picture of Thoreau's late antislavery politics, acknowledging the racial implications of his ecologism also amends this picture by underscoring the proto-posthumanism of his late politics. In *The Politics of Nature,* Bruno Latour spells out the distinction between an environmentalist politics that aims to renaturalize human life and preserve nature from human encroachment, and an outlook (what I am calling posthumanism, and Latour calls "political ecology") that begins from the nonhumanist assumption of humanity's naturalness.[10] There is nothing intrinsically redemptive in this latter synthesis: by contrast to what is sometimes presented as environmentalism's romantic aspiration to overcome human alienation and reunite with nature, posthumanism's sense of the always-already imbrication of social and natural processes is not ethical but ontological. Bearing this distinction in mind, I explore how, in addition to his environmentalist appeals to preserve wildness in both our exterior and interior landscapes, Thoreau's late work also elaborates a speculative theory of embodiment that attenuates his political commitments to liberal individualism and conscientious action. If Thoreau's late naturalistic research lent support to monogenist theory and thus bolstered his longstanding antislavery views, it also profoundly reorganized his theory of antislavery activism by remapping political reform onto the vast and diffuse populational, multigenerational, and not-quite-voluntary mechanisms of evolutionary change.

Against Agassiz: Thoreau's Development in Context

The story of Thoreau's evolution from social to environmental activist hinges upon the *Journal,* and the transformation it records as Thoreau's observational methods grew progressively less Transcendentalist and more empiricist over the course of the 1850s. The story I have to tell about Thoreau's development from individualism to posthumanism via environmental racial theory also begins with the renovation of his observational practice in the *Journal,* which I propose to characterize somewhat differently. For while I am fully persuaded that the *Journal* demonstrates Thoreau's gradual renunciation of Emerson's mode of reading nature as a symbolic text, I would like to suggest that it should also be read as registering his increasing resistance to another towering figure of antebellum natural philosophy, Louis Agassiz. Readers of the prior chapter will recall that Agassiz was a featured contributor to *Types of Mankind;* he was also, in the late 1840s and 1850s, a looming presence in Thoreau's larger social circle: the celebrated head of Harvard's brand-new Lawrence Scientific School, a driving force behind the professionalization of American science and the chief architect of the theory of "special creation," which upholds the immutability of species and rejects the notion that races develop in response to their environments. When read in light of Thoreau's opposition to Agassizian science, the *Journal* begins to appear as a more consistently empirical project. As I shall argue below, even in its "poetic" mode of the early 1850s, the *Journal* demonstrates Thoreau's deliberate investigation, *pace* Agassiz, into nature's power to materially influence and thereby plastically transform life.

Louis Agassiz arrived in Boston in 1846 during the second year of Thoreau's residence at Walden Pond. He had been invited to give the prestigious Lowell Institute lectures in Boston and planned to spend two years touring the New World; as it happens, he never left. The buoyant Swiss naturalist so impressed American audiences with his encyclopedic knowledge and dynamic showmanship that his celebrity was soon being compared to Jenny Lind's, and by the end of 1846 Agassiz was offered a professorship at the head of Harvard's brand-new Lawrence Scientific School, slated to open in 1847.[11] The creation of the Lawrence School indexes the rising prominence of natural science in antebellum America. When Thoreau had attended Harvard in the mid-1830s, scientific study, such as it was, was an afterthought to the classical education on offer.[12] But the appointment of Agassiz to helm this new school is also telling in its own right. For as it was initially conceived, the Lawrence School was designed to offer instruction in practical sciences that would directly support "the pursuit of commerce, manufactures, and the mechanic arts."[13] After Agassiz's spectacular popular success in 1846, however, the Lawrence School's major donor, cotton manufacturer Abbot Lawrence, was so captivated that he decided to pursue Agassiz, a theoretical scientist, for the school's top post. Agassiz's appointment thus gave the Lawrence School a newly theoretical mandate, attesting to the rising cachet of science not just as an applied practice but also as an episteme.

At Harvard, Agassiz consolidated this cultural shift by tirelessly working to institutionalize and professionalize American science. In 1847, he founded the American Association for the Advancement of Science (of which Thoreau soon became a member), and in 1853 he began to lay plans for opening the nation's first museum of natural history. That same year he announced his intention to bring out the first comprehensive survey of North American natural history, soliciting subscriptions among his influential friends, who by this point included Senator Charles Sumner, Henry Wadsworth Longfellow, Ralph Waldo Emerson, Oliver Wendell Holmes Sr., and James Russell Lowell. But perhaps Agassiz's most profound influence on American science consists of his teaching: Agassiz trained the first generation of professional scientists in America. When he arrived in the United States, there was not a single domestic institution equipped to educate natural historians; by the end of the century, Agassiz's former student William James would observe, "there is hardly one now of the American naturalists of my generation whom Agassiz did not train."[14]

From his immensely influential position, Agassiz propagated a version of natural history organized on the theory of special creation.[15] His research on glaciers in the 1830s, before his emigration to the United States, yielded the breakthrough hypothesis that the earth has undergone a number of ice ages, each of which caused a mass extinction event. From this insight, Agassiz developed his theory of special creation, arguing that God serially scrubs the earth clean with glaciers in order to repopulate the earth with more advanced and complex versions of the prior world's species. This theory of speciological change allowed Agassiz to account for a fossil record that kept turning up extinct species that nonetheless bore striking resemblances to extant species without requiring him to conclude that such fossils indicate that species are inherently changeful. Instead, the theory of special creation holds that only God has the power to change nature: in his apparently growing wisdom, God periodically revises species, but species themselves are static, undergoing no physical change between ice ages and remaining fixed in the geographical place to which God assigned them. On this theory, then, the resemblance between fossil species and present-day species is strictly typological: these species are not materially related, Agassiz asserted, but rather represent sequential iterations—an early and a later, superior draft—of a single divine thought. Agassiz thus roundly rejected the "developmental hypothesis" advanced by men like Jean-Baptiste Lamarck, Étienne Geoffroy Saint-Hilaire, and Robert Chambers. To the contrary, he argued that "there is nothing in [organized beings] which depends in the slightest degree upon the nature or the influence of the physical conditions in which they live."[16] Such physical "agents have never been observed to produce anything new, or to call into existence anything that did not exist before," he maintains, concluding (in a line that might have made the early Emerson proud) that "the whole Creation is the *expression of a thought*, and not the *product of physical agents*."[17] Like stop-motion animation, Agassiz's world only appears to move. God, and not change, is the author of the world that we see, and this syntactical world presents us with a "vast picture in which each animal, each plant, each group, each class, has its place, and from which nothing could be removed without destroying the proper meaning of the whole."[18]

From their first contact, it was clear that Agassiz's scientific premises and methods were not Thoreau's. In 1847, while he was still living at Walden Pond, Thoreau received an invitation to contribute birds to Agassiz's North American collection. Collecting and classifying specimens was a cornerstone of Agassiz's scientific method. Since he did not believe that species are influenced by their environments, he saw no value in studying species *in situ*; instead, he sought to comprehend the divine "thought" of creation by collecting as many extant species as possible and organizing these specimens into typological groupings—dividing them into the "four great branches of the animal kingdom" (Radiata, Mollusks, Articulata, Vertebrata), and then ordering them within these branches according to "their superiority or inferiority in regard to others."[19] In 1847, Thoreau had not yet begun to study natural history in earnest; however, he was already convinced of the importance of studying life in context. In response to Agassiz's request for bird specimens, he wrote of his "squeamishness on the score of robbing [bird] nests" and suggested that there was, in any case, a wider variety of birds to be found near Harvard, since he had "noticed that in an open country where there are but few trees, there are more attractions for many species of birds than in a wooded one."[20] Thoreau's distaste for killing life in the name of studying it (he signs off, "Trusting that you will feather your own nest comfortably without stripping those of the birds quite bare") was thus not only an ethical position. For Thoreau, any worthwhile study of North American birds must not only be able to identify different species but must, more importantly, be able to describe their distinctive ways of being—to understand how birds interact with their habitats and how habitat change (for instance, Cambridge's deforestation) might induce populational migration (attracting more birds to Agassiz's suburban campus than to Thoreau's woods). It is, after all, not the shape but the *life* of the body that intrigues us.

Already in this brief first encounter, it's clear that Thoreau's interest in the lived interaction between organisms and their environments sets his approach to the study of nature apart from Agassiz's. Laura Dassow Walls describes this difference as a fault line that divides the field of romantic science more broadly. As she argues, early nineteenth-century science was dominated by two competing attitudes toward local particularity. On one side were the "rational holists" (including Emerson and Agassiz) who viewed nature's diversity as the expression of an anterior ordering principle that is itself immaterial—law, spirit, thought, God, the One. Alternatively, "empirical holists" (including naturalists like Thoreau and Alexander von Humboldt) held that nature's diversity is "moved and animated by *internal* forces," that nature unfolds itself through the dynamic interaction of its myriad parts. These differing premises led romantic era science in two different directions: rational holists identified patterns in nature in an effort to elucidate the underlying and eternal ordering principle or moral law manifested therein; empirical holists endeavored to discern nature's interconnectivity—to observe the "infinity of mechanical forces and chemical attractions" through which climate, topography, and vegetation, as well as human economies, languages, and cultures, variously combine and impinge on one another to create the forms of life distinctive to that place.[21] The result of this latter epistemology, Walls suggests, "could be called a kind of situated knowledge," a mapping of local complexity that also traces this local assemblage's connections to natural phenomena farther flung in space and time.[22]

In the late 1840s and early 1850s, Thoreau's pursuit of "situated knowledge" was chiefly driven by his interest in something that Agassiz's science strictly prohibited—the possibility of human development. Agassiz believed that humans *demonstrated* development in the sense that, for instance, the "white race" characterized "man in his highest development," whereas other races embodied various aspects of humankind's "early stages of development."[23] Nonetheless for Agassiz, humans did not possess an intrinsic *capacity* for development; only an act of God—an exterminating ice age and total new creation—could change the nature of the races and advance humankind toward moral and physiological perfection. By his own account, Thoreau came to understand his sojourn at Walden Pond as an effort to prove the opposite hypothesis: that humans are indeed impressible, that "physical agents" in our environments can so alter our moral natures that we might come to "live with the license of a higher order of beings."[24] Thus though he may have originally conceived of his move to Walden as an experiment in removal—a demonstration of the freedom afforded by renouncing one's social environment—by the end of revising *Walden* in 1854, Thoreau had come to frame it as an experiment in self-transformation, embracing (as William Rossi persuasively documents) a transmutationist theory of evolution that allows him to conclude that "there is an incessant influx of novelty into the world."[25] If we would only go out into nature and open ourselves up to its creative force, we might find that these are "but the spring months in the life of the race," he warrants.[26] In

"Walking," an essay he first delivered in 1851, while he was still revising *Walden*, Thoreau formulates this thought in the form of an overtly anti-Agassizian credo: "I believe that climate does thus react on man—as there is something in the mountain air that feeds the spirit and inspires. Will not man grow to greater perfection intellectually as well as physically under these influences?"[27]

But the site of Thoreau's most rigorous and sustained experiment in environmental self-cultivation is the journal that he turned into a laboratory of situated empiricism in 1850. In November, Thoreau began to write in his journal every day. From that point forward the *Journal* became the instrument of a *practice*—what Walls describes as "a tool for seeing."[28] Thoreau's entries in this period demonstrate his ambition not only to record observations of flora and fauna around Concord but, moreover, to refine his capacity for perception—to discover how his own life is environed and, through this effort of attention, to thereby make himself more receptive to the influence of this environment. "Why should just these sights and sounds accompany our life?" he wonders in an entry for April 18, 1852, which serves as a kind of mission statement for this new *Journal* project:

> Why should I hear the chattering of blackbirds, why smell the skunk each year? I would fain explore the mysterious relation between myself and these things. I would at least know what these things unavoidably are—make a chart of our life—know how its shores trend—that butterflies reappear & when—know why just this circle of creatures completes the world. Can I not by expectation affect the revolutions of nature, make a day to bring forth something new?
>
> As Cawley loved a garden, so I a forest. Observe all kinds of coincidences—as what kinds of birds come with what flowers.

Fascinated by nature's "coincidences" (such as "what kinds of birds come with what flowers"), Thoreau frames his *Journal* project as an effort to map the various elements of his environment so that he might "explore the mysterious relation between myself and these things." What he wants to assemble, then, is not simply an Agassizian survey that will index all of the species that appear in Concord through the cycle of a year. For in addition to being able to list "what these things unavoidably are," Thoreau hopes to make "a chart of our life"—to identify the material relations *between* these myriad phenomena and his lived experience so as to understand how "just these sights and sounds" produce just this kind of life. Moreover, Thoreau hopes that by studying this interrelation he can transform it—can "make a day to bring forth something new." His project is thus not simply documentary but creative: it is not only knowledge but also development he is after.

In her still peerless analysis of the *Journal*, Sharon Cameron highlights how this passage signals Thoreau's break from the symbolic analytic of nature he had learned from Emerson, and which he employs so frequently in *Walden*. In his Emersonian mode, Thoreau "reads" natural phenomena as parables that are morally edifying, but here, Cameron argues, Thoreau's natural phenomena "evade morals or interpretations." For, as she explains, "morals are fixed" and universal whereas the natural phenomena Thoreau mentions here are "fugitive" and particular—historical rather than exemplary, desultory instants and not instantiations of a transcendent moral order. Indeed, Thoreau even suggests that this nature is unfinished, that it is still capable of bringing forth "something new." Accordingly, Cameron concludes that "the sustained documentation of the *Journal* [is] the strategy for writing about nature that resists being symbolic": convinced that this world is still in the making, the *Journal* sets out to record natural phenomena without mining them for timeless moral truths.[29]

While I share Cameron's sense that this passage indicates Thoreau's conversion to an analytic of "nature that resists being symbolic," I want to suggest that this change nonetheless did not put an end to his conviction that nature is morally edifying. When Cameron writes that the *Journal* is satisfied "by the very act of observing contrasts, disassociated from story, progression, from anything at all"—or again, when Buell suggests that the *Journal* tracks Thoreau's progress "from homocentrism to biocentrism"— we are tempted to conclude that nature, in the *Journal*, is wholly indifferent to human meaning.[30] But if nature is not a divine text—a message for humans ciphered in bark and feathers—this need not mean that it therefore bears no relation to human thought. Throwing aside hermeneutics, Thoreau's *Journal* proceeds on the understanding that the material environment *conditions* Thoreau's perception of it. In other words, I suggest that the admittedly desultory notes that these entries collect—their apparently haphazard shifts between observations on the weather, flora and fauna, and the thoughts or reflections that these spring in Thoreau—will only seem to be a record of "relentless discontinuousness" if we discount what I take to be the *Journal*'s founding premise: that the various natural and mental phenomena it registers are materially interconnected.[31]

On my reading, Thoreau's early *Journal* sets out to study the sensuous relations between his mind and nature, determined to identify the as-yet "mysterious" mutuality through which "just this circle of creatures completes" or convokes his thought of the world. The contours of this argument will be easier to comprehend by way of example. In his journal entry for July 21, 1851, Thoreau reports,

> When I am against this bare promontory of a huckleberry hill, then forsooth my thoughts will expand. Is it some influence as a vapor which exhales from the ground, or something in the gales which blow there, or in all things there brought together agreeably to my spirit? The walls must not be too high . . . the trees must not be too numerous nor the hills too near bounding the view.[32]

Here Thoreau describes an experience of what we might call inspiration atop a huckleberry hill. However, instead of relaying the content of his dilated thoughts, as we might expect, Thoreau is strictly interested in the physical circumstances surrounding their occurrence. Thus he takes note of the precise arrangement of walls (not too high), trees (not too numerous), and hills (not too near) in an effort to account for the fact that just *this* composition of objects has the power to cause his thoughts to spontaneously "expand." This subjective experience is the result of "some influence," he proposes, and if the mechanism at work is more complicated than the miasmic local vapor he first suspects, it nonetheless retains for him all the predictability and reproducibility of a physiological reflex: "When I am against this bare promontory . . . my thoughts *will* expand." However ephemeral or ethereal it may seem, this experience of mental illumination is, for Thoreau, a legibly material and embodied phenomenon.

This moment echoes others in the *Journal*, which doggedly tracks the movements of Thoreau's thoughts of nature. We can see this, for instance, in Thoreau's fascination with the correlation between the character of his thoughts and the seasons in which they arrive. For Thoreau, winter had a kind of incubating effect, its emptiness bringing his thoughts to fruition: "The winter was made to concentrate and harden and mature the kernel of [man's] brain, to give tone and firmness and consistency to his thought," he writes. "Then is the great harvest of the year, the harvest of thought."[33] And if "winter with its inwardness" of blank days causes thoughts to take final shape, spring is, for Thoreau, the season of new freshets of inspiration.[34] "When the frost comes out of the ground, there is a corresponding thawing of the man," he reports.[35] It would be easy to mistake these observations for analogies; however, Thoreau repeatedly indicates that the relation he means to invoke is not comparative but causal. Thus, for instance, when he observes that "the distant view of the open flooded Sudbury meadows, all dark blue, surrounded by a landscape of white snow, gave an impulse to the dormant sap in my veins," we are at first tempted to imagine that his

feeling of revival manifests as a kind of mystical sympathy with the re-
awakening earth in this early spring thaw. But the entry goes on to explain that his quickening pulse is more specifically the result of
anticipation: offering the first "placid reflecting water" to be seen since the
ponds and rivers froze over months earlier, the flooded meadows direct his
gaze upward to the sky, where he expects, on the "promise of the morrow,"
to see the arrival of new avian life (birds come to fish those newly reopened
waters). The flooded spring meadows thus produce a stirring in Thoreau
because they indicate the return of activity after a long dull winter. "I must
be on the lookout now for the gulls and the ducks," he eagerly concludes;
"this is the sap of which I make my sugar after the frosty nights."[36] Reflections like these help to bring the *Journal* into focus as an instrument for
studying the sensuous and affective relations by which natural phenomena incite physiological responses and excite mental phenomena. By faith-
fully documenting these coincidences, the *Journal* enables Thoreau to
observe himself observing nature. In the retrospect that it provides, he can
scrutinize his experience for clues to the specific mechanisms by which
"climate does thus react on man."

It is therefore not only the mutability of natural phenomena that marks
the *Journal*'s departure from Emerson's and Agassiz's static naturalism;
Thoreau's heresy also inheres in his embodied conception of mind. Indeed,
as Branka Arsić observes, Thoreau's ambition to think "the origin of
thought . . . outside of the self" presumes a recursive relationality between
mind and world that is at odds with the image of a "self-posited reflexive
mind representing the external and material world." The *Journal* practices
an empiricism that begins from the assumption that the mind is not autonomous but rather inextricable from the external and material world
it perceives—not mystically fused in some "vague and dubious quasi-
ecological" way but ordinarily and unavoidably immersed by virtue of its
embodiment and ongoing, sensuous impressibility.[37] On this reading, then,
what changed as Thoreau's conception of nature became progressively less
Transcendentalist and more empiricist in the 1850s is not his sense *that* nature is morally instructive but his sense of *how* this edification takes place.
If, for Emerson and Agassiz, nature's order is symbolic (a catechism of law
in rocks and stones and trees), in Thoreau's *Journal* nature increasingly appears as a shifting array of physical agents that work us over, impressing
us sensuously and materially impinging on our minds through mechanisms
Thoreau was determined to discover.[38]

This intermediation of mind and environment makes for an unusual scientific practice: Thoreau understands his perceptual experience to be a

facet of the material phenomenon he is observing. Thus while Agassiz was training up the first generation of American scientists in the methods of strict objectivity (a mode of seeing Walls describes as a "crystalline purity . . . emptied of self"), Thoreau was developing an experimentally meta-observational practice that would not have passed muster at the Lawrence Scientific School.[39] As he would protest, however, his own method was arguably more rigorously empirical than the alternative. Thus, in a memorable journal entry for Christmas Day, 1851, he complains:

> I witness a beauty in the form or coloring of the clouds which
> addresses itself to my imagination, for which you account scientifically
> to my understanding, but do not so account to my imagination. . . .
> You tell me it is a mass of vapor which absorbs all other rays and
> reflects the red, but that is nothing to the purpose, for this red vision
> excites me, stirs my blood, makes my thoughts flow, and I have new
> and indescribable fancies, and you have not touched the secret of the
> influence.[40]

Lamenting the poverty of conventional science, Thoreau calls for an expanded practice that would take into account the whole phenomenon of sunset—both the observable light *and* the sensuous effects of that light on its observer. "This red vision excites me, stirs my blood, makes my thought flow," he insists, pointing to the fact that this light has not only passed through the vaporous body of a cloud, but also through the medium of his own body, striking his eye and exciting his pulse and mind. Although it would be another thirty years before the invention of an instrument to measure changes in blood pressure, and even longer before the invention of a means to measure blood flow to the brain, Thoreau knows these as-yet-unmeasurable physiological phenomena to be materially real nevertheless, and he insists that they must be counted among the empirical phenomena that compose the multidimensional event we call "sunset."

On this reading, then, when Thoreau suggests that science is in need of a poetic supplement, he is not voicing the commonplace romantic assertion that poetry has access to a higher moral truth to which empiricism's prosaically earthbound materialism is blind. For Thoreau, "poetry" refers to experience—the same authority to which empiricism is, ostensibly, committed. Thus when he despairs at the deficiency of an "objective" science that purges subjective experience from its frame of reference, he is not exposing the inherent limitation of empirical knowledge so much as he is accusing conventional science of failing to live up to its empiricist creed. "There is no such thing as a pure *objective* observation," Thoreau protests, since "the sum of what the writer of whatever class has to report is simply some human experience."[41] A truly materialist empiricism must therefore acknowledge the mediating presence of the observer's subjectivity. Indeed, he suggests that insofar as "objective" science fails to incorporate human perception within the frame of the natural world it scrutinizes, it not only lies about the empirical conditions of its operation but moreover condemns its inquiries to inconsequence. For by expunging the observer from the scene of observation, science precludes itself from examining what must be, tautologically, the most interesting facet of any natural phenomenon: its human interest. Thus Thoreau objects, "I think that the man of science makes this mistake . . . that you should coolly give your chief attention to the phenomenon which excites you as something independent of you, and not as something as it is related to you. The important fact is its effect on me. . . . The point of interest is somewhere *between* me and them (i.e., the objects)."[42] There is, in other words, no such thing as intrinsic significance: we study that which excites us, and facts are only ever facts *for* someone.

But if it is thus a phenomenological rather than a poetic correction to science that Thoreau envisions, poiesis remains, in a different sense, the central concern of his alternative empiricism. As he insists, the aim of observation is not simply to document a fact but to register its effect on us in the event of perception. In this subjective science, the "poetry" or inventiveness of Thoreau's descriptions stems from the creativity of the perceptual encounter itself—watching a sunset generates a new experience in him. Hence he insists, "After all the truest description & that by which another living man can most readily recognize a flower—is the unmeasured [?] & elegant one which the sight of it inspires—No scientific description will supply the want of this though you should count & measure & analyse every atom that seems to compose it."[43] What may seem like the inventiveness of Thoreau's "poetic" descriptions of nature—their "unmeasured" embellishments, their interest in the effect and inspiration that natural objects can excite, and not simply in their measurable "atoms"—is in fact an insistence on the documentary. Our relations themselves are creative, sensuously, physiologically, and mentally transformative, and it is this— the poiesis of perception—that Thoreau's prose attempts to get down. "A true description growing out of the perception & appreciation of [a fact]—is itself a new fact . . . indicating [its] highest quality . . . the relation to man."[44] The world invents and reinvents Thoreau, and the poetry of the *Journal* is just another kind of geological record the world leaves.

This therefore suggests that if Thoreau's reflexive science anticipates late twentieth-century critiques of scientific positivism—if, like Bruno Latour or Karen Barad, Thoreau insists that scientific knowledge is subjectively and culturally mediated—his science also points up a connection between positivism and racialist ideology. Thoreau's situated or relational scientific practice stems from his sense that bodies, minds, and even landscapes are *alive*, processual, susceptible to development: perception is an embodied event, and the viewer (at least) is altered by these encounters. His science therefore does not propose to tell us what an object *is* but, rather, how it *moves* us; it is the calculus to positivism's algebra, a science not of identity but of change. As such, Thoreau's critique of positivism is also a critique of racialism's essentialist view of the body. From the perspective of his lively science of a world in flux, the positivism of biological identity is untenable. Like Agassiz's science of still specimens and fixed orders, racialism's nomenclatural grid of human difference must inexorably be belied by the slow flow of embodied change.[45]

In fact, by the mid-1850s, Thoreau's accumulating *Journal* record had led him to expand his intuitions of development into a nascent theory of speciological change. In 1856, on a visit to Horace Greeley's farm in New York, Thoreau described to Greeley his hypothesis that plant species do in fact migrate and colonize new territories through the agency of seeds, which are variously dispersed by wind, water, and animals.[46] Although the mobility of plants may be a phenomenon that seems wholly unrelated to the question of human development and racial difference, to midcentury naturalists this connection, on the contrary, went without saying. Information regarding the (im)mobility or (im)mutability of plant and animal species was universally understood "to throw light," as Agassiz affirms, "upon the very origin of the differences existing among men."[47]

Thoreau's effort to substantiate his theory of speciological development presented him, however, with a new problem of scale. For whereas he could hope to observe his own experiences of natural transformation, the processes of seed dissemination and populational succession that now occupy him are phenomena that unfold at temporal and geographical scales not directly available to human experience. The mechanisms by which this kind of natural change is accomplished are at once too small—too dispersed and incremental—and too large—too attenuated in space and time—to register in our attention without the aid of careful, longitudinal records. It is therefore not coincidentally around the time of Thoreau's disclosure to Greeley that his *Journal* starts to become less consistently self-reflexive, focusing less and less on his perceptual experience as he becomes progressively more intent on systematically documenting the incremental mechanisms of populational change.

I am therefore suggesting what we have taken to be the newly "empirical" or "scientific" nature of Thoreau's late *Journal* might also, and maybe
even more accurately, be described as its newly racialist imaginary. The
early *Journal* was already empirical—indeed, William James might say,
"radically" so—and its idiosyncratic empiricism grew out of Thoreau's
desire to investigate the possible natural mechanisms of individual development. What changes in Thoreau's final years is his determination to
investigate the mechanisms of natural development at the level of biological populations—a scalar shift that turns his attention from the drama of
personal reform to the epic sweep of speciological change. But if this means
that his subjective experience now takes a backseat to more "objective"
methods, it should be clear that Thoreau's late science remained ripe with
human interest and even political controversy.

On the Dispersion of Species: Race in Thoreau's Population Studies

In 1853, Thoreau grieved privately to his *Journal* that he might never find
an audience for his natural historical research. He had recently received a
survey from Agassiz's American Association for the Advancement of Science, to which he felt unable to respond frankly: "I felt that it would be to
make myself the laughing stock of the scientific community to describe or
attempt to describe to them that branch of science which specially interests me, inasmuch as they do not believe in a science which deals with the
higher law. . . . How absurd that, though I probably stand as near to nature as any of them, and am by constitution as good an observer as most,
yet a true account of my relation to nature should excite their ridicule
only."[48] If Thoreau's *Journal* remained a largely private enterprise in the
early 1850s, this may be because his project presumed what Agassiz's influential science strictly precluded: that environmental agents impinge on
the body, and that individuals, races, and species are susceptible to change.
This theory of natural development at the heart of the *Journal* and the
unorthodox observational methods Thoreau developed to test it put Thoreau so far outside of the scientific mainstream Agassiz was then consoli-
dating around himself that Thoreau did not dare to share it. A few years
later, however, as he began to pursue these mechanisms at scale—tracking
not his own personal development but the mechanisms of dispersion, succession, and adaptation in plant populations over time—Thoreau's research
became more legible (if still unpalatable to Agassizians) as a direct contribution to mainstream monogenist science.

In this section I suggest that two events in the latter half of the 1850s were instrumental in spurring Thoreau to brave ridicule by preparing his naturalistic research for publication. The first of these was the publication, in 1857, of the long-anticipated first volume of Agassiz's projected masterwork, *Contributions to the Natural History of the United States of America*, which contains Agassiz's definitive statement of the theory of special creation, "An Essay on Classification." The second event was the publication, in late 1859, of Darwin's *On the Origin of Species*, which sparked a long season of controversy in Boston scientific circles and marked the beginning of the end of Agassiz's preeminence. As I shall argue, reading Thoreau's late naturalistic writings in light of these catalytic events draws out their polemical investment not only in ecological systematicity and the politics of environmental protection, but in human ecology and the politics of human difference on the eve of the Civil War.

Despite dining with Agassiz at Emerson's in 1857, the year *Contributions* came out, Thoreau did not get around to reading Agassiz's book until the following year. But if Thoreau was not overly eager to read the long-anticipated volume, it nonetheless seems to have had a major effect on him. As Robert Richardson reports, upon finishing *Contributions* Thoreau commenced a "major reading campaign in zoology," for which "Agassiz's volume seems to have been the initiating impulse."[49] At the same time, Thoreau's antagonism toward Agassiz's theory of special creation becomes more palpable in his *Journal*. In March, he objects that "No science does more than arrange what knowledge we have of any class of objects" (a jibe particularly aimed at the typological emphasis of Agassiz's static science).[50] Later that summer, observing toad spawn in a small pool atop Mount Monadnock, Thoreau dryly quips that "Agassiz might say that they originated on the top."[51] Thoreau's account of a trip that Emerson took with Agassiz to the Adirondacks is likewise laced with condescension for both men: apparently Emerson bought a gun, shot a bird for Agassiz's collection, and then proceeded to shoot at bottles for fun. "It sounds rather Cockneyish," Thoreau sniffs. "Think of Emerson shooting a peetweet (with shot) for Agassiz—& cracking an ale bottle (after emptying it) with his rifle at six rods!"[52] Ultimately, however, Thoreau's dissent is most forcefully expressed in the form of counterevidence: as Richardson notes, in the spring of 1859, the *Journal* is particularly "filled with observations on the interconnectedness and interdependence of things in nature."[53] In the fall of that year, Thoreau began the major undertaking of culling his *Journal* notes in order to compose the manuscript that would become *Wild Fruits*.

Wild Fruits can be read as a tacit riposte to Agassiz's *Contributions*. A regionally specific guide to the identification and, above all, *appreciation* of New England plants, *Wild Fruits* is the situated antithesis to Agassiz's grand national typology. Thus whereas Agassiz promises to "[bring] together an extensive museum of purely American specimens," magisterially parading the nation's radically diverse fauna before us, Thoreau begins by suggesting that his purpose is to drive us out into nature, to bring us into closer contact with the vegetation immediately surrounding us.[54] "Most of us are still related to our native fields as the navigator to undiscovered islands in the sea," Thoreau observes. "We can any afternoon discover a new fruit there which will surprise us by its beauty or sweetness."[55] Most important, for Thoreau the value of this local knowledge has to do with the transformative moral effect it can have on us. "The value of these wild fruits is not in the mere possession or eating of them, but in the sight and enjoyment of them," he tells us. The child who goes huckleberrying "is introduced into a new world, experiences a new development, though it brings home only a gill of berries in its basket." Thus whereas Agassiz's volume is founded on the understanding that the value of comprehensively studying the immutable order of species is to decipher the vast "thoughts of God" encoded therein, Thoreau's guide is premised on his conviction that it is important to observe these local fruits because "the fruits of New England . . . educate us and fit us to live here." Thoreau promises us not an image of eternal order but an opening onto change: "The value of any experience is measured, of course . . . by the amount of development we get out of it." The chief interest of the species he will proceed to list is not the "finite" place they occupy in an orderly cosmos unmoved by physical forces, but the dynamic "part they play in our education."[56]

But it is not only humans who develop in Thoreau's manuscript. In *Wild Fruits's* standout essay, "Wild Apples," which Thoreau first delivered as a lecture in February 1860 (a month after perusing Darwin), Thoreau describes the development of a new variety of apple, explaining how an imported varietal near him has, through generations of migration and environmental adaptation, become feral and self-propagating, its flesh transformed into "the choicest of all its kind."[57] The striking thing about this little fable of re-wilding is just how mechanically specific it is. This is, as David Robinson notes, "a very Darwinian narrative" of speciation, highlighting how this new variety has arisen through the agencies of dissemination (its seed has strayed the orchard into unprotected new fields) and local pressure (aggressive browsing by its "bovine foes" has forced it to adapt new "tactics" for survival).[58] Thus if Thoreau's prefatory promise of "development" to the reader who would stray into her "native fields" seems hazily unspecific, the development this apple undergoes by its wandering (or what *Walden* might call its "extravagance") is unmistakably evolutionary, involving a physiological and characterological transformation. Indeed, it is no accident that Thoreau's word for this fruit's peculiar flavor is "racy," an adjective he uses three times in this essay but apparently nowhere else in his corpus.[59] While ostensibly highlighting the fruit's piquant taste, he clearly favors "racy" for its ability to underscore the fruit's distinction as a new breed. For Thoreau, the bracing flavor of this apple's flesh is a speciological trait that is also a kind of moral virtue, expressive of what he will ultimately describe as its uniquely American character. This is, he suggests, "*our* wild apple": a transplanted and once-colonized fruit that "strayed into the woods from the cultivated stock" to assert its independence, annex new territories, and gradually become a "superior" new type. With "Wild Apples," Thoreau brings his critique of Agassiz's science into high relief, underscoring the raciological implications of his theory of environmental adaptation and development.

The other catalytic event that seems to have emboldened Thoreau to publish his naturalistic research was the publication of *Origin of Species*. Thoreau first read *Origin* in January 1860, just five weeks after its publication and one month before he first delivered "Wild Apples" as a lecture. In the ensuing months, Darwin's book became a flashpoint of controversy in Boston scientific circles, particularly between Agassiz and his Harvard colleague Asa Gray. Gray had shared research with Darwin as Darwin was composing *Origins*, and he had even begun to introduce Darwin's ideas on evolution to Boston audiences (possibly including Thoreau) as early as 1858.[60] Between February and April 1860, Agassiz, Gray, and other prominent men of science debated evolution in a series of meetings before the Boston Society of Natural History, the American Academy of Arts and Sciences, and in the pages of the popular and scientific press. Thoreau may have attended one or more of these debates—his *Journal* indicates that he traveled to Boston on the day that at least one of them took place (February 6, 1860). But of course, as we have seen, unlike many in those Boston circles, Thoreau had not been persuaded by Agassiz's speciological theory to begin with; whereas Darwin's thesis struck other midcentury readers with the force of a detonation, Thoreau was already sympathetic to the idea that populations adapt and develop under the influence of their local environments.

What was new to Thoreau, in Darwin's book, was the theory of natural selection. According to this theory, speciation occurs when the natural variation within a species produces an anomalous trait that affords its carrier a competitive advantage, allowing that trait to proliferate down through ensuing generations. As Gray notes in his review of *Origin*, what made Darwin's theory worrisome was its ambivalence on the score of natural selection's progressivism ("Only let us hope that it always works for good," Gray writes). Moreover, Gray anticipated that this theory might be greeted with popular resistance—not only because it rules "the Negro and the Hottentot our blood-relations," but moreover because it puts the human race in "a closer relation" with the "quadrumanous family" (primates), and even ultimately traces "the evolution of the human no less than the lower animal races out of some simple primordial animal."[61] In short, Darwinian monogenism upheld the common origin not just of all humanity but, moreover, of all life.

However, as Darwin himself acknowledged, his theory still suffered from blind spots, and it is here that reading *Origin* may have been particularly productive for Thoreau by helping him to recognize the vital and timely importance of his own seed studies. In his concluding chapter, Darwin observes that "the chief cause of our natural unwillingness to admit that one species has given birth to other and distinct species, is that we are always slow in admitting any great change of which we do not see the intermediate steps."[62] In particular, he confessed, he was as yet unable to demonstrate the "intermediate steps" by which species migrate (as his theory required him to hypothesize) from one region to another:

> Turning to geographical distribution, the difficulties encountered on the theory of descent with modification are grave enough. All the individuals of the same species, and all the species of the same genus, or even higher group, must have descended from common parents; and therefore, in however distant and isolated parts of the world they are now found, they must in the course of successive generations have passed from some one part to the others. We are often wholly unable even to conjecture how this could have been effected. . . . We are as yet profoundly ignorant of the many occasional means of transport.[63]

Thus, as Michael Berger has demonstrated, Thoreau's studies of seed dispersal are not just related to Darwin's work but "directly support one of the weakest links in Darwin's argument for evolution."[64] Whereas Darwin was forced to simply assert that populations have gradually migrated to the "distant and isolated parts of the world [where] they are now found," Thoreau had laboriously observed the "infinitely . . . extensive and regular" system by which plants—which are the most emphatically rooted and thus apparently immobile of all the species—are broadly disseminated by wind, water, and animals.[65] His seed studies were thus poised, as Berger argues, to provide crucial support for Darwin's embattled thesis.

In the fall of 1860, on the heels of a long summer of evolutionary debates, Thoreau delivered his lecture on "The Succession of Forest Trees." Modestly addressing the enigmatic yet common occurrence that when a pine forest is cut down, an oak stand may spring up in the clearing, "Succession" sets out to demonstrate that this phenomenon is the result of the movement of seeds. Thanks to a vast and somewhat haphazard network of environmental mechanisms, Thoreau argues, even the heaviest seeds "will be found to be winged or legged," able to wend their way across vast distances and even seemingly insurmountable topographical barriers without the aid of divine intervention.[66] In the weeks after delivering "Succession," Thoreau threw himself into the task of elaborating this account by beginning work on a book-length manuscript, *The Dispersion of Seeds,* which compiled years of his naturalistic research to offer an even more comprehensive inventory of the mechanisms of seed migration and populational succession.

Thoreau's impressively detailed grasp of interspecies mutualism and environmental dynamism in "Succession" has led contemporary critics to praise this essay's proto-ecological understanding of nature. The essay is much less often read as an argument for racial unity and yet, coming as it did on the heels of months of evolutionary controversy, it would have been clear to Thoreau's audience that his argument for speciological mobility bore directly upon the question of environmental adaptation at the center of the debate between Darwin and Agassiz. Indeed, the fact that "Succession" was the most widely reprinted of all of Thoreau's essays—excerpted in several publications and republished verbatim in three, including Horace Greeley's *New-York Weekly Tribune*—suggests that editors and readers appreciated its germaneness to the headlining questions of evolution and racial difference.[67]

As if to ensure that we recognize the anthropological dimensions of his botanical thesis, Thoreau prefaces his essay with a humorous sketch of the ecology of racial migrations. "Every man is entitled to come to a Cattle-Show, even a transcendentalist," he quips to his audience at the Middlesex Agricultural Fair; "and for my part I am more interested in the men than in the cattle."[68] In the paragraph that follows he describes the pleasure he takes in people-watching:

> I wish to see once more those old familiar faces, whose names I do not
> know, which for me represent the Middlesex country, and come as
> near being indigenous to the soil as a white man can. . . . It is true,
> there are some queer specimens of humanity attracted to our festival,
> but all are welcome. I am pretty sure to meet once more that fellow . . .
> who prefers a crooked stick for a cane; perfectly useless, you would say,
> only *bizarre*. . . . He brings that much indulged bit of the country with
> him, from some town's end or other, and introduces it to Concord
> groves.

As Walls notes, readers today tend to take these prefatory remarks on the fair as "witticisms" and "throwaway literary asides."[69] Against that assumption, Walls observes that they also situate Thoreau as a speaker, exploding "the illusion of an invisible omniscient 'I.'"[70] But in addition to resisting the pretense of objectivity, these humorous remarks also cagily point to the connection between nonhuman and human ecologies. Reminding us that humanity is also a subject of the naturalist's scrutiny, Thoreau anticipates the essay's analysis of populational mobility and secondary growth among tree species by noting that the typologically "familiar" population of Middlesex County is nonetheless not original to this place but rather has migrated and adapted to this "country," becoming "as near being indigenous to the soil as a white man can." He further suggests that the features of this local race are not fixed, taking note of how one or two "queer specimens of humanity," recently arrived from elsewhere, are even now introducing "bizarre" new variations "to the Concord groves." Here again, Thoreau's horticultural pun ("bizarre" being a term for splashy, variegated varietals of flower) and his metaphorical substitution of Concord's "groves" for its society both insist that the ecology he is about to describe applies interchangeably to oak stands, cattlekind, and the human race.[71]

When read in the context of Agassiz's and Darwin's landmark midcentury publications, the racial import of Thoreau's late naturalistic writings is more visible. But if there is still any question about the racialism implicit in Thoreau's studies of dissemination, Thoreau's "Indian Notebooks" help us to see that Thoreau explicitly understood the migration of seeds and migration of races to be conceptually of a piece. Thoreau's second-largest undertaking in this decade, after the *Journal*, the "Indian Notebooks" consist of twelve commonplace books that together comprise what Richard Fleck calls "the largest body of knowledge on American Indian cultures in the nineteenth century."[72] In these books, Thoreau transcribed passages from his wide-ranging reading of travelogues, missionary reports, land surveys, and ethnologies relating to the indigenous peoples of North America, and their record indicates that in the late 1850s he also began to compile research on the question of Native American racial origins.[73] Although Thoreau's bibliography on this subject was catholic (he read works of both polygenist and monogenist science), evidence suggests that he was most persuaded by the theory that indigenous Americans did not originate in North America (as polygenists argued) but, rather, migrated to this continent from Asia. Indeed, his transcriptions from polygenist works betray an impish instinct to catch them in moments of conceptual impasse.[74] By contrast, in 1856 Thoreau approvingly transcribed Benjamin Smith Barton's thesis "that the Americans are not, as some writers have supposed, specifically different from the Persians, and other improved nations of Asia," affirming the likelihood of Smith's thesis in his *Journal* the following year, where he observes that "It is most . . . in accordance with the natural phenomena, to suppose that North America was discovered from the northern part of the Eastern Continent, for a study of the range of plants, birds, and quadrupeds points to a connection on that side. . . . Men in their migrations obey in the main the same law."[75] In keeping with this thesis, in the late "Indian Notebooks" Thoreau pursues cross-racial commonalities by reading travelogues not only of North America but also of the Middle East, Greenland, Australia, the East Indies, the Arctic, and several regions of Africa. As he confessed to the *Journal* in 1859, "It is the spirit of humanity—that which animates both so-called savages & civilized nations, working through a man, and not the man expressing himself, that interests us most."[76] Here again, Thoreau's interest in animation—in the migratory and mutational dynamism of life—leads him to reject the typological episteme embraced by Agassiz's science and by racialism's ideology of identity and difference.

Thoreau was thus well aware that his own research on speciological migration and development, published in "Succession" and "Wild Apples," was proposing to contribute to an ecological science that was inseparable from racial theory in his antebellum moment. But if we can therefore discern this work's connection to racial theory, defining their racial *politics* remains a different and far more speculative task. As readers of the prior chapter will remember, monogenist racial theory was deployed in both pro- and antislavery arguments, and in support of both racist and egalitarian views. In analyzing Thoreau's writings, a number of scholars highlight the racial chauvinism and settler colonialism implicit in these (and other) essays' visions of a new "racy" flavor of white transplants who are, like the wild apple or Middlesex farmer, becoming "near indigenous to the soil" of their appropriated home. As these critics note, such a vision effects a double displacement of Native Americans, anticipating their geographical expulsion and cultural appropriation by a "superior" new race of nativized white Americans.[77] On the other hand, critics who have focused on Thoreau's studies of Native Americans—including his anthropological and ethnographic research in the "Indian Notebooks" and his accounts of traveling with Penobscot guides in *The Maine Woods*—suggest that by the late 1850s Thoreau had developed a far more nuanced admiration for Native American cultures, expressing a desire to learn from them that did not amount to a desire to impersonate or displace them.[78]

While holding this line of inquiry open, I would like to propose that Thoreau's engagement with racial science may also have shaped his politics in a very different way. I have been arguing that Thoreau's interest in ecological change is inseparable from his interest in human development and the question of racial history more broadly. I would now suggest that the theory of speciological development—its biologism, contextual mechanisms, and the vastly expanded scale at which it operates—reinflects Thoreau's theory of social reform, as evidenced in the last antislavery essays of his career, written in defense of John Brown. As I shall discuss in the next section, the naturalization of Thoreau's late antislavery thought registers in the way he accounts for conscientious disagreement (which now appears to be a matter of embodied differences) and in his abandonment of immediatism (Thoreau now suggests that moral reform requires generations to unfold). In particular, I suggest that this alteration in Thoreau's thought registers as a problem of attenuated human agency that his late essays introduce. In this regard, Thoreau's late antislavery essays encapsulate both the power and the limitations of the political ecology that emerge out of his final writings.

Weird John Brown: The Revolutionary as Racial Anomaly

Thoreau's last antislavery essays are coeval with his late natural historical manuscripts; between 1859 and 1860 he moved back and forth between his political and ecological writings. In October 1859 Thoreau had just begun to draft *Wild Fruits* when news of John Brown's raid on Harpers Ferry reached Concord.[79] Eleven days later, on October 30, he delivered "A Plea for Captain John Brown" at the Concord Town Hall, reprising his speech twice more that week (once in Boston as a stand-in for Frederick Douglass, who had sailed to England to avoid being arrested in connection with Brown). On December 2, Thoreau delivered a short eulogy for Brown at a memorial service he had organized at Concord. In early January 1860, Thoreau was reading Darwin, and in early February he drew up final proofs of "A Plea" as he prepared to deliver "Wild Apples" for the first time. In the ensuing spring and summer months, as the Darwin-Agassiz debate played out, he chiefly worked on the manuscript of *Wild Fruits*, but he also wrote a substantial second essay, "The Last Days of John Brown," which he sent to be read at a July Fourth memorial service for Brown in North Elba and which was subsequently republished in the *Liberator*. Two months later he delivered "Succession" at the Middlesex County Fair and began to compose *The Dispersion of Seeds*, his most comprehensive case for speciological migration and adaptation.

As a rule, critics have tended to describe these months of Thoreau's life as a time of intellectual bifurcation, characterizing his essays for Brown as a temporary distraction from his main task of composing his late natural historical manuscripts.[80] My claim here is that his thoughts on Brown are better understood as extensions and translations of his naturalistic research, for the theory of change he formulates in *Wild Fruits* and *The Dispersion of Seeds* is the same one that animates the account of political reform he sketches out in his essays on Brown, which envision social change as a process of intergenerational succession that is no less operational and inexorable for being difficult to discern in the moment.

Thoreau's essays in praise of Brown entered a public sphere in which even abolitionists denounced Brown's violent methods and popular consensus held that he was insane. Against the tide of this public opinion, Thoreau's essays not only seek to justify Brown's cause but advance the strikingly counterfactual claim that this would-be revolutionary—thwarted, arrested, and slated to die—has succeeded. To the neighbors who tell him Brown "threw his life away," Thoreau responds: "Such do not know that like the seed is the fruit, and that, in the moral world, when good seed is planted, good fruit is inevitable, and does not depend on our watering and cultivating; that when you plant, or bury, a hero in his field, a crop of heroes is sure to spring up. This is a seed of such force and vitality, that it does not ask our leave to germinate."[81] To justify his faith in Brown's ultimate success, Thoreau leans on the logic of natural succession that he was just then working out in his other manuscripts. His metaphor here frames political change—in this case the proliferation of abolitionist sentiment—as a process that operates through mechanisms akin to those by which the wild apple's new race came about. As he tells us in "Wild Apples," the remarkable thing about that "chance wild fruit" is that its seeds are "hardier" than those of the cultivated stocks from which this apple diverged, able to "plant themselves in distant fields and forests" without the assistance of human tending.[82] That this fruit can germinate "in woods and swamps and by the sides of roads," and even survive the grazing herds of "bovine foes," is evidence of what Darwin would term its natural advantage.[83] This apple is, as Thoreau more colloquially puts it, "good seed"—a natural variant whose anomalousness affords it a higher rate of survival and thereby allows it to propagate a new breed. And this is how Thoreau now proposes to explain why Brown's words and deeds need not fall on sympathetic ground for his beliefs to "germinate": some beliefs have "such force and vitality" that they can withstand our indifference and proliferate among us without our "leave."

According to the more standard view, which holds that morality is a set of positions we consciously assent to, there is something unsettling in this notion that a belief might propagate itself without the aid of our consent. And of course, one might also note that this disconcerting idea that moral truth has its own kind of endemic force is an article of Transcendentalist faith that recurs throughout Thoreau's political writings. "What force has a multitude?," he observes in his 1849 essay, "Resistance to Civil Government. "They only can force me who obey a higher law than I."[84] But if moral truth emboldens those who choose to become its champions, what seems to have changed in this late essay is that here moral truth apparently has the power to move through populations of its own accord. Looked at differently, then, we can see that Thoreau's vision of Brown's propagative power marks a profound shift from an individualistic to a populational conception of morality. That is, whereas in 1849 Thoreau's rhetorical question "What force has a multitude?" was meant to contrast the multitude's physical force with the superior moral power of the conscientious individual, Thoreau's late writings now conflate moral and physical compulsion. Brown's moral force is the same as his propagative capacity; moral force can now be measured by demographic success—by the multitudes that it produces with or without "our leave." Brown has not simply done something heroic; he embodies a superior, heroic race.

And hence, although Thoreau takes comfort in projecting a future race of John Browns, his conflation of moral and raciological identity might well give us pause. The essentialism it implies results in an attenuation of moral agency. This problem becomes clearer in "Wild Apples" when Thoreau reverses his metaphor: if Brown was "good seed," here he suggests that good seeds are heroic individuals. Turning the emergence of the variant wild apple into a parable of human progress, Thoreau writes that among men, too, "only the most persistent and strongest genius defends itself and prevails, sends a tender scion upward at last, and drops its perfect fruit on the ungrateful earth. Poets and philosophers and statesmen thus spring up in the country pastures, and outlast the hosts of unoriginal men."[85] Beyond illustrating how topologically entwined Thoreau's late naturalist and political writings are (they use the same metaphors), we can also notice that in both projects Thoreau is working through the same philosophical problem: how to understand agency within a materialist system. One can, for instance, read this passage as a lesson about the singular importance of the exceptional individual. According to both the "great man" theory of history and the evolutionary theory of development, one heroic specimen—one anomalous individual, one unusually bovine-resistant seedling—has the power to change the course of history (human or natural) going forward. On the other hand, this parable also works to naturalize—to render embodied and involuntary—the heroic individual's contribution. Here greatness is not an accomplishment so much as it is an identity—an embodied "genius" for persistence that allows him to "outlast" his "unoriginal" peers. Indeed, that word "genius," etymologically related as it is to "genus" and "gene" via their shared root in the Latin word for the male spirit of a familial or tribal line, conjures an exceptional character that is specifically raciological—inborn like the wild apple's distinctive hardiness.[86] To praise the virtue of such a man—as, indeed, Thoreau praises the character of the wild apple—is to congratulate the beneficiary of biological luck.

Of course, as the second epigraph to this chapter attests, this is not the first time that Thoreau has suggested that moral character might be determined by one's embodied "nature." However, in the context of his late empirical research, and in this case arriving in the midst of a story about the wild apple's racial speciation, his invocations of natural succession carry a new kind of weight. At this point in Thoreau's career as a naturalist, we can no longer dismiss the biologism of his metaphors as purely rhetorical. Taking these figures seriously therefore also entails acknowledging that the problems of human agency that they introduce are very real. The possibility that we are not responsible for the beliefs that we hold pervades Thoreau's defense of Brown in "A Plea." It lingers, for instance, around Thoreau's suggestion that Brown is a new breed of American: "the most American of us all," he does not typify Americans ("He was too fair a specimen to represent the like of us") but rather instantiates its new type. Thus Thoreau insists that "Brown could not have been tried by a jury of his peers, because his peers do not exist." Instead, he rises "above [his ac-cusers] literally *by a whole body*"—a grim visual pun which transforms Brown's hanging corpse into the measure of not just his moral but also his *corporeal* superiority (a distinction Thoreau underlines in italics and by his insistence that he is speaking "literally"). And by this same embodied logic, in "A Plea" Thoreau argues that Brown's detractors are "half-brutish," suffering from "a difference of constitution, of intelligence, and faith." "They pronounce this man insane, for they know that *they* could never act as he does, as long as they are themselves," he complains, under-scoring the existential nature of this disagreement—they are *constitution-ally* incapable of sympathizing with him; they could not think or act as he does and be "themselves."[87]

This essentialism becomes loudest in Thoreau's second essay for Brown. Written in the spring or summer of 1860, in the midst of the public de-bate over Darwin's challenge to Agassiz, "The Last Days of John Brown" is even more insistent that Brown's critics are not just morally but physi-ologically inferior to him. "The man who does not recognize in Brown's words a wisdom and nobleness," Thoreau submits, is "not willfully but con-stitutionally blind." As he continues,

> I was not surprised that certain of my neighbors spoke of John Brown
> as an ordinary felon, for who are they? They either have much flesh, or
> much office, or much coarseness of some kind. . . . Several of them are
> decidedly pachydermatous. I say it in sorrow, not in anger. How can a
> man behold the light who has no answering inward light? They are
> true to their *sight*, but when they look this way they *see* nothing, they
> are blind. For the children of the light to contend with them is as if
> there should be a contest between eagles and owls. . . . It is not every
> man who can be a Christian, even in a very moderate sense, whatever
> education you give him. It is a matter of constitution and tempera-
> ment, after all. He may have to be born again many times. . . . It is not
> every man who can be a freeman, even.[88]

In deeming his neighbors "pachydermatous," Thoreau recasts the racist trope that Black bodies are insensitive—naturally impervious to heat, over-work, and emotional hardship.[89] Simulating the essentialism, biological chauvinism, and even the dermatological fixation of racist science, Tho-reau finds his neighbors condemned to moral blindness by an insensibility that is congenital ("not willfully but constitutionally" acquired) and phys-iological ("a matter of constitution and temperament, after all"). He even indicates that *Homo pachydermatous* may be another species—benighted "owls" to the diurnal "eagles" who sympathize with Brown—and in doing so he affects the same condescending regret ("I say it in sorrow, not anger") that Nott and Agassiz express when they come to similarly heretical conclusions. At once echoing and indicting Agassiz's patronizing proposition that "the best education to be imparted to the different races" must account for "their primitive difference" by not attempting "to force the peculiarities of our white civilization . . . upon all nations of the world," Thoreau suggests that resistance to the truth of human equality proves that not every white man "can be a Christian . . . whatever education you give him."[90]

But as gratifying as this satirical skewering of polygenism is, its biologism also injects Thoreau's last antislavery essay with a fatalism uncharacteristic of his prior politics. In earlier essays like "Resistance to Civil Government" (1849) and "Slavery in Massachusetts" (1854), Thoreau rails against what he describes as our conscientious enslavement to the slaveholding power, and urges us to "for once and at last serve God . . . by obeying that eternal and only just CONSTITUTION which He, and not any Jefferson or Adams, has written in your being."[91] In these earlier essays, moral redemption is within everyone's reach: their own quaking resolve is the only obstacle standing between them and moral perfection. But by the John Brown essays, the moral "constitution" Thoreau invokes has taken on a fleshy materiality and embodied diversity that makes it operate very differently, so that now moral reform may be beyond my power: "It is not every man who can be a freeman, even." Of course, it is clear that Thoreau does not intend to wholly limit the scope of our moral agency. These essays still press us to overcome our torpidity and live up to the promise of our natures: "If this man's acts and words do not create a revival, it will be the severest possible satire on the acts and words that do. . . . [Brown] has already quickened the feeble pulse of the North, and infused more and more generous blood into her veins and heart."[92] But different, here, is these essays' new sense that we may be working within organic limits, that the "constitution and temperament" that dictate our conscience, though technically still given us by God, may afford us greater or lesser moral insight depending upon the luck of our birth.

But if Thoreau therefore seems to accede to a kind of moral fatalism, his resignation is leavened by his correspondingly redoubled faith that moral progress is nevertheless on its way. Both "A Plea" and "Last Days" conclude by affirming Brown's future redemption, expressing a degree of optimism that is unusual in Thoreau's political writings. In professing this faith, Thoreau invokes a newly capacious sense of political time. When in "Slavery in Massachusetts" his choice was between Jefferson's Constitution or God's, his options were to live within the fallen time of human history or to immediately assent to the timeless order of higher law inscribed in his conscience. Now, however, Thoreau seems to imagine moral reform as a gradual rather than millennial process. Brown himself is a product of history here: "such a man as it takes ages to make, and ages to understand."[93] Likewise, Thoreau now figures Brown's vindication as an outcome that will arise not through our instantaneous moral conversion but by the intergenerational march of succession: as we have seen, Thoreau expects "a new crop of heroes" to spring from Brown's fecund "good seed" and disseminate his legacy to the future. It is thus by turning to the timeline of speciological change that Thoreau can conclude that even though Brown's raid did not incite the hoped-for slave insurrection, it nevertheless engendered "the possibility, in the course of ages, of a revolution."[94] "I foresee a time when the painter will paint [the] scene" of Brown's martyrdom, Thoreau confidently closes "A Plea." "The poet will sing it; the historian record it; and . . . it will be the ornament of some future national gallery, when at least the present form of Slavery shall be no more here."[95]

One possible name for this optimistic patience is passive resistance. This, at least, is the term Wai Chee Dimock invokes to describe what she calls the logic of "slow translation" subtending Thoreau's faith in Brown's eventual success. "Is an action still meaningful if the outcome transpires far beyond the life span of the actor?" she hears Thoreau's essays for Brown asking. "Just how far can deed and consequence be strung out?" As Dimock argues, Thoreau's answer—*really far*—works to expose the fact that our tendency to judge political actions by their immediate results puts a premium on violent acts, whose consequences are "instantly adducible and demonstrable." Against that bias, Thoreau's philosophy of passive resistance challenges us to expand our sense of the scale at which politics happen. In contrast to war's "bluntly truncated" temporal timeframe, the enlarged horizon of passive resistance allows us to discern the operation of far more subtle methods and processes of political change.[96] From this perspective, Dimock suggests, Brown's posthumous agency now becomes visible in the legacy he has "given over to the care of others . . . who will go on to write" about him and catalyze new activism.[97] Under the sign of passive resistance, we may begin to trace the "luxuriance of outcome" that exfoliates from more indirect and minimal political actions like antislavery essays, withheld consent, the "will to disarm," and other acts of nonviolent civil disobedience.[98]

But what led Thoreau to adopt this vastly expanded view of political change? The cascading ramification of minimal events that Dimock observes here describes the thesis of *The Dispersion of Seeds*, which sets out to demonstrate that natural change occurs not by spontaneous generation or the violence of divine apocalypse but by the ongoing operation of myriad minor agencies. This gradualism describes Thoreau's "faith in a seed":

> For many years the daily traveler along these roads—nay, the proprietor himself—does not notice that there are any pines coming up there . . . but at last his heir knows himself to be the possessor of a handsome white-pine lot, long after the wood from which the seed came has disappeared.
>
> We need not be surprised at these results when we consider how persevering Nature is and how much time she has to work in. . . . A great pine wood may drop many millions of seeds in one year, but if only half a dozen of them are conveyed a quarter of a mile and lodge against some fence, and only one of these comes up and grows there, in the course of fifteen or twenty years there will be fifteen or twenty young trees there, and they will begin to make a show and betray their origin.
>
> In this haphazard manner Nature surely creates you a forest at last, though as if it were the last thing she were thinking of. By seemingly feeble and stealthy steps—by a geologic pace—she gets over the greatest distances and accomplishes her greatest results.

Like Dimock, Thoreau suggests that by dilating the scale of our vision we may begin to perceive the "slow translation" of a world that otherwise appears, to our immediate senses, as a fixed order that can only be changed by violent catastrophe. Thus Thoreau explains how the "seemingly feeble" and "haphazard" agency of seeds, breezes, and felicitous fence posts are sufficient to move whole forests, albeit at a "geological pace." Though this process may be too gradual and protracted to witness personally, he insists that it should give us faith that ours is a mutable world: "We find ourselves in a world that is already planted, but is also still being planted as at first."[99]

By calling the philosophy of minor agencies she finds in the Brown essays "passive resistance," Dimock suggests that the theory of change these essays introduce is of a piece with Thoreau's earlier political writings (the term "passive resistance" is, after all, most closely identified with "Resistance to Civil Government"). On my reading, however, his thinking in the John Brown essays derives more immediately from his late naturalistic studies, and in fact marks a significant departure from his earlier antislavery thought. What Thoreau discovered as his early naturalistic interest in personal moral growth became an interest in speciological succession and development is that, from the perspective of ecological systems, the agency of any given individual is singularly hard to parse. A lone pine seed may be decisive or expendable to the generation of a new pine stand, and although Thoreau describes the results of this process as intentional (the coyly realized plan of a personified "Nature"), up close, he confesses, its indirect and dilatory operation looks anything but purposive. The transference of this ecological model of change into his antislavery writings inspires his expanded conception of political action, and the result seems less an elaboration than a displacement of his earlier politics' emphasis on the revolutionary power of individual moral agency and the possibility of immediate political conversion. Resituating Brown's action at Harpers Ferry within the much larger history of this raid's diffuse future legacy allows Thoreau to assert Brown's eventual success, but it does so by minimizing the scope of Brown's intentional agency. The actions Brown conscientiously took—his raid and speeches—are dwarfed by comparison to the posthumous cascade of consequences his life has triggered and which are, Thoreau attests, what will ultimately bring his revolution to fruition.

This subsumption of individual agency into systemic complexity drives Thoreau's final conclusion, at the end of "Last Days," that Brown's death is nothing, his execution inconsequential: "He is more alive than he ever was." Having compared Brown's martyrdom to Christ's, Thoreau now punningly naturalizes that metaphor by comparing Brown to the sun, proclaiming that today Brown "works in public, and in the clearest light that shines on this land."[100] His unconcern for Brown's death underscores that it is not Brown's actions but his influence, the series of aftereffects his life will have touched off, that are poised to transform us. At the same time, the image of Brown's influence as a kind of sunlight conjures Thoreau's early *Journal* studies of the mechanisms of light's influence, the way it impinges on us and subtly transforms our thoughts. "I have new and indescribable fancies, and you have not touched the secret of the influence," he wrote of that sunset on Christmas Day.[101] Thus though Brown's legacy will no doubt, as Dimock argues, carry forward via the discursive mechanisms of cultural transmission, in this case, Thoreau's rhetoric refuses to care about the distinction between cultural influence of the sort Dimock cites (whose mechanisms require voluntary human action and consent) and environmental influence (whose mechanisms do not). Brown is now an element of our environment like the light, and that environment has the power to gradually yet radically transform whole populations, whether they wish to be changed or not.

Thoreau's antislavery materialism is thus surprising for two reasons. First, in this racial scientific moment, the predictable antislavery move would have been for Thoreau to deploy his monogenist theory of speciological development to defend human equality and uphold the brotherhood of all races. But though he voices this thesis elsewhere in his work, Thoreau's essays for John Brown spurn the discourse on racial origins and instead draw upon his empirical studies to frame a profoundly expanded theory of political change. In doing so, they move away from the individualism and immediatism of his earlier politics, and hence the second surprise here is that in amending his sense of the timeline and mechanisms of social reform, Thoreau's ecologism leads him to take a deeply qualified view of human agency. Where his earlier writings spoke to our will and resolve, these late writings speak of our condition. Thoreau imagines us as embodied beings who are not fully in control of our moral identities: we are sometimes "willfully" but other times "constitutionally" immoral, and if we are individually and collectively evolving this change seems to occur less by choice than by adaptation, as we affectively and physiologically respond to natural and social environments that work us over.

In this sense, Thoreau's antislavery materialism divorces his late politics from a Western humanist tradition that defines human nature by its moral autonomy and sovereign agency (the freedom of conscience and freedom to enact it that are so crucial to Thoreau's early antislavery work). Thoreau's empirical studies led him to reimagine all of nature as an imbricated and generative process: "The development theory," he observes in *Dispersion*, renders nature "equivalent to a sort of constant new creation."[102] In place of racism's static hierarchy of biological life, Thoreau's ecological politics emphasize life's mutability, a view he came to from his early faith in the human mind's susceptibility to environmental influences.

In theorizing the intermediation of social and biological life, and refusing any final distinction between politics and nature, Thoreau's antislavery materialism anticipates key aspects of contemporary posthumanist theory. Like many posthumanist theorists, Thoreau offers his vision of worldly processualism as a response to the problem of political oppression: the changefulness he uncovers bespeaks a worldly susceptibility to "constant new creation" which promises that the future need not reproduce the wrongs of the present (such as slavery). More specifically, the scope and complexity of this processualism makes his view newly empowering to minor agencies in ways reminiscent of recent posthumanist theories of political affect. Promising that even apparently inconsequential actors (a gust of wind, a peckish cow, a failed revolutionary) can unleash effects that snowball into significance—that just one splinter can derail vast trains of power—Thoreau evinces an optimistic faith in the transformative power of minor agencies that resonates, for instance, with William Connolly's account of the vulnerability of neoliberal order to grassroots activism. Connolly insists on the volatility of even the most hegemonic-seeming institutions in the face of the sheer complexity, and hence unpredictability, of the diverse forces that shape our lives. "Creative processes flow through and over us, and reflexivity doubles the creative adventure," he observes, arguing, "If you join attention to differing degrees of creativity in the domains of human culture, nonhuman force fields, and culture-nature imbrications to a critical account of the expansion, intensification, and acceleration of neoliberal capitalism, you may be brought face-to-face with the fragility of things today."[103] With Connolly, as with theorists like Brian Massumi and John Protevi, we can see how assemblage theories of political affect shift our attention from the question of what's right to the question of how (rather than should) a given set of affects, dispositions, beliefs, and, ultimately, institutions may come to be supplanted by another.[104]

Like Thoreau's essays for Brown, then, posthumanist theories of political affect and assemblages offer something like an ecological model of moral change that challenges us to acknowledge the distinctly nondeliberative, subhuman, nonhuman, and suprahuman forces that shape our political landscapes. Unlike Thoreau, however, these contemporary theories do not tend to flag the ways in which the unmanned "creative processes" they describe threaten to relegate us to political passivity by contracting the scope of individual action and intentionality. As we have seen, in relaxing the distinction between human intentionality and involuntary change, Thoreau's late ecological vision rescales our sense of political time from the tight rhythms of electoral cycles to the slow roll of geophysical change. One effect of this scalar shift is that it makes the role of conscientious action seem comparatively slight, so that Thoreau's late political theory seems at once optimistic that slavery will be abolished and pessimistic about the prospect that abolition will be the result of principled and concerted human effort. By contrast, as Mark McGurl observes, posthumanist discourse often chooses not to emphasize the dispossession of human agency that is implicit in its scaled-up view of systemic complexity. In posthumanist work, "even in its gloomier modes, there is a widespread sense, if not of hope, then at least of an opening, a breach" that is born of its certainty that "to see just how much of the total energy in the universe lies beyond the grasp of human beings . . . is also to witness the profound contingency and frailty of contemporary social and economic institutions." Nonetheless, McGurl asserts, whether or not posthumanists acknowledge it, in making human agency "visible as something nested in forces beyond its control," posthumanism confronts us with "the terrifying nature of our ethically unconscious selves."[105] In this regard, the unsettling fatalism that tinges Thoreau's late ecological politics may yet have something to teach posthumanism about the political stakes of its materialist ontology.

Thus both Douglass's and Thoreau's antislavery materialisms bring moralism and materialism together in ways that unsettle the rational, agential, and self-determining moral subject of Western humanism. In doing so, they also redefine the politics of embodiment framed by midcentury racialist thought. In place of a biological hierarchy running from "fully" human to nonhuman life, these authors' materialisms point to the imbrication of human and nonhuman agencies and the co-constitution of political and ecological processes. If Douglass's antislavery materialism thereby confronts us with our "animal" automaticity, and Thoreau's discloses the chasteningly attenuated nature of our agency—underscoring the radical passivity of passive resistance, its paradoxically posthumous life—Whitman, as the next chapter shall explore, exposes the unintentionality of our words and, indeed, the illegibility of the identity that utters them.

CHAPTER 3

Whitman's Cosmic Body: Bioelectricity and the Problem of Human Meaning

The preceding chapters have suggested the need to expand our familiar understanding of the debate over slavery and racial equality in the run up to the Civil War. Stepping back from the confrontation between racist science and antislavery liberalism, we can discern the emergence of a somewhat different disagreement. My readings of Douglass and Thoreau have thus aimed to show that the antebellum debate over racial equality was not solely a conflict between racist materialism and antislavery universalism, but it also involved a struggle within materialism itself over biologism's political entailments. If the political clout of racist science rested at least in part on the growing authority of biological conceptions of the human, Douglass's antislavery appeal to the autonomic instinct for self-preservation and Thoreau's antislavery faith in the morally progressive tendencies of speciological change both point out that biological conceptions of the human do not necessarily support proslavery or racist views. At the same time, as we have seen, their antislavery materialisms also create problems for longstanding humanistic assumptions about human autonomy and individual agency that were structurally central to the liberal mainstream of antebellum antislavery thought.

If nothing else, then, the preceding chapters have offered a lesson in the difficulty of mapping the antebellum moment according to our well-worn opposition between materialism-racism-slavery and idealism-liberalism-antislavery. Arguments that we have thought of as liberal (because antislavery), like Thoreau's and Douglass's, can turn out to be materialist in ways that complicate or even undermine the very possibility of liberalism. Inversely, arguments we have understood as materialist (because racist) can prove deeply invested in defending the premises of liberalism. After all, the animalized and hyper-embodied Black body of mid-nineteenth-century racist doctrine was designed to throw the inherent autonomy of the "fully" human (white, male) liberal subject into sharper relief. We have a working version of this thought in the now common observation that the primary function of Blackness in Western culture has been to consolidate and purify the concept of whiteness. In the context of racist science more specifically, embodying or racializing Blackness allowed for the comparative disembodiment of whiteness. When racial scientists cast the white race as the original and standard human form, or the most intellectually and morally advanced human form, they rendered the white body neutral or negligible to white humanity, thereby working to preserve the white subject's bona fides as a transcendently autonomous liberal subject.

As part of my effort to show that antebellum debates over slavery and racial difference thus became a front (indeed, arguably one of the most historically important fronts) in a broader and still ongoing cultural negotiation of the political entailments of materialism, I turn now to a set of questions that, at least at first, may seem far removed from these antebellum debates. This chapter explores Whitman's relation to two strains of antebellum embodied thought—one liberal and one more radically materialist—both of which were unstably conjoined within the American Spiritualist movement. Born in 1848, the Spiritualist movement rapidly gained popularity in the 1850s by propounding what it described as the first empirically grounded "religion of proof." Drawing upon research into the role of electricity in the body, Spiritualist doctrine held that the human soul is materially real—that it exists as a bioelectrical phenomenon—and that this material soul persists beyond the dissolution of the corporeal body, guaranteeing the immortality of the discrete, individual self. Thus though Spiritualism was not chiefly concerned with questions of racial difference, Spiritualist orthodoxy was like racist science in this limited sense: it, too, articulates a materialism that labors to preserve the integrity—that is, the boundedness and self-possession—of the liberal subject. As this chapter will argue, however, the bioelectrical self that Spiritualism constructed was theoretically unstable. At odds with Spiritualist orthodoxy, Spiritualist practices of mediumship highlighted the bioelectrical self's physiological receptivity—its vulnerability to ambient material influences including communications from other material spirits. The porous communicativity of the bioelectrical self thus threatened to belie rather than to immortalize the boundedness of the Spiritualist subject. As I shall argue, this alternative, monistic, and open-ended bioelectrical self was an important inspiration for *Leaves of Grass.*

Whitman's relation to Spiritualism allows us to track the ways that biologism circulated through the antebellum cultural imagination beyond discourses explicitly associated with racial science. Panning out from the immediate fray of the debate over slavery and equality, this chapter focuses on the difficulties that the antebellum embodied subject posed to the figure of the liberal subject more generally, and to the democratic politics that subject sustains. As we shall see, these difficulties were in some cases finessed or simply repressed whilst elsewhere they rise more immediately to the surface—perhaps nowhere more insistently, as I shall suggest, than in Whitman's groundbreaking antebellum poetry. The reading to follow begins by tracing Whitman's inheritance from Spiritualism's bioelectrical theology. I argue that the "body electric" that pulses at the center of his early poetry departs from Spiritualist orthodoxy, which distinguished the vulnerable earthly body from the indestructibly material soul, by instead conjuring a bioelectrical subject who is originally relational, granted identity not despite but because of the body's nervous entanglement with the world. Whereas Spiritualism promised to square the messy dependencies of human materiality with the transcendental integrity of the liberal individual, on my reading Whitman's poetry lays bare contradictions that are inherent to that project.

Indeed, I argue that Whitman's theory of nervous entanglement not only informs his poetic topoi but moreover structures his theory of poetic communication. That is, I propose that in addition to its thematic prominence in the early *Leaves*, the body electric furthermore provides the philosophical ground from which Whitman developed what I describe as the uniquely "embodied poetics" of his highly experimental first volumes. This novel poetics emphasizes the physiology of poetic communication over and against poetry's propositional content, challenging some of our most basic assumptions about what poems do and how they mean, as well as about the nature of the subjects between whom those poems and meanings pass.

As we shall see, Whitman's embodied poetics ultimately stress the constitutive indeterminacy of both the propositional poetic subject and the embodied human subject. Touting the body's entanglement in a procreant "reality . . . . materialism first and last imbueing," Whitman attempts to engender a wholly new poetry adequate to a cosmos thus monistically and processually reimagined.[1]

In our present critical moment, it is tempting to read Whitman's porous and processual self through the lens of posthumanist and specifically new materialist models of the human. Like Whitman's, these latter-day materialisms position the material body as a correction to the idealism of the liberal subject. But while this chapter will acknowledge intriguing parallels where they arise, I will ultimately suggest that Whitman's materialism remains something distinct. On my reading, Whitman's bioelectrical subject confronts us with the failure of attempts—both by antebellum era movements like Spiritualism and by posthumanist theory today—to reconcile the processual materialist body with a legibly liberal politics of democratic pluralism. For Whitman's bioelectrical self is finally so spectacularly indistinguishable from the cosmos that flows through his nervous body (plastically "quivering [him] to a new identity") that it is impossible to assign content—that is, anything like a stable meaning or essential identity—to this subject. To be sure, Whitman does not always acknowledge, let alone embrace, the effacement of identity that his poetry enacts. Nonetheless, as I hope to demonstrate, the erosion of personal particularity in his work is inescapable, at once glaring and programmatic, arising at the level of both form and content in the early *Leaves*.

In its final movement, then, this chapter turns from the poetics of Whitmanian embodiment to consider the racial politics that this unidentifiable bioelectrical body encodes. Returning to the infamous slave auction scene in "I Sing the Body Electric," I show how Whitman's bioelectrical ontology gives rise to a highly idiosyncratic defense of racial equality that leaves the basic premises of liberal individuality and equality behind. If Whitman's materialism generates a powerful vision of racial unity here, its egalitarianism nonetheless bears little resemblance to the individualistic and pluralistic democratic politics that we conventionally attribute to his work—and that Whitman, himself, claimed to celebrate. As I argue, the tension between Whitman's processual bodies and the more conventionally liberal politics of mainstream antislavery discourse resurfaces in contemporary calls for a more radically pluralistic posthumanist democracy today, raising questions about the racial politics implicit in the posthumanist project. I will turn to those questions, investigating the friction between posthumanism's fluid ontology and its recognizably liberal politics, in Chapter 4.

God Vibrations: The Bioelectrical Soul in Theory and Practice

In his 1860 review of *On the Origin of the Species*, Asa Gray confesses that the unraveling of liberal selfhood haunts midcentury science. Anticipating that many readers will find Darwin's theory objectionable because it conjoins human races and ultimately "makes the whole world kin," Gray points out that this unifying vision nonetheless harmonizes with the prevailing currents of modern scientific thought. After all, he observes, the "principle triumphs" of modern science "have consisted in tracing connections where none were known before, in reducing heterogeneous phenomena to a common cause or origin, in a manner quite analogous to that of the reduction of supposed independently originated species to a common ultimate origin." Indeed, Gray continues, the "scientific mind" now "contemplates the solar system as evolved from a common, revolving fluid mass . . . has come to regard light, heat, electricity, magnetism, chemical affinity, and mechanical power as varieties or derivative and convertible forms of one force . . . and . . . speculates steadily in the direction of the ultimate unity of matter."[2] However much Darwin's vision of speciological unity "discomposes us," then, Gray warns that our preference for separateness, difference, and hierarchy voices a doomed resistance to the model of physical reality that nineteenth-century science was progressively unveiling: that of a monistic cosmos unified by a fretwork of past and ongoing material interrelations that belie categorical distinctions between races, species, and ultimately even between physical bodies.

If it was obvious to Gray that modern scientific materialism was poised to engulf white racial—and ultimately human—exceptionalism in one vast, monistic soup, not all antebellum materialists concurred with this projection. Darwin's polygenist and monogenist detractors obviously understood themselves to be giving an empirical account of reality and so, too, did antebellum Spiritualism, the movement to which I turn in this chapter. As I shall argue, Spiritualism's distinctive brand of materialism forms an important cultural context for *Leaves of Grass*: in addition to popularizing the divinized "body electric" that would prove so powerfully inspiring to Whitman, Spiritualist discourse housed two contradictory views of materialism whose tensions help to illuminate the complex role of embodiment in Whitman's work.

Officially, Spiritualist doctrine espoused a kind of onto-theology that held that spirits are empirically real (comprised of bioelectricity) and that promised that we persist as materially embodied and autonomously individual spirits beyond the grave. In practice, as we shall see, the communicative performances associated with Spiritualism—in which mediums claimed to channel spirits and speak in the voices of the dead—point to a very different conception of the bioelectrical self, flaunting its susceptibility to external forces and the porosity of the border between one self and another. The vulnerability and fungibility of the bioelectrical self in Spiritualist mediumship was thus at odds with the discretely bounded individualism of the bioelectrical soul espoused in Spiritualist doctrine. In this opposition, Spiritualist doctrine bears a structural resemblance to antebellum racist science's resistance to Darwinian monogenism in that it, too, framed a materialist account of the human that worked to defend the figure of the liberal subject against encroachment from more radically conjunctive materialisms. Ultimately, Spiritualism's internal contradictions make it a particularly vivid example of just how uncertain materialism's relation to liberal individualism was in this moment.

Unfolding in proximate relation to "professional" science (the prior chapter should give some indication of how tenuous such borders were in this era), the American Spiritualist movement rose to popularity in the 1850s promulgating what it described as a rigorously scientific "religion of proof." Its ostensibly empirical theology centered on the uniquely ambivalent substance of electricity, that invisible yet material stuff that "sparks" the body into life. Indeed, despite decades of empirical investigation, electricity remained at midcentury a phenomenon stubbornly resistant to scientific disenchantment.[3] Stymied by its oscillation between object and event, materiality and impalpability, chemists dubbed it an "imponderable fluid," and since the late eighteenth century, when its role in galvanizing the nervous system was first experimentally established, bioelectricity had inspired a series of popular therapeutic movements, including mesmerism and phrenology. When it first arose in 1848, then, Spiritualism was the latest face of what was already a vibrant constellation of bohemian bioelectrical movements.[4] Drawing upon both scientific and peri-scientific discourses, Spiritualism proclaimed electricity the missing link between the ineffable human spirit and its effable body. As one phrenologist put it, bioelectricity revealed the "godlike department of our nature reduced to DEMONSTRABLE CERTAINTY": it furnished, in short, the perceptible matter of the soul.[5]

Spiritualists stressed the scientism of their faith, confident that the measurable materiality of bioelectricity would soon lead scientists to verify the empirical reality of the spiritual world. Arguing that mind "is a substance—an element—as really so as air or water," they insisted that the body's electrical mechanisms furnish "sensuous evidence" of the soul.[6] Indeed, the soul was so utterly substantial in Spiritualist discourse that questions like "how much does a soul weigh?" were seriously entertained while traditional theological teachings about the "*immateriality* of the spirit" were roundly dismissed as "the most consummate nonsense."[7] Spiritualists thus took pains to distinguish their own rationalist theology from what they saw as the baseless mysticism of other religions. As the movement's first major codifier, Andrew Jackson Davis, protested, "If men do not consult Nature and Reason, and 'try the spirits' by the rigid righteousness of those immutable principles . . . there can not be any limits set to the wild fanaticism and superstitious absurdities into which the honest seekers after truth and spirituality will not assuredly plunge themselves."[8] Whatever else Spiritualism may have been—a theatrical entertainment, profitable quackery, a program for consoling the bereaved—it was also a site of metaphysical speculation, propounding the materiality of the spirit and, conversely, the intrinsic spirituality of matter.

One of the specific attractions of Spiritualism's fusion of science and religion was its claim to have reconciled the dispiriting facts of human materiality with continued faith in the individual's transcendent autonomy. Whereas other biologisms seemed to sentence the self to contingency by suggesting that our minds and moral characters are merely by-products of the bodies we are born with, the bioelectrical soul allowed Spiritualism to conceive of identity as the expression of a spirit that is independent of the corporeal body (just like the classically Christian soul) and yet demonstrably material nonetheless. This compromise funded Spiritualism's chief consolatory promise: that heaven and the afterlife are just as real and materially substantial as our spirits. Thus Andrew Jackson Davis taught that death does not spell the end of the body nor of individual subjectivity but rather works as a kind of "cleansing process" that purifies our earthly bodies of "their transient imperfections." On this embodied account, death looks less like a miraculous translation from one ontological state (flesh) into one wholly other (spirit) and more like an accelerated form of evolution that instantaneously perfects each individual body according to what Jackson characterized as a "beautiful . . . law of progress."[9]

In her best-selling Spiritualist novel, *The Gates Ajar* (1868), Elizabeth Stuart Phelps paints a vivid picture of this embodied heaven populated by immortal yet fully material individuals. Bereaved by the death of her brother, the novel's heroine, Mary Cabot, finds no solace in her minister's account of the afterlife as a state in which all individuality melts away, bearing off with it all "selfish affections" such as love for one's family to leave only a bliss that "glow[s] with holy love alike to all other holy hearts."[10] Mary's Spiritualist preceptor, Aunt Winifred Forceythe, shudders at this vision of spiritual communion, objecting that it "would destroy individuality at one fell swoop. We should be like a man walking down a room lined with mirrors, who sees himself reflected in all sizes, colors, shades, at all angles and in all proportions . . . til he seems no longer to belong to himself."[11] "The truth is," she concludes, "the ordinary idea [of heaven], if sifted accurately, reduces our eternal personality to—*gas*."[12] What Phelps's characters find unacceptable in orthodox Christian doctrine, then, is the prospect of a spiritual existence that annihilates the liberal self, dissolving her into a "great blank ocean" of celestial community "which shall swallow up, in a pitiless, glorified way, all the little brooks of our delight."[13] By contrast, the great appeal of Spiritualist theology for these characters is its promise that, since "the spiritual body is real, is tangible, is visible, is human," we shall therefore still very much "be *ourselves* in heaven," retaining all of our personal affections (those "little brooks of our delight") and our private possessions—including, most importantly, the particular and particularizing bodily "sizes, colors, shades" that encode our (gendered and racial) identities and that allow us, Aunt Forceythe suggests, to belong to ourselves.[14] Indeed, Aunt Winifred triumphantly insists that we shall even continue to live in private houses with our nuclear families—both of which, she confesses, will undergo "many differences and great ones" in the process of purification, yet ultimately will remain recognizably "*mine* just the same."[15] In place of a gaseous oneness with God, Aunt Forceythe's Spiritualist afterlife looks more like the idealized brochure for a new suburban community, promising everything the liberal individual's possessive heart had ever desired in life.[16]

Spiritualism's materialist reconceptualization of the soul thus allowed it to guarantee the integrity of liberal personhood even after the decomposition of the mortal body. In this specific sense, Spiritualist materialism echoes racist science in that both offer their adherents an embodied account of the human that simultaneously works to preserve the singularity and autonomy of the liberal subject. For the many Spiritualists who also identified as abolitionists, as well as for Spiritualist practitioners of color, the similarity likely stopped there: unlike racist materialism, Spiritualist materialism did not propose that only some (white, male) persons qualify as truly ensouled or autonomous.

But if it was not systematically racist, neither was Spiritualism programmatically antiracist. Indeed, despite deep cultural connections to the abolitionist and feminist movements, many prominent Spiritualists did suggest that the bioelectrical soul was most fully developed in the white race. Thus, for instance, Andrew Jackson Davis asserted that the phenomenon of Spiritual communication (the practice in which a Spiritualist medium, endowed with exceptionally refined powers of nervous "receptivity," channels electromagnetic transmissions from the spirit realm, speaking for the dead) first emerged in the mid–nineteenth century because it was only just then enabled by the evolutionary advancement of the white race. As Davis argued, the "miracles and spiritual disclosures of this era flow *naturally* and *consequently* from the state of mental and moral development to which the Anglo-Saxon portion of the human race has generally attained."[17] In light of a statement like this, Spiritualism's individualistic afterlife (complete with gendered and raced bodies, domestic spaces, and nuclear family units), stands out more clearly as a markedly conservative vision—a rejection of the undifferentiated communalism of the "gaseous" afterlife Phelps's characters deplore. Indeed, Davis proclaimed that heaven is in fact partitioned into six hierarchical societies, "each being characterized by a different race of spirits . . . in different stages of moral culture," and by the late 1860s Spiritualist cartographies uniformly mapped heaven as a racially partitioned space in which "every race and nation . . . enjoyed its own unique heaven peculiarly suited to its individual needs and desires."[18] If Phelps's heaven seems like a suburban paradise, Davis's shared the dream of segregation that would fund the suburbanization of America a century later.

As individualistic as this doctrine seems, however, Spiritualism's bioelectrical self was also a philosophically unstable entity. Much like the paradoxically insubstantial electrical substance that inspires it, the Spiritualist subject oscillates between singularity and diffusion thanks to the inherently communicative function of bioelectricity. This instability was spectacularly on display in the practice of Spiritualist mediumship, which was the movement's main means of demonstrating its bioelectrical faith and recruiting converts from audiences who arrived by turns skeptical and curious. As Davis explains, spirit communications are made possible by the fact that we exude a "general electric atmosphere," breathing our spiritual electricity into the space around us like a cloud of perfume. When the mind is properly relaxed, "these electrical elements flow down from the brain into the nerves, and into all the infinite ramifications of the nerves, and

thence into the atmosphere which we breathe," generating a uniquely refined electrical field "through which communications [between souls] can
be made."[19] In the event of communication, the medium conducts the electrical emanations of another soul into his or her own body, allowing that
soul to speak and even act through the medium's nervous circuits.

The Spiritualist medium, then, conjures a very different view of the bioelectrical self. Unlike the corporeally defined and possessive Spiritualist
subject whom Davis and Phelps project into heaven, the Spiritualist medium is chiefly distinguished by her capacity for nervous receptivity and
sympathetic affinity: porous and possessed, she is a conduit of sympathetic
connection with souls not her own. The fluidity of identity modeled by
Spiritualist mediums injected the movement with radical tendencies not
legible within its conservative account of a bounded and individualistic afterlife. Thus, for instance, in what Molly McGarry describes as the
"amorphous sexual matrix" opened up by the practice of mediumship, Spiritualist men and women were free to perform other genders in ways corrosive to the strictures of mid-century gender ideology. Spiritualist séances
and demonstrations provided a sanctioned space in which Spiritualist practitioners could "reimagine their gender through practices ranging from
cross-dressing to defying the vocal ranges equated with sexual difference."[20] For female mediums in particular—often young and poor—this
license to command an audience and speak in the tongue and tones of dead
presidents afforded unprecedented access to a public authority otherwise
forbidden to them in both church and state. Indeed, Spiritualism was
closely associated with the feminist movement: as Anne Braude notes,
"While not all feminists were Spiritualists, all Spiritualists advocated
women's rights."[21]

But if mediumship allowed women to performatively lay claim to the
"masculine" virtues of liberal agency and autonomy, the important point
here is that it did so by spotlighting the fictionality of that liberal self. In
this sense, Spiritualist feminism is a curiously double-edged sword, insofar as mediumship enabled female practitioners to assert a liberal autonomy via a practice that tacitly gainsaid it. Beyond sanctioning trans-gender
and cross-class performances, then, the larger unorthodoxy of Spiritual
mediumship inheres in its public demonstration of a bioelectrical self whose
borders are permeable and whose subjectivity is curiously multiple—
sympathetic, affiliative, and uncannily networked with other minds. Instead
of conferring individual identity (as Phelps imagines that our distinctive
bodily "sizes, colors, shades . . . and proportions" do), the medium's

nerve-riddled body is the site of bioelectrical exchanges that attenuate individual identity, capitulate autonomy, and blur the boundary between subjects. Along these lines, John Lardas Modern describes the Spiritualist subject as someone who is alternately "in control yet susceptible to human influences, both past and present," and in this way uncertainly poised between contingency and autonomy, "docility and freedom."[22] Similarly, Stephanie LeMenager has shown how the bioelectrical body's susceptibility was also understood to extend to climatic influences, which Spiritualists believed could variously enhance or hinder conductivity between spirits, vitalizing or vitiating the bioelectrical self. As LeMenager notes, this climactically tuned Spiritualist subject seems perpetually at risk of dissolving "within a network of energetic actors" in the "atmospheric soup" of the environment.[23]

Thus, while Spiritualism's main selling point was its claim to have successfully fused corporeal materiality, liberal individuality, and Christian immortality, the bioelectrical subject who effected this grand détente simultaneously seemed to belie the model of selfhood it stood for. As the critics above suggest, the sympathetic susceptibility and communicativeness that characterize the bioelectrical self light up an invisible dimension of embodied being, extending selfhood beyond the border of our electrically conductive skin. In this way, Spiritualist discourse generated two contradictory visions of self and world: a recognizably liberal-individualist one, in which the bioelectrical soul guarantees the persistence of individual identity after death and heaven is a segregated space; and a monistic one, in which the bioelectrical soul blurs the bounds of identity and the universe is materially interconnected.

That this internal contradiction does not seem to have troubled Spiritualist discourse may be attributable to the fact that both versions of the bioelectrical self seem to agree upon its central revelation of humanity's empirically supernatural nature. And yet the logics of transcendence underpinning these two visions are philosophically quite distinct. For Spiritualist expositors like Davis and Phelps, the supernaturalism of bioelectricity derives from the occult nature of electricity itself, poised as it was between thingy materiality and celestial imponderability. Thus, glossing Saint Paul's assertion that "There is a natural body, and there is a spiritual body," Davis explains that, indeed, "the spiritual body is a substance" that is moved by "a fine force" or spirit that "flows through [the] nerve-sensations." In short, for Davis, the ethereality of bioelectricity (the rarified fineness of its "force") allows it to occupy two ontological statuses (material and spiritual) at once, thereby manifesting the human body's inherently otherworldly endowment: "the invisible presence of the Divine in the visible human."[24]

By contrast, as I have suggested, the practice of spiritual mediumship foregrounds a rather different conception of bioelectricity's transcendentalism. (Ostensibly) demonstrating the bioelectrical subject's susceptibility to external forces—to "human influences, both past and present" as well as to atmospheric influences in the nonhuman environment—the spectacle of spiritual communication highlights both the nervous self's permeability and its extension beyond the bounds of its skin. But though the latter version of bioelectrical transcendentalism therefore contends that our beings are not wholly contained in our bodies, it does not explicitly insist upon being's supernaturalism. Charles Taylor's distinction between "enchanted" (ensouled) and "buffered" (secular) selves is helpful for drawing out this discrepancy. On Taylor's description, the peculiar quality of "enchantment" that the concept of the soul has traditionally named refers to the idea that there is some aspect of human being that transcends the body and renders it susceptible to supernatural forces beyond human ken or command.[25] Clearly, the Spiritualist medium's bioelectrical porosity bears a structural resemblance to Taylor's enchanted self. This similarity, however, depends upon a conceptual sleight of hand, for the medium is susceptible to forces that are represented as material rather than supernatural—he is affected by electrical emanations and climactic influences, manifesting the body's porosity to a physical world that impinges on his senses at every instant. Although these material forces may be so various and complex as to be practically incalculable, they are not, like supernatural forces, *essentially* incalculable. This is, in other words, a transcendentalism that does not leave the realm of the natural world—bringing it closer to Asa Gray's empirical vision of "the ultimate unity of matter" than to Phelps's and Davis's Spiritualist accounts of an individualistic afterlife. Indeed, in stark contrast to Phelps's disdain for "gaseous" communion, this monistic tendency within Spiritualist practice ultimately envisions us as part of a vast embodied commons, or what Robert Cox calls a "social physiology," in which all bodies are woven "into the fiber of a sympathetically united nation in precisely the same way that the nerves, organs, and tissues were integrated within the organic body."[26] At odds with Spiritualism's doctrinal commitments to the possessive and autonomous liberal self, then, the bioelectrical physics of mediumship threatened to explode this integral subject by rendering it finally indistinguishable from a larger and fluidly networked material world.

The Poet as Nervous Medium

Spiritualism's transcendental materialism and adhesive individualism were attractive to Whitman and are important contexts for his thinking about embodiment and sexuality.[27] The movement's influence on the early *Leaves of Grass* is particularly unmistakable in Whitman's unorthodox assertions of the body's divinity. "If the body were not the soul, what is the soul?" he demands. Although he treats this as a rhetorical question, the burden of explanation is obviously Whitman's. In prefatory notes for the first edition of *Leaves*, he offers an initial defense of this statement, writing:

> We hear of miracles, but . . . tell me then, if you can, what is there in the immortality of the soul more than this spiritual and beautiful miracle of sight? . . . . I open two pairs of lids, only as big as peach pits, when lo! the unnamable variety and whelming splendor of the world come to me . . . though rocks are dense and hills are ponderous, and the stars are away off sextillions of miles.[28]

This note can read as a familiar enough defense of the wonders of the human body: sight instantaneously ferries "ponderous" objects across even cosmic distances in order to reveal mountains and starlight to us. In his 1802 *Natural Theology* (required reading when Thoreau was at Harvard), William Paley famously points to the intricacy of the eye as evidence that it, along with the rest of nature, must have been purposively designed, thus proving the existence of God. (Indeed, the intuitive force of Paley's argument was such that in, 1860, after publishing the treatise that would ring natural theology's death knell, Darwin confessed to Asa Gray, "The eye to this day gives me a cold shudder.")[29] In drawing our attention to the marvel of eyesight, then, Whitman might be making a Paleyan claim, pointing to the phenomenon of sight as empirical proof of the body's divine origin.

By the time this note made its way into the preface to the first edition of *Leaves of Grass* (1855), however, Whitman had refined his characterization of sight's miraculous nature. In the preface, he observes,

> What is marvelous? what is unlikely? what is impossible or baseless or vague? after you have once just opened the space of a peachpit . . . and had all things enter with electric swiftness softly and duly and without confusion or jostling or jam.[30]

Whitman's restatement clarifies that it is not the *fact* of sight that impresses him (isn't it amazing that we can see?) but more specifically sight's bioelectrical physiology that he finds so improbable: in the moment of perception, "things enter" the eye "with electric swiftness," inscribing impressions on the nervously receptive body. For Whitman, then, there is something distinctly miraculous—"marvelous," "unlikely," "baseless or vague"—about the way the body's bioelectrical mechanisms render us permeable, revealing our physiological porosity to "all things."

As we have seen, Whitman was hardly alone at midcentury in discerning something tantalizingly like "the immortality of the soul" vouchsafed by nervous electricity. More specifically, we are now in a position to note how Whitman's account of the bioelectrical soul echoes the earth-bound transcendentalism implicit in the Spiritualist practice of mediumship, and at odds with Spiritualist orthodoxy. It is, after all, not the inherent divinity of electricity but the bioelectrical body's permeability—its ability to reach beyond itself and to be, in turn, suffused by things not itself—that elicits Whitman's wonder and prompts his conclusion that the body is enchanted, itself a soul. Again, as I have argued, this gloss of transcendentalism involves an elision or misdirection insofar as it asks us to substitute the body's nervous porosity to *material* forces for the susceptibility to supernatural forces that has historically distinguished the enchanted self. Insofar as the former state can be called transcendental, the susceptibility it names delivers us not into an electro-spiritual afterlife but rather into a physiologically conjoined cosmos, disclosing a self suffused not by the immanent presence of the divine so much as by the immanent presence of the world—a vast yet mundane communion.

To be sure, Whitman will also inherit Spiritualism's contradictions, most spectacularly displayed in the way his speaking persona veers between egotistical particularity and impersonal collectivity—occasionally in the same breath ("Walt Whitman, an American, one of the roughs, a kosmos"). The reading I will be offering here, however, proposes that *Leaves of Grass* programmatically foregrounds the latter. That is, despite Whitman's claim to have been "the poet of the self," I submit that his poetry consistently foregrounds the self's dispossession and identity's constant dissolution, celebrating the ways in which the nervous system's sensuous receptivity interpellates us within a vast network of earthly communication and embodied sociality. In this section I will examine key moments in which the early *Leaves* thematizes bodily porosity and the dissolution of individual identity, and I will suggest how reading these moments in light of midcentury bioelectrical discourse can usefully expand and reinflect our discussions of sexuality in Whitman's work. In the following section, I explore how Whitman's interest in bioelectricity shows up not only at the level of content but moreover in his signature poetic forms, and in what I describe as the embodied poetics that give rise to those forms. Across both sections I shall argue that if Spiritualism's popularity in the early 1850s supplied Whitman with the trope of the body electric and of the sanctified physical body, its shadowy strain of monistic materialism was decisive for Whitman's thinking about both the ontology of the self and the ontology of poetry.

Just as Spiritualism's bioelectrical body wavered between autonomy and dispossession, transcendence and susceptibility, so too does Whitman's bioelectrical self pulse in and out of formlessness. This oscillation forms the crux of one of the most haunting passages of "Song of Myself." The uncharacteristic brutality of this passage accentuates the threat that bioelectrical embodiment poses to liberal personhood. "Mine is no callous shell," it begins:

> I have instant conductors all over me whether I pass or stop,
> They seize every object and lead it harmlessly through me. . . .
> Is this then a touch? . . . . quivering me to a new identity
> Flames and ether making a rush for my veins,
> Treacherous tip of me reaching and crowding to help them,
> My flesh and blood playing out lightning, to strike what is hardly
> > different from myself
> On all sides prurient provokers stiffening my limbs. . . .
> The sentries desert every other part of me,
> They have left me helpless to a red marauder,
> They all come to the headland to witness and assist against me.
>
> I am given up by traitors;
> I talk wildly . . . . I have lost my wits . . . . I and nobody else am the
> > greatest traitor,
> I went myself first to the headland . . . . my own hands carried me there.

This violent scene is generally read as depicting a sexual encounter, and critics have been divided as to whether that encounter is homoerotic or autoerotic. In his masterful reading of this passage, Mark Maslan argues for their indifference. As he points out, mid-nineteenth-century sexual hygiene literature routinely figured sexual desire as an external force that invades and overmasters unwary men. On Maslan's reading, this passage draws out a conclusion implicit but unacknowledged in that literature: namely, that "when men's masturbatory and heterosexual urges are defined as forms of surrender to an invading force, *all* male desire begins to look homoerotic."[31]

Without detracting from this account of Whitman's "audacious molding" of hygienic theory into queer desire, we might nonetheless consider what happens to this passage when we take its accusation against "villain touch" more literally. That is, if we read this passage as a complaint not against sexual desire specifically so much as against the fact of sensuousness more generally, its narrative of incursion and ravishment begins to read differently. Spotlighting how our nervous physiology renders all sensation a form of penetration—as nerves "seize every object" they encounter, shepherding them into our bodies via storms of bioelectrical "lighting"—the passage draws our attention to the impossibility of self-sovereignty in light of the manifest un-callousness of our shells. The speaker's panic in the face of this incursion is that of a liberal subject who has presumed the integrity of his physiological borders and his absolute possession of the body they delimit. Hence he experiences the mundane physiology of touch as a radical betrayal—not only is he susceptible to this "red marauder" of sensation but worse, it is aided and abetted by the "treacherous tip" of his own sensuously receptive skin—which he now finds does not act as a border or islanding "headland" at all, but rather as an eager network of "instant conductors."

On this reading, onanism would be exactly the wrong way to think of this scene, since its larger point is that self-stimulation is structurally unavoidable given our nervous architecture: in every waking moment, our senses are working to arouse and provoke us. Indeed, more broadly, I worry that to gloss the invading force here as specifically *sexual*, as distinct from sensual, in nature risks minimizing or missing entirely the polemic against the liberal self this passage otherwise encodes. For whereas the discourse on sexuality stresses object choice and is directed toward typological identification, sensuality is indiscriminate and (as this passage luridly illustrates) belies our individuation. Thus though we might be tempted (as the speaker initially was) to view this scene of overmastery as a threat to be resisted, the passage ultimately instructs us to accept that dispossession is a feature inherent to bioelectrical subjectivity because the body is a sensitive medium of communication and change. "I and nobody else am the greatest traitor": for Whitman, to be a nervously embodied self is to testify, involuntarily (of course) and at all times, against the doctrine of individual autonomy and identity.

But while this passage exposes the fiction of autonomy, unlike more recent denunciations of the liberal subject (such as those coming out of deconstruction, posthumanism, and affect theory), its mood is not strictly celebratory. Instead, the violence of Whitman's imagery and anxiety of his speaker task us to acknowledge the sacrifice this shift in outlook entails. To be sure, as we have also seen with Spiritualist mediumship, the porosity of bioelectrical embodiment works to reunite self and world in a single system of continuous mutual exchange (hence our speaker here finds that his senses "strike what is hardly different from myself"). But if the bioelectrical body therefore stands to release us from the burden of singularity, relieving our sense of alienation from the world, by the same token it also threatens to do away with our sense of being anyone in particular at all. For although Whitman admires that sensations move through us "harmlessly," he also makes clear that they are not without consequence. To the contrary, sensuous perception materially alters this speaker, "quivering [him] to a new identity." Indeed, since there is no disembodied soul to serve as a separate locus of identity in the version of bioelectrical embodiment Whitman invokes, all material alterations to the body therefore constitute changes at the level of being.[32] More pointedly, then, if every sensuous perception is a touch, and every touch quivers us to a new identity, then in what sense can we—inscribed and revised by each passing experience— still lay claim to something like an identity at all? If this scene feels like a rape, it is because of its attention to the violence its monistic ontology does to the speaker's sense of selfhood. Brought face to face with his susceptibility to the world and the continuous existential renovation embodied experience wreaks, this speaker becomes, like his identity, incoherent: "I talk wildly . . . . I have lost my wits . . . ." Indeed it would seem that talking wildly is inevitable now since the no longer tenable fiction of a self-representing "I" has been displaced by a babbling bioelectrical "we"—I, my hands, their nerves, villain touch, and the "red marauder" of sensation that tethers me to other bodies "hardly different from myself." If the porosity of embodiment gains us the world, this passage observes that it also costs us that thing we have heretofore known as the self.

Indeed, across the pages of *Leaves*, embodied selves and other objects freely dissolve and coalesce again in Whitman's intermittently liquefying gaze, enumerated in one moment and in the next proving composite or dispersed beyond recognition. Individual bodies are ramified by all that exists around them: you are "your person and every particle that relates to your person."[33] And these horizontal relations of association and interaction also extend longitudinally across time, as Whitman indicates when he describes himself as an index of the earth's entire history: "Before I was born out of my mother generations guided me, / My embryo has never been torpid. . . . For it the nebula cohered to an orb. . . . Monstrous sauroids transported it in their mouths and deposited it with care."[34] Moreover, he also understands each thing to be an index of everything that will unfold from its body after its death: "I effuse my flesh in eddies and drift it in lacy jags/I bequeath myself to the dirt to grow from the grass I love,/If you want me again look for me under your bootsoles."[35] Despite the presence of nouns and proper names, then, Whitman's bodies are perpetually in transit—processual, ongoing—and thus belie any name we would give them. In Michael Warner's acutely succinct words, Whitman "makes the phenomenology of selfing a mess."[36]

Despite the continuous transformations implicit in its processual ontology, however, *Leaves* will not sustain the elegiac awareness of self-loss it registers in the violence of the foregoing long passage. More commonly Whitman is, like his posthumanist counterparts, optimistic that the body's integration with the world does not entail the dispossession of the self so much as its heroic dilation. Perhaps Whitman's most ecstatic articulation of this thought comes at the very outset of *Leaves*, in the poetics he lays out in the 1855 preface. Here Whitman defines the poet as a particularly talented medium, someone who can make himself a channel of the whole nation, conducting the panoply of its influences into his receptive and plastic body:

> The American poets are to enclose old and new for America is the race of races. . . . he gives them reception . . . he incarnates [his nation's] geography and natural life and rivers and lakes. Mississippi with annual freshets and changing chutes, Missouri and Columbia and Ohio and St. Lawrence with the falls and the beautiful masculine Hudson, do not embouchure where they spend themselves more than they embouchure into him. . . . When the long Atlantic coast stretches longer and the Pacific coast stretches longer he easily stretches with them north or south. . . . On him rise solid growths that offset the growths of pine and cedar and hemlock and liveoak and locust and chestnut . . . with flights and songs and screams that answer those of the wildpigeon and highhold and orchard oriole and coot and surf-duck. . . . To him the hereditary countenance descends both mother's and father's. To him enter the essences of the real things and past and present events—of the enormous diversity of temperature and agriculture and mines—the tribes of red aborigines . . . the first settlements north or south—the rapid stature and muscle—the haughty defiance of '76 . . . the wharf hem'd cities and superior marine . . . the free commerce—the fisheries and whaling and gold-digging—the endless gestation of new states. . . . For such the expression of the American poet is to be transcendent and new. . . .

[He] sees the solid and beautiful forms of the future where there are
now no solid forms.[37]

No ordinary panorama, this catalog collects sights that ostensibly enter the
poet's body and transform him, so that it is the poet, not his poem, that
ultimately "incarnates" this landscape.[38] Whitman's preface thus breaks
with the oracular tradition of Romantic poetics that preceded him, and that
cast the poet as a visionary who prophetically sees through the material
world to lay bare "the soul of the thing" (Emerson), unveiling the "spirit
of its form" (Shelley).[39] Leaning on the bioelectrical body, Whitman reimag-
ines poetic perception as an event in which the poet does not see penetra-
tively through objects but is himself penetrated and inscribed by them. He
does not write a great poem; he *is* one.

And thus in the climax to his discourse on "the curious mystery of the
eyesight" in the 1855 preface, Whitman promises that by reading his poetry we, too, can become embodied poems. "Read these leaves in the open
air every season of every year of your life," he instructs, "and your very flesh
shall be a great poem and have the richest fluency not only in its words but
in the silent lines of its lips and face and between the lashes of your eyes and
in the very movement and joint of your body."[40] The fungibility of bodies
and poems in Whitman's thinking points to a broader translation between
the poetics of embodiment I have been examining here and what I will call,
in the next section, his embodied poetics. Although his suggestions that
poetry impinges on a reader's body directly have alternately been denounced and embraced as pure "mysticism," in the next section I will explain why Whitman's embodied poetics—with its persistent conflation of
bodies and poems, and perversely counterfactual claims to be able to touch
the bodies of its readers—must be understood in relation to the historically
specific form of materialism propagated by midcentury bioelectrical discourse.[41] Via the nervous impressionability of the bioelectrical body, Whitman came to rethink poetry as a site, first and foremost, of haptic
communication—a means of transferring not meanings but transformative
physical effects via an intimate sensuous encounter called reading.

Causal Encounters: The Meaningless Intimacies
of Embodied Poetics

Inspired by bioelectrical physiology, in the 1855 *Leaves* Whitman constructs a novel poetics—a new semiotic theory about what poetry is, how
it communicates, and by extension, what kinds of things *subjects* (as in per-

sons and as in poetic propositions) are. As I shall argue, this new poetics abjures poetry's propositional subject in order to foreground its materiality as a medium of communication, and this inversion generates many of the idiosyncrasies typical of Whitman's early style, including his penchant for deictics and second-person address, his strangely diffuse yet resolutely embodied persona, and his signature early form, the catalog. But more disconcertingly, I suggest, Whitman's bioelectrical media theory also engenders the eccentricity of his overt disdain for hermeneutics ("these leaves conning you con at peril") and his audacious renunciations of authorial intent ("you will hardly know who I am or what I mean"). Put simply then, I will be tracing here how the dissolution of the liberal subject we have just observed also entails, on Whitman's bioelectrical theory, the dissolution of the subject—the meaning—of poetry.

To understand how bioelectrical discourse might have influenced Whitman's sense of what poetry is and does, it will first help to understand how Spiritualism's onto-theology also functioned as a media theory. Through their popular (if perhaps spurious) demonstrations of bioelectrical communication (sometimes described as "spiritual telegraphy"), Spiritualist mediums drew attention to the material mechanisms by which thought is transmitted from one mind or soul to another. This aspect of Spiritualist theory is spelled out for us in the following excerpt from an editorial published in *Harper's* in April 1852, which, if skeptical about Spiritualism's claim to communicate with the dead, is nonetheless persuaded by its bioelectrical account of communication. As this editor explains,

> Is not the communication from soul to soul literally, as well as figuratively, *tele-graphic*, that is, *far-writing*, or *writing from afar?* An identity might, perhaps, be shown in the very medium of communication, so far as the process has a material medium. There is no difficulty, and no danger, in admitting that the electric fluid may be the agent in the cerebral and organic transmission, as well as in the galvanic battery. . . . The soul, by its own spiritual energy, first turns the emotion or feeling into a thought. It translates the thought from the abstract to the concrete, from the intuitional to the conceptive. It brings it down into the soul's chamber of imagery, and imprints it on the brain. In other words, the message is reduced to writing and given to the clerk at the station-house, who translates it into telegraphic signals. The more immediate transmitting power is now set in operation. An influence is imparted from the brain to the nerves (or wires) of the vocal organs. It is continued to the lungs, and sets in motion a current of air. This impinges on the outward atmosphere,

and is carried on through successive undulations until it reaches the other station for which it was designed. It enters the office-chamber of the ear, communicates with the other cerebral battery, and then writes off from the auditory nerve or wire, the signals which, by the other logical and linguistic faculty, or the clerk at the second station, are translated into the pictorial symbols understood by all, and thus written on the second brain.[42]

According to this bioelectrical model of communication, thought is always materially instantiated. Originating when the "spiritual energy" of the soul converts a "feeling" or "intuitional" impulse (what we might now term an affect) into a "conceptive" piece of mental "imagery," thought is serially transposed: first it is "reduced to writing;" then it is "translate[d] into tele-graphic signals" that shoot through the nerves; next it is translated by the vocal chords into "a current of air" (or, spoken language) and ferried through "the outward atmosphere," at which point it begins the process of reverse-translation into nervous "signals" and thence into "pictorial sym-bols" in the listener's brain.

Two things are particularly worth noting about the account of commu-nication this editorial describes. The first is how its focus on the physiol-ogy of transmission shifts our attention from hermeneutics to the haptics of language. There is little interest in anything like meaning, representa-tion, or interpretation here, and the serial translations this model entails (from "emotion" into "thought;" brain "imagery" into nervous "writing;" and from these "telegraphic signals" into spoken "currents of air;" etc.) oc-casion no concern about the distortion or loss of an original message. What counts as "understanding" or the achievement of "meaning" here therefore shows up not as the product of an act of interpretation, but instead simply coincides with the closing of the communicative circuit: the message is successfully received when this series of energetic transfers arrests in the brain or soul of the listener.

The second thing to notice about this account is how its bioelectrical model of communication effaces the difference between bodies and texts. According to its physics of information, thought is always materially in-stantiated—as "pictorial symbols" in the brain, electrical "signals" in the nerves, "a current of air" on the lips, and rippling "undulations" in the at-mosphere. And yet, as we have just seen, despite its emphasis on thought's material embodiment, at no point does this account worry that informa-tion is being lost, added, or simply reshaped by its translation from one medium to another. In her landmark study of informatics, N. Katherine

Hayles describes this indifference to medium specificity as the symptom of an outlook in which information has "lost its body."[43] But a more Whitmanian way to put this might be to say that, on this account, bodies have become information: manifesting electrical "writing" in the states of its brain and nerves, this bioelectrical body is *readable*: a fleshy text.[44]

In this regard, the bioelectrical account of communication opens up fresh perspectives on Whitman's habitual conflation of poems and persons, and on the distinctive (sometimes even aggressively presumptuous) erotics this conflation lends to his theory of poetry. "Come closer to me. . . . I pass so poorly with paper and types . . . . I must pass with the contact of bodies and souls."[45] Through deftly misdirectional deictics and the unearned familiarity of second-person address, *Leaves* doggedly presses its body to us, interpellating us into an intimate encounter when we thought we were reading alone. Whitman's penchant for conflating poems with bodies, and reading with caressing, has been critically interpreted in a number of different ways. To poststructuralist critics it has often seemed like an infuriating flaw, exposing an "archaic belief in the magical power of naming."[46] By contrast, ecocritics have recently embraced this "mysticism" as a laudably ecopoetical attempt to communicate the "unsaid and unsayable" essence of being without falling back on the anthropocentric biases of human language.[47] Alternatively again, queer theoretical readings have suggested that Whitman cannily courts the contradiction between language and touch in order to generate rhetorical "intimacy-effects" that light up queer desire's "world-making power" to unite "vast networks of virtual strangers" into a nation."[48] But even champions of Whitman's counterfactually embodied poems confess that while he might have wished to write poems that touch us, he was perfectly aware of "the impossibility of doing so literally," and thus they conclude that this gesture is best understood as a kind of rhetorical trick (Michael Moon calls it "planned catachresis") designed to recruit our complicity in Whitman's fantasies of physical immediacy.[49] Along these lines, Helen Vendler argues that Whitman wished to make reading "something closer to a blood transfusion or an infusion of semen," although of course at best this dream could only exist as a speculatively "envisioned mutuality" between himself and his audience.[50] A poem obviously can't actually touch us; Whitman just wants us to *think* about bodies and their exquisite erotics, and in doing so maybe cozen us into feeling aroused by an intimacy he can only pretend to be sharing with us.

As we've just seen, however, from a bioelectrical perspective there is nothing inherently mystical or metaphorical about the claim that reading impinges on us physically: bioelectrically speaking, all communication is embodied. When Whitman complains that he "must pass with the contact of bodies and souls," he is therefore stating a bioelectrical truism: even our prosaic *Harper's* editor agrees that linguistic communication "literally" involves physical contact between bodies and (embodied) minds or souls ("Is not the communication from soul to soul literally, as well as figuratively, *tele-graphic*, that is, *far-writing*, or *writing from afar?*"). By the same token, (and as this editor's ambivalent formulation suggests), bioelectrical theory does not imagine that this embodied "communication from soul to soul" is the opposite of writing or any other ostensibly more mediated mode of communication. For bioelectricity is itself a medium, and thus bioelectrical theory treats all touch as a kind of inscription. By contrast to poststructuralist logic, then, according to which the preference for embodied immediacy over linguistic mediation invariably stems from a specious metaphysics of presence, Whitman's impatience with "paper and types" expresses a frustration at distance or attenuation, not absence. From a bioelectrical perspective, the difference between textual and bodily inscriptions is a matter of degree and not kind: as compared to writing on paper, the nervous writing that is touch is simply temporally closer to the event—the cognitive moment—of meaning. Read this way, Whitman's conflations of body and text no longer appear so deluded or strategically misleading; instead they remind us of the material conditions of our reading.

To this end, Whitman's characteristic use of deictics and second-person address could be understood as attempts to direct us not toward a mystical or purely rhetorical intimacy but to a concretely embodied one. Like Magritte's self-denying still life ("ceci n'est pas une pipe"), this line's reflexive reference to itself as "paper and types" drives my attention from the poem's representational register to its materiality, throwing its ontic there-ness into relief. Suddenly I am acutely aware of the nap of the paper under my thumb, or the edge of the iPad digging into my palm, and in this way Whitman returns me to my body and foregrounds the physical encounter I am at that moment having with his text. In this moment we do, indeed, find ourselves rhetorically interpellated into a scene of intimacy, but one that is neither purely notional nor quite interpersonal: we are recalled to our immediate sensuous encounter with the nonhuman body of the poem itself.

But perhaps even to note the distinction between interpersonal and object relations is to miss Whitman's point. Peter Coviello argues that Whitman invokes a more-than-genital sexuality as "the ground note of *all* human attachment," forming "the engine that drives the human capacity for relation to others."[51] For Coviello, this non-normative sexuality allows Whitman to envision "a kind of *seriality*" embodied in the "queer progeny" of his affectionate future readers—a vision that replaces "generational time, marked by the pairing of children and futurity," with a style of "queer world-making, and indeed queer future-making."[52] In reading Whitman's solicitations of intimacy as efforts to foreground our haptic encounter with the text, I am suggesting that this analysis might be expanded. Beyond even more-than-genital sexuality, *sensuality* is the embodied phenomenon that, for Whitman, grounds our attachment to and generative interaction with all the bodies (human and otherwise) around us.[53] The good news is that literally everything in the room is flirting with you.

Whitman's bioelectrical poetics moreover also shed light on his perverse yet persistent hostility to the idea that the goal of reading is interpretation. Whitman's early editions of *Leaves* are emphatically anti-hermeneutic: "Have you practiced so long to learn to read?," he taunts us right out of the gates; "Have you felt so proud to get at the meaning of poems?"[54] The 1860 *Leaves* doubles down on this rebuke, warning: "These leaves conning you con at peril . . . for it is not for what I have put into it that I have written this book, / Nor is it by reading it you will acquire it."[55] Instead of "conning" his words, Whitman wants us to be assailed by them, wants them to communicate as physical *rather* than linguistic objects. Thus he consistently figures his work as an involuntary emission—unpremeditated as any "ejaculation" or "barbaric yawp," his words are "belched" sounds, "wafted with the odor of his body or breath," exuding organically from his body like that live-oak "uttering joyous leaves all its life" by biological fiat. In one magnificent riff in "Song of Myself," we are serially informed that instead of reading a poem we are in fact being impregnated, jetted with the stuff of arrogant republics, dilated with tremendous breath, embraced and possessed, fetched flush to Whitman's body, and thrummed by the orotund sound of his voice. "Behold I do not give lectures or a little charity," he expounds; "What I give I give out of myself." And lest we mistake him to simply mean he speaks sincerely ("out of myself" as in "from the heart"), he commands us: "open your scarfed chops till I blow grit within you."[56] Whitman relentlessly insists that his poems are touching us. And in describing his poems, *in* his poems, as not-poems, he turns the representational register of his poetry against itself. Cross-dressed as nonlinguistic objects—performing what Michael Warner terms a kind of "metadiscursive queerness"—these poems verbally profess that they have nothing to say.[57]

Indeed, for all our hand-wringing over the (apparent) counter-factualism of Whitman's staged intimacies, we have been strangely unperturbed by the fact that this rhetorical pose arguably renders poetic communication unintelligible. For if, as Vendler argues, Whitman wishes to make poetry "closer to a blood transfusion or an infusion of semen," we might well ask how such an intimate physical exchange (counterfactual or not) could be a model for something that we would still recognize as poetry. How does one "read" a mouthful of grit, an injection of blood, or an "infusion" (in Vendler's delightfully chaste phrase) of semen? And if, after all, it's not "the meaning of poems" we are meant to "get at" by reading *Leaves*, then what *is* the point of reading it? Put differently, if object-poems are simply meant to affect us physically, the way grit and semen and other nonlinguistic objects do, then how will we know a poem from a handsy poet or a mouthful of sand when we see one?

At the risk of stating the obvious, most of us operate under the assumption that all poems are objects but not all objects are poems. We conventionally distinguish between the expressly communicative objects that are texts (or works of art) and, conversely, nontextual objects (hammers, grit, grass, the joints of our bodies) that may in some sense be expressive but that we do not take to be expressly trying to tell us something. Perhaps no critic writing today has had more to say about the costliness of ignoring this distinction than Walter Benn Michaels, who has extensively critiqued the idea that we might "read" nonlinguistic objects, treating objects as if they were signs. According to Michaels, the problem with this "fantasy of meaning without representation," this dream of a "text written in blood," is that unlike signs, objects (blood, grass, leaves, bodies) are not intentional and hence, although they may communicate effects or experiences (can bruise us, excite us, give us a cold), they cannot be said to communicate *meanings*.[58] The difference between experience and significance, he explains, is that experience has to do with the effect the object in fact has on us (and this is not a matter for interpretation, only attestation, the question of our individual experiences of the object), whereas significance has to do with the effect the object intends to have on us (and this is the object of interpretation, the question of the object's meaning).[59] For Michaels, then, *intention* is the additive by which we may distinguish between a text's meaning and its merely incidental effects—between its significance and what Derrida might call its "trace," or what William Wimsatt and Monroe Beardsley describe (in a phrase gratifyingly resonant with my present discussion) as our "psycho-galvanic reflex" to the text.[60] As Michaels argues, "Once we turn the meaning of the poem into our experience of it"—

that is, once we treat the poem as identical to the event of our reading it—"we begin to treat the poem as if it had no meaning."[61]

A reader like Michaels must therefore object that Whitman's embodied poetics is strictly meaningless. For Michaels, it is only insofar as the things Whitman makes are precisely *not* simply objects that they can qualify as poems in the first place. *Leaves'* bioelectric poetics would thus seem to lead poetry up a blind alley: its emphasis on the physicality of reading empties poetry of anything that would count, for Michaels at least, as meaning. By treating poems as material objects that corporeally (or "psycho-galvanically") affect us, Whitman makes poetry indistinguishable from any other species of object in the world. I might just as well "read" anything at all—by its own lights, "Song of Myself" has no more claim to my attention than the surface it's printed on, the dog snoring at my side, or the Mississippi River rolling somewhere out there in the darkness.[62]

But as fatal as it may seem to the project of poetry, Whitman is nothing short of explicit (i.e., thoroughly intentional) about his poetry's lack of intention. He scolds us that we are doing poetry all wrong when we set out "to get at the meaning," and insists that whatever it is that his poetry exists to convey "eludes discussion and print,/It is not to be put in a book . . . . it is not in this book."[63] Laying out his program for poetry in the 1855 preface, he argues that a poem requires neither interpretation nor comprehension to be a success:

> To speak in literature with the perfect rectitude and insousiance of the movements of animals and the unimpeachableness of the sentiment of trees in the woods and grass by the roadside is the flawless triumph of art. . . . You shall not contemplate the flight of the graygull over the bay or the mettlesome action of the blood horse or the tall leaning of sunflowers on their stalk or the appearance of the sun journeying through heaven or the appearance of the moon afterward with any more satisfaction than you shall contemplate [the poet]. The greatest poet has less a marked style and is more the channel of thoughts and things without increase or diminution, and is the free channel of himself. . . . Let who may exalt or startle or fascinate or sooth[e] I will have purposes as health or heat or snow has and be as regardless of observation.[64]

Despite his reference to "speak[ing] in literature," the modes of expression to which Whitman compares poetic utterance here—the movements of animals, the sentiment of trees—are not only neither literary nor spoken; they're not human. The "triumph of art," he asserts, is to attain an inhuman indifference to human understanding. "Let who may exalt or startle or fascinate or sooth[e]," he sniffs; perlocutionary effects are not the essence of poems. Nor are authorial intents: "I will have purposes as health or heat or snow has," he explains, which is to say that his poetry will not have purposes but rather consequences. For—and this is Michaels's point—health and heat and snow cannot be said to purpose or *mean* what they do, since their effects (invigorating, heating, cooling) are unintended. Neither reducible to authorial intent nor to readerly reception, the Whitmanian poem aspires to exist among us like graygulls and blood horses and tall, leaning sunflowers—that is, as things that shape our world without speaking to us, things that "enter" us and imprint themselves on us but that we do not propose to interpretively "understand." It is in this sense that the poem can afford to be "regardless of observation"; freed from the obligation to successfully convey a specific meaning, the poem becomes, like a horse or snow, something that does not depend upon our comprehension to be realized as an effectual or even transformative part of our shared world. As he predicts at the close of "Song of Myself," "You will hardly know who I am or what I mean,/ But I shall be good health to you nevertheless,/ And filter and fibre your blood." Following Whitman's bioelectric logic through, therefore, lands us at the perplexing conclusion that Whitman's interest in embodied poems—in the bioelectrical physiology of reading and the textuality of bodies—stems from a theory of poetic intimacy and physicality that is, in the end, indifferent to poetic meaning.

Embodied Poetics and the Problem of Recognition

It may be useful at this point to take a moment to distinguish Whitman's anti-intentionalism from other varieties of anti-intentionalism in poetry and poetic theory. In the early twentieth century, for instance, Imagist poets maintained that art's value is independent of its capacity to mean. "A poem should not mean/ But be," Archibald MacLeish announced in 1926, elaborating his "Ars Poetica" in lines evocative of Whitman's preface: "A poem should be wordless/ As the flight of birds. . . . A poem should be equal to:/ Not true." Like much of *Leaves*, MacLeish's poem has a kind of self-canceling didacticism, clearly outlining in verse a program *for* verse to be not only non-didactic but also not meaningful. In the vein of Michaels's critique, Robert Pinsky faults Imagism for conveying "the powerful illusion that a poet presents, rather than tells about, a sensory experience."[65] And yet for Imagism, as MacLeish would later specify, the point of the object-poem is "not to recreate the poet's emotion in some one else. . . .

The poem itself is finality, an end, a creation."[66] If the poetry of meaning is valuable insofar as it is instructive to readers (tells them something), the poetry of being needs no readers because being is an end in itself.

Whitman does not share MacLeish's belief in poetry's autonomy or intrinsic value; on the contrary, for Whitman every poem is inherently unfinished. For Whitman, it is neither what poetry is nor what poetry teaches us but what (or really, *whatever*) it does to us that makes it valuable.[67] As he argues, poetry is not self-contained but, rather, lives through its readership:

> A great poem is no finish to a man or woman but rather a beginning. . . .
> The touch of [the poet] tells in action. Whom he takes he takes with
> firm sure grasp into live regions previously unattained . . . . thenceforward
> is no rest. . . . They two shall launch off fearlessly together till the new
> world fits an orbit for itself and looks unabashed on the lesser orbits of
> the stars and sweeps through the ceaseless rings and shall never be
> quiet again.[68]

Here, poetry's value is not intrinsic but, rather, lies in its catalytic capacity, its power to transform us. Indeed, despite his "firm sure grasp" of the reader, the poet is not in control of his poem's explosive effects. Instead, he is merely a co-traveler launched "together" with his reader on a journey of "ceaseless" transformations—a process so endless (so hermeneutically pointless) that Whitman's description loses sight of it as it ripples past the known galaxy, "never [to] be quiet again." This is poetry as black market jetpack: it works by quickening readers, although it claims no responsibility for their resulting trajectories.

For some readers, including Michaels, this euphoric renunciation of authorial control more accurately marks the extinction, as opposed to the ideal, of poetic communication. But although Whitman's anti-intentionalism can seem like a promiscuous willingness to mean *anything* ("an indiscriminate hurrahing for the Universe" is how William James once characterized *Leaves*), I think we do better to recognize it as a studied critique of the idea of intentionalism, a critique that flows logically from his embodied poetics.[69] From a materialist perspective, intentionalism looks like a willfully limiting description of poetry's actual effects in the world: it would limit us to counting only those effects its author predicted, bracketing out a whole range of real, if merely "accidental" or subjective, effects that ripple out incalculably farther than the horizon of any author's original desire. From this perspective, when Whitman suggests that poetry launches "into the unknown," he is not irresponsibly denying paternity of his work but realistically acknowledging the impossibility of predetermining the shape of its future offspring.

Thus I suggest that in asking us to recognize that poems are not just intentional communications but also radically disseminative events, Whitman opens our eyes to the unavoidably indiscreet conditions of poetry's material existence. Like Thoreau with John Brown, Whitman's sense of his poetry's value asks us to take a broader and much longer view of poetry's action—of the real if diffuse and unpredictably proliferating effects it will have unleashed. In this sense, his embodied poetics frames a theory of agential externalities, of the ungovernable aureole about every action (every touch, every utterance, every poem) that obscurely, unpredictably, and at the same time unarrestably links the present moment to outcomes and others invisible to us. And though we may well wish to codify rules— such as intentionalism in hermeneutics, for instance, or tort in the law— that carve out zones in which predictability and responsibility might more locally hold, Whitman's embodied poetics challenges us to embrace the empirical life of poetry, in all its wanton creativity.

Another way to say this might be to point out that Whitman's embodied poetics is just that—a poetics rather than a hermeneutics. As Daniel Tiffany argues in *Infidel Poetics*, poetry has always been uniquely concerned with language's sensuous dimensions (its sounds and rhythms), and this interest in the "cadaverous materiality" of language's body drives poetic language toward obscurity.[70] Sketching the history of lyric obscurity from ancient riddles and charms through the "difficulty" of high modernist poetry, Tiffany argues that a principled defiance of transparency or even intelligibility lies at the very heart of the poetic project. Indeed, for Tiffany, poetry's obscurity grounds its peculiar sociality: "Obscurity," he writes, "rather than being the principle impediment to poetry's social relevance, would provide the key to models of community derived specifically from the nature of lyric expression."[71] Thus, what might otherwise seem like the obstacle to poetry's ability to communicate—its opacity, its elliptical difficulty—is, for Tiffany, the grounds of its uniquely "negative sociability."[72] Poetry under this description does not communicate so much as it convenes, gathering speakers and hearers, authors and readers, around the incomprehensible lyric object.

Like Imagism's theory of poetic autonomy, Tiffany's theory of lyric obscurity bears some illuminating parallels to Whitman's embodied poetics, but in the end remains distinct. For Tiffany, lyric obscurity is best "regarded principally as an *event* or deed" rather than as an encrypted message, and poetry's sociality inheres not in *what* it communicates but, rather, in its power to solicit us into this scene of (obscure, even contentless) communication.[73] Under this understanding of lyric, we might conclude that Whitman's embodied poetics—his denial of poetry's meaning and insistence on its physiological eventfulness—is not, in fact, antipoetic but, rather, articulates the terms of the poetic project tout court.[74] However, to see Whitman as an exemplar of Tiffany's lyric theory may be to narrow the claims that Whitman is making about obscurity. For Tiffany, the obscure objects that are poems constitute a unique class of objects—poems are especially obscure, or obscure in some special (poetic) way. For Whitman, however, obscurity is not a feature particular to poetry; it is, rather, a condition endemic to all embodied life. In other words, obscurity is not an effect of Whitman's lyrics (it is hard to imagine clearer, more prosaically candid lines than his) but rather Whitman's poetry is *about* obscurity: he is trying to articulate the philosophical problem of the obscurity of embodied being. When he says that he "cannot tell how my ankles bend . . . . nor whence the cause of my faintest wish," he's not telling a riddle; he's telling us about the riddle that ankles and wishes *are*.[75]

More precisely, Whitman is noting the mystery of the way ankles and wishes work—the hows and whences of their bendings. This specification is an important one, since the real and fundamental source of ontological obscurity for Whitman is the fact that bodies are open-ended: receiving and disseminating effects, perpetually undergoing reinscription, they are materially although not metaphysically transcendent. If most of us do not wonder about our bends and bents, it is because we take these things to be expressions of our willful intentions. But as we have seen, on Whitman's bioelectric theory intentions are a kind of optical illusion. At best, they describe a misleadingly thin slice of a material history that in fact engulfs intention in its cascade of preceding causes and unpredictably sprawling effects. The lyric obscurity that he is talking about, then, and that makes him unable to say what a poem finally means (even just what it finally *causes*) is the consequence of a condition that poetry shares with literally everything: every embodied *thing* is, for Whitman, a thing in flux. To say "who I am or what I mean," one would have to find a way to stand outside of time and space, looking back from their ends, in order to catalog the finally completed sequence of material history that passed through a given body or poem. One must write a tremendously long catalog, and even then, the catalog would not contain itself.

Put differently, there is an important difference between something that is unsayable because its meaning is encrypted (as in lyric obscurity, or as in the hermetic value of Imagism's poem-of-being) and something that is unsayable because its meaning is *unfinished*—because the thing itself is still unfolding. And therefore, unlike the obscurity of Tiffany's occulted subjects or the self-sufficiency of MacLeish's autonomous ones, Whitman's embodied subjects (lyric, human, or otherwise) confront us with a problem of recognition that is unique to his poetics. As I shall explore in the next section, the ineffability of Whitman's processual bodies—what I have described, in the prior section, as the self-loss or identity-lessness of his continuously evolving subjects—lands us in a world in which recognition of the other would seem to be impossible because the other is perpetually changing. Accordingly, the next section asks, if the bioelectrical body does not so much confer identity as efface it by tracing our lineaments out through the vast network of our sensuous attachments, then what does this do to Whitman's conception of racial difference and human equality? And what kind of democracy can subsist in a world of such indiscrete individuals?

Infinity at Auction: Interracial Sympathy in Whitman's Democracy

Reviving one of Spiritualism's preferred terms for bioelectrical communication, Jane Bennett reads Whitman's porous bodies as, above all, *sympathetic* ones. Thus she argues that Whitman's interest in sensuous susceptibility highlights "sympathy's capacity to imprint or act upon the flesh," alerting us to the ways in which sympathy moves as "a more-than-human or natural force" between bodies that are "continuously affecting and being affected by each other and by atmospheres."[76] In this way, Whitman challenges us "to form a conception of sympathy that is more than a dynamic of 'identification' between two or more (aspirationally) sovereign individuals," and in doing so, Bennett suggests, Whitmanian sympathy avoids the most glaring ethical flaw in sympathy as it has conventionally been conceived. Saidiya Hartman explains that this flaw arises when "in making the other's suffering one's own, this suffering is occluded by the other's obliteration"; in other words, in the act of identifying with the other, we risk overwriting the other's identity with our own.[77] By contrast, Bennett suggest that Whitman helps us to imagine a form of sympathy that is not premised upon an imagined projection (which is also an erasure) but is instead embodied, grounded in "a trans-individual model of receptivity, affectivity, and sociality."[78] On this reading, sympathy names a bodily susceptibility that reveals not simply our notional similarity or speculative equality with the other, but our material involvement with—our dependence upon and constitution through—the body of the other.

In this section, I propose to both extend and critique this conception of Whitmanian sympathy by examining how its substitution of mutuality for equality informs Whitman's antislavery argument in "I Sing the Body Electric." If the human body, as Whitman conceives of it, is the ever-shifting tally of an ongoing and hence ineffable creative process, then how can the politics of recognition proceed? What happens to the phenomenon of interracial sympathy when neither the subject nor the object in a given scene of identification can be identified? What, indeed, could a democratic politics without discrete persons even look like? The processualism of Whitman's embodied poetics challenges us to shift our attention from individuals and the drama of their interpersonal interactions, to systems and the ecology of their material intra-relations. In this section I propose to consider the political affordances and limitations of this embodied ontology, particularly as it informs Whitman's antislavery thought.

Although neither an ardent nor even a particularly consistent antislavery advocate, Whitman provides at least one clear enunciation of his opposition to slavery in the climactic slave auction scene of "I Sing the Body Electric."[79] As its title (appended in 1867) suggests, this poem is a paean to bioelectric embodiment, and ultimately it reproduces the contradiction of antebellum Spiritualist theology, asserting the divinity of the nervous body while pointing to the paradoxically mundane physics of its purely processual transcendence. ("The man's body is sacred and the woman's body is sacred," Whitman affirms; "Each has his or her place in the procession / All is a procession, / The universe is a procession with measured and beautiful motion.")[80] The poem famously closes with a scene in which Whitman's speaker "helps" at a slave auction by clambering up onto the auction block to take over the work of enumerating the features of the Black bodies for sale. He does so in order to assert that every life is invaluable and that "each belongs here or anywhere just as much as the well-off . . . . just as much as you." This message of inclusion has earned the poem the reputation of being a celebration of "a fully inclusive and egalitarian democracy."[81] As Martin Klammer, Betsey Erkkila, Karen Sánchez-Eppler, and Jimmie Killingsworth variously argue, the poem mounts a powerful "defense of black personhood" (Erkkila) and reaffirms the "sacred" nature of every body (Killingsworth).[82]

Things get complicated, however, for the very notion of "personhood" as this poem mounts its defense of the invaluable body. Whitman affirms at the poem's outset that "the expression of the body of man or woman balks account" and its concluding scene, in which the speaker takes over the work of accounting from an auctioneer who "does not half know his business," offers a strikingly literal demonstration of this statement. Whitman's own, better calculus unfolds in a series of catalogs that demonstrate the absurdity of buying and selling persons:

Gentlemen look on this curious creature,
Whatever the bids of the bidders they cannot be high enough for him,
For him the globe lay preparing quintillions of years without one animal
                                                                    or plant,
For him the revolving cycles truly and steadily rolled.

In that head the all-baffling brain,
In it and below it the making of the attributes of heroes.

Examine these limbs, red black or white . . . . they are very cunning in
                                                          tendon and nerve;
They shall be stript that you may see them.

Exquisite senses, lifelit eyes, pluck, volition. . . .

Within there runs this blood . . . . the same old blood . . the same red
                                                              running blood;
There swells and jets his heart . . . . There all passions and desires . . all
                                                  reachings and aspirations. . . .

This is not only one man . . . . he is the father of those who shall be
                                                        fathers in their turns,
In him the start of populous states and rich republics,
Of him countless immortal lives with countless embodiments and
                                                                enjoyments.

How do you know who shall come from the offspring of his offspring
                                                        through the centuries?
What might you find you have come from yourself if you could trace back
                                                      through the centuries?[83]

By the end of this extended catalog, we would still be hard-pressed to identify the enslaved man at its center (is he old? young? tall? short?). In place of an individualizing portrait, Whitman gives us a natural history of this man's body. The polemical force of this move is that it allows Whitman to underscore how deeply entangled this ostensibly solitary figure in fact is in the material fabric of the shared world.[84] If the institution of slavery has left this man kinless, Whitman's catalog reminds us that his genealogy is nonetheless epically long and unbroken, that his body is the product of a cosmic history: first the earth cohered from a nebula, then soils crumbled from bare rock, and finally myriad stages of development brought us the "cunning" design of this man's limbs and the human passions of his blood. Thus Whitman affirms that the slave's story is a branch of humanity's history as a species, and extends even farther back through the larger material history of the earth and stars. If this asserts the shared history of all bodies, it also insists on each body's limitlessness: in Whitman's eyes, this man is the index of an unimaginably long history ("quintillions of years") that culminates in him, and of a future that exfoliates out from him (in "countless immortal lives") whose horizon is equally unforeseeable. Hence Whitman concludes, "This is not only one man"; the only seemingly singular figure we see is an integral part of a recombinatory and creatively unfolding physical cosmos.

No ordinary slice of antislavery rhetoric, then, this passage argues that no bid could be high enough for this enslaved man because no one can say precisely what it is that they are bidding on in the first place. "How do you know" what the true scope of his life will turn out to have been? And if you cannot know, how dare you presume to assess the value of something with such unknown parameters—to put a price on an open-ended process? If the slave auction scene is uncomfortable—and it is in a number of ways—this is not least because Whitman's critique of slavery refuses to explicitly condemn the immorality of selling persons. The objection this passage raises is not that human life is priceless because it is "sacred" (i.e., morally exceptional to materialist systems of value); it is, more specifically, that the value of any body is *inestimable*. This man "balks account" because he is the temporary individuation of an unfolding cosmos, the momentary instantiation of a material and social process so awesomely boundless that it enfolds both his and our pasts and futures in its vast transhistorical sweep. "All is procession," Whitman exclaims in the lines that introduce this scene: "The universe is a procession with measured and beautiful motion." Within this processual plenum, it is impossible to circumscribe being into discrete objects, to tell where one body ends and another begins.

Critics have not always looked kindly on Whitman's emulsifying vision. D. H. Lawrence famously accused Whitman of substituting the sloppiness of "merger" for the delicate mutuality of interpersonal sympathy.[85] More recently, Sánchez-Eppler faults Whitmanian sympathy, in terms that echo Hartman's critique of sympathy, for failing to inspire a truly interracial sympathy. Whitman simply "dissolves the bodies" of both slave and spectator, Sánchez-Eppler observes, effacing the enslaved man's specificity in the process of uniting slave and spectator into an undifferentiated, transpersonal whole.[86]

We may now be in a position to see how this "failure" is not just integral to this scene but structural to Whitman's poetics and its underlying ontology. Indeed, one now begins to see why Whitman volunteers for the auctioneer's job, for he has done more than any other poet to show how the auctioneer's catalog might be a kind of spiritual (even Spiritualist) exercise—a kind of chanting hymn to the transcendental nonsingularity, the finally uninumerable multiplicity, of any one thing. A solitary slave at auction is also a prehistoric globe, revolving seasonal cycles, rich republics, and countless future lives; a poet is also a book of poems, a leaf of grass under our bootsoles. Everything exceeds its immediate body and in this sense, equally enmeshed in a sympathetically united cosmos, everything is ultimately one. But what could equality look like in this sprawling, heterogeneous unity? Is the sameness of two things that are conjoined (one) the same as the sameness of two things that are comparable (equal)? That is, is asserting our universal material mutuality really tantamount to establishing our universal moral equality? What would it mean to be equal to something that is, in the final analysis, not just *like* but *part of* yourself?

Thus we may begin to appreciate the nonhumanism of Whitman's argument with slavery, and the extent to which it undermines the metaphysics of personhood in which democracy and racial equality have both traditionally traded. In the liberal humanist tradition enshrined in the U.S. founding documents, "all men are created equal" and are vested with certain "unalienable Rights." From this premise, as Douglass saw, the question of whether or not slavery is consistent with this principle of equality before the law depends upon establishing whether or not slaves should be recognized as "men," and as such endowed with what Chief Justice Taney, in his *Dred Scott* decision, terms "rights which the white man was bound to respect." And thus, as I have suggested across the preceding chapters of this book, the effort to establish the humanity of the slave is how race, as a system of visible differences and attitudes toward those differences, came to seem so important. Look at this hair, this skin, the turn of this hip: do you, white American, recognize this body as categorically like yours, or different? Can you see yourself in this body, feel sympathy for it?

Whitman moots these questions of recognition; in the ontology that he articulates and makes the marrow of his revisionary poetics, equality operates by a very different logic. As the auction scene in "I Sing the Body Electric" makes clear, there can be no politics of recognition for the Whitmanian self because this self is fundamentally unrecognizable—it is impossible to even determine the shape of the phenomenon that it (they?) is (will have been?). Instead, the egalitarian ethos of his verse, such as it is, turns on the notion that the sameness of material *contiguity* (you are physically connected to me) can be seamlessly substituted for the sameness of moral *equality* (you are as good as me). *Leaves* flirts with this conversion from its outset: "Every atom belonging to me, as good belongs to you," it begins, provocatively refusing to choose between the moral claim that you and I are of equal worth (your atoms are as good as mine) and the empirical claim that you and I share matter (my atoms may one day be yours—check your bootsoles).[87] Indeed, throughout his first three editions, Whitman continually works the slippage between material mutuality, affective intimacy, and moral equality, but however closely he conflates them, it is not clear that these modes of imagining political community are interchangeable. The fluidity of the Whitmanian person defies the calculus of equality, dissolving the units (here persons) that equality compares into an undifferentiable unity. His defense of the Black body's equality is thus arguably useless in the same way that his poetics is, strictly speaking, useless: both highlight the illimitable natural history of bodies and poems, but since empirical expansiveness is a feature of every object in Whitman's ontology, it does not suggest how or why these objects *specifically* ought to be valued.[88] What legal rights are due to human bodies as opposed to grass or blood or a poem? Why should we read a poem as opposed to blood or grass or a human body?

Like his antihermeneutic poetics, then, Whitman's materialist account of persons is anti-identitarian. Stripping both poems and persons of conventional subjecthood (individual identity or intentional meaning), he returns them to us as empirically infinite processes, entangled aspects of a procreant "reality . . . . materialism first and last imbueing."[89] At once disconcertingly modest and astoundingly epic, this processualism does away with identity by proliferating it such that both poems and persons threaten to lose their normative or ethical force. We are no longer tasked with recognizing what they "truly" mean, who they "really" are. Instead, Whitman's politics follow his poetics in inviting us to marvel at the ineffable (although not otherworldly) wonder of interconnected being, to acknowledge how "every spear of grass and the frames and spirits of men and women and all that concerns them are unspeakably perfect miracles all referring to all."[90]

The force of this admirably ecological vision—the truly exquisite complexity of the relational world it discloses—is therefore also what seems to render it politically inert. For without discrete units it is not clear that there can be either democracy or equality as we know them; there is only, and always already, attachment and unity. Moreover, even if we permit ourselves to act *as if* the temporary organizations of matter we call bodies were countably distinct, the fact remains that, by Whitman's lights, literally every material body (whether human, animal, vegetable, mineral, or textual) is incalculable, and thus invaluable. This confronts us with the problem of a moral polity constituted by literally everything. Conceived in terms of its material interinvolvement, this polity displaces the question of its constituents' similarities and differences and thus bypasses the politics of representation and recognition that subtend the politics of race, class, gender, sexual orientation, physical ability, and species rights as we currently know them. As I shall discuss in Chapter 4 and the Coda, the problem of making this processual ontology speak to the concerns of embodied specificity and racial difference continues to trouble contemporary posthumanism today.

In the foregoing three chapters I have been excavating a materialist strain of antislavery thought that began to crystallize in the writings of Douglass, Thoreau, and Whitman in the 1850s as an embodied alternative to biological racism. This antislavery materialism coalesces in their work neither as a consistent political platform nor as an explicitly codified theory but, rather, as a tendency of thought arising from their efforts to reimagine "the human" in light of burgeoning midcentury discourses of human embodiment. Departing from both mainstream abolitionism (which largely denied the relevance of bodily difference to human equality) and biological racism (which argued that certain bodies—Black, native, female—are biologically determined and hence naturally inferior), these authors embrace the materiality of human being and use it to dismantle the notion of biological hierarchy. In doing so, their writings invoke a physical cosmos whose dense interdependencies preclude the erection of racial and speciological hierarchy (Douglass), in which the ceaseless drift of evolutionary change belies racial and speciological essentialism (Thoreau), and in which the processual becomings of our permeable bodies blur the distinction between entities (Whitman). In place of racial science's static typological system, these antebellum materialisms give us an anti-essentialist ontology in which identity is contingent and fluid, shaped by the dynamic interrelation of biological and cultural forces.

In navigating this third way between disembodied antislavery and biological racism, these authors invite us to radically rethink the category of the human. This effort was, at least in part, strategic: a response not only to the rising cachet of empirical science but also to the mutual support liberal and racist ideologies lent each other in the nineteenth century. Indeed, as we have seen, although liberal humanism's universalism and racism's hierarchism would seem to be antithetical, biological racism in fact quite happily invoked liberal humanism's account of the human as a form of being that is uniquely independent of the material order. The figure of the autonomous, disembodied liberal self funded midcentury racism's hierarchical distinction between "fully" human white persons (whose characteristic racial trait is to be rationally independent of their bodies) and "lesser" forms of racialized, gendered, bestialized, and objectified beings, whose identities are biologically predetermined. Thus despite its ostensible materialism, antebellum racism shared liberalism's fundamental assumption that the most fully human was the least embodied; meanwhile, despite its ostensible universalism, antebellum liberalism needed the fatally embodied form of life racism supplied in order to secure its own self-definition. As Russ Castronovo observes, this reciprocal exchange yields a singularly deathly episteme: between the human citizen whose body is effaced by the purifying fires of liberal universalism and, by contrast, the dehumanized noncitizen who is sentenced "to excessive and lethal embodiment," this modern liberal-raciological order proves singularly hostile to embodied life.[91] Stepping outside the deadly either/or of a disaffectedly abstract liberal personhood on one side and a dehumanized materiality on the other, Douglass, Thoreau, and Whitman demonstrate that empiricism's entry into antebellum political reasoning in fact afforded a wider range of embodied discourses than these two alternatives allow. Insisting upon the materiality of all humans, these authors frame a tentative and experimental but provocative counterdiscourse that resists biological racism and points beyond liberal humanism's conception of the human.

At the same time, as I have tried to show, this revisionary materialism was not without cost to these authors insofar as their forays into embodied thinking undermined aspects of the progressive liberalism and romantic individualism with which they are broadly associated. Their incipient materialism often appears as a subversively contrapuntal theme in their thought, at odds with the liberal commitments they elsewhere espouse. Douglass's strategic embrace of animality is, for instance, in tension with his determination to establish beyond doubt his race's claim to the rights and privileges of full humanity. Thoreau's appeal to evolution as an agent of moral change conflicts with his faith in the power of the conscientious individual to effect profound personal and political reform; and Whitman's sense of himself as an expansively interconnected material plenum ("a kosmos") is disconcertingly at odds with his sense of himself as a discrete and self-possessed liberal subject ("Walt Whitman") and representative of a class ("an American, one of the roughs"). This is to suggest, then, that there is a distinctly illiberal tendency in the materialist swings of these authors' thought—that their explorations of human ontology undermine their appeals to human rights, agency, and selfhood as liberal humanism constructs them. This heretical tendency marks the opening of their work onto radically new modes of imagining the human—to alternative epistemes that are not only antiracist but whose antiracism moreover transforms our conception of human being and its modes of community from the ground up.

In the modern politics of democratic pluralism, the effort to end racism and other exclusions based on embodied identity involves a struggle at once *for* inclusion and against incorporation into a disembodied universalism that ignores or denies the embodied difference of these lived identities. The challenge of this pluralistic politics of sympathy is thus to insist upon individual and embodied specificity while also asserting the equality of humans and universality of human rights. The material processualism that subtends these antebellum antislavery materialisms can light up the difficulty of making contemporary posthumanist discourses of ontological fluidity—in assemblage theory, new materialism, and "affirmative" biopolitics, for instance—speak to discourses of racial and social justice. As I shall explore in Chapter 4 and the Coda, although like Douglass, Thoreau, and Whitman many posthumanists today understand themselves to be working toward an expanded democratic politics and in the service of a more radically egalitarian and inclusive ethics, it is not clear that the materialist ontology they embrace can support the redeemed democracy they envision. At the very least, I shall suggest that this conversation, already begun, is one that we now need to be having.

CHAPTER 4

Posthumanism and the Problem of Social Justice: Race and Materiality in the Twenty-First Century

In this chapter I would like to explore the present-day status and stakes of the epistemic overhaul that I have been tracing through the antislavery materialisms of Frederick Douglass, Henry David Thoreau, and Walt Whitman. The preceding chapters have suggested that these authors' embodied accounts of the human bear certain affinities with the materialist turn of contemporary posthumanist theory. There is, of course, a kind of knowledge and also a kind of pleasure to be had in recognizing the slant rhymes of historical recurrence. However, this chapter starts from the premise that antebellum antislavery materialism should be interesting to us now not simply because of its shadowy prescience of posthumanist theory, but also because its divergence from contemporary theory can help to light up absences and aporias in posthumanist discourse today.

The absence that antebellum antislavery materialism makes conspicuous is the missing term of race in contemporary posthumanist theory. As I have argued, the proto-posthumanism that Douglass, Thoreau, and Whitman developed in the 1850s was triggered by the rise of racial science and the consolidation of modern biological racism. Race is the founding proposition around which their antislavery materialisms gather, like so many antibodies, to wrest human materiality away from its conscription by racist ideology. Against the backdrop of this history, the marginality of race in contemporary posthumanist discourse is puzzling. In this regard, examining the transhistorical echoes between antislavery and contemporary posthumanist materialism can help to bring the latter's undertheorized relationship to histories of racism and social justice into sharper focus. In doing so, I hope to amplify demands that posthumanism's current critics are already making for a fuller accounting of posthumanism's racial politics.

Indeed, a growing number of critics now suggest that the absence of race from posthumanist theorizing constitutes a considerable theoretical and ethical failure. This absence registers most notably in what Zakiyyah Jackson describes as posthumanism's "resounding silence" on the subject of racism, which remains one of the most powerful and resilient technologies for delimiting and policing the border between the "fully" human and the "nonhuman."[1] Race's absence furthermore registers in the posthumanist archive's general neglect of theorists of color whose analyses of "the tight bonds between humanity and racializing assemblages in the modern era" prefigure posthumanism's critique of Western humanism's abjection of the nonhuman. As Alexander Weheliye points out, black feminists like Sylvia Wynter and Hortense Spillers began calling for revisionary "genres" or conceptions of the human long before contemporary posthumanism picked up this refrain.[2]

To be fair, most critics working under posthumanism's large tent understand themselves to be advancing a critique of humanism's exclusions that is sympathetic to antiracism while seeking to go beyond the anthropocentric terms it offers. For these critics, posthumanism is a liberatory project that proposes to radically extend the democratizing efforts that antiracism and antisexism pioneered. Thus when Bruno Latour proposes that the exclusion of nonhuman being from moral and political consideration "will soon appear . . . as extravagant as when the Founding Fathers denied slaves and women the vote," he identifies posthumanism as the successor to antiracism: a related but ultimately distinct political struggle.[3] Whereas antiracist and antisexist movements speak up for the equality of what they construe as dehumanized humans, posthumanism's "flat ontology" makes the case for the ethical and political standing of nonhuman being, human or otherwise.

At its broadest, this chapter proposes that this distinction between dehumanized and nonhuman beings—a distinction that insists that "human" is not just a biological but a natural moral identity—lies at the root of racism's marginality in posthumanist discourse, as well as the marginality of speciesism in antiracist discourse. Although theorists from both of these schools insist that "the human" is an ideological construct—a moral category whose borders have been willfully drawn and redrawn throughout Western humanism's history—both schools nevertheless regularly naturalize the human by conflating this moral category with the biological category *Homo sapiens*. Thus, for instance, when posthumanists denounce human exceptionalism and defend nonhuman rights, they generally understand themselves to be speaking up for non–*Homo sapiens*. But in conflating the human with *Homo sapiens*, their critics observe, posthumanists ignore the long and ongoing history of racism that has systematically demoted targeted populations of *Homo sapiens* to the status of "nonhuman." Meanwhile, if posthumanism fails to acknowledge that "the nonhuman" may include some *Homo sapiens*, for their part antiracist theorists also tend to argue that this inclusion is a heinous category mistake. That is, when antiracist critics document the genocidal consequences suffered by those to whom Western humanism has denied human status, they tend to insist that this moral category *is* in truth natural: that all *Homo sapiens* are human and ought, therefore, to be accorded equal human rights. Between posthumanism's biologization of the moral category, "human," and antiracism's moralization of the biological category, *Homo sapiens*, the artificiality of "the human"—something both discourses, in other moments, quite compellingly flag—recedes from view.

To argue that the human is not synonymous with *Homo sapiens* is to observe something so simple, so very basic to posthumanist and antiracist theorizing, that it sometimes strikes me that I might be embarrassing myself. Forging ahead nonetheless, this chapter aims to demonstrate that the slippage between the human and *Homo sapiens* (or, conversely, between the nonhuman and non–*Homo sapiens*) is persistent in posthumanist and social justice criticism and contributes to their mutual alienation. The first two sections below will therefore rehearse some of the most trenchant objections and correctives to posthumanist theory offered by recent antiracist and social justice criticism. Although this discussion is bound to offer a critique of posthumanist theory, it is not meant to condemn the posthumanist project tout court but, on the contrary, to strengthen it by suggesting how posthumanism might productively engage with antiracist and social justice theory going forward. As I shall suggest, a closer collaboration between posthumanist and social justice theories can help to clarify the broad common ground that they in fact share.

Toward this end, my third and final section will highlight posthumanism's resonance with the work of the anticolonial and Black feminist theorist,

Sylvia Wynter. I focus on Wynter's work because, more than any other critic now writing on Blackness and justice, Wynter insists that overcoming racism is not simply a matter of redeeming liberal humanism but rather commits us to inventing new "genres of the human" that look beyond Western humanism's episteme of "Man." Wynter's work, then, frames social justice as an explicitly post*humanist* project—a project of moving beyond Western humanism—and as such it offers the most fertile site for discerning crosscurrents between posthumanist and social justice projects. This third section therefore lays out my vision for the partial reconciliation and future collaboration between posthumanist materialisms and post*humanist* social justice theories. One major advantage of this collaboration, I suggest, is that read through one another, these theories speak each other's lapses, illuminating blind spots the other cannot see. Thus I show how each attempts to preserve a central feature of the episteme they ostensibly oppose: posthumanism remains committed to liberalism's individualist politics while even Wynter's social justice theory remains invested in Western humanism's philosophy of human exceptionalism. Thus I propose that, taken together, these theories spur each other to live up to the transformative potential of their epistemic challenge to liberal humanism's construction of "Man."

At the same time, however, I shall argue that the clarified posthumanism this collaboration yields also makes the limitations of this project more visible—limitations that, I argue, antislavery materialism anticipates and therefore can help us to anatomize. Above I have suggested that the antebellum materialism I have been outlining lights up absences and aporias in its latter-day counterpart; if the absence is race, the aporia we arrive at here has to do with what I shall describe, in my Coda, as posthumanism's romanticism. This chapter's detour through twenty-first-century posthumanisms thus ultimately leads us back to the antebellum sources with which it starts. In the Coda I will return to Douglass, Thoreau, and Whitman in order to suggest how their antislavery materialism helps us to confront the vestiges of romantic naturalism within modern posthumanism and presses us to reimagine what a future posthumanist politics might look like.

Lastly, a note on methodology: these final chapters depart from the broadly historicist and textual approach of my foregoing chapters to engage in a more abstractly philosophical discussion of recent critical theory. They are nonetheless written with a number of different potential readers in mind: from scholars of the nineteenth century who have little or no familiarity with contemporary critical theory, to critical theorists with little or no interest in nineteenth-century literature. I have therefore tried to describe the theories treated in these final chapters in terms that rely as little as possible upon the idioms or critical jargons characteristic of each. To some readers this decision may seem to express a degree of skepticism or estrangement from these critical schools, but my aim is clarity in the hopes that making these discourses accessible to new readers—and more mutually accessible to each other—will contribute to their further development.

Myopias of the Anthropocene: Human ≠ Homo sapiens

Posthumanist materialism confronts us with our inhumanity—our animality, materiality, and irreducible alterity to ourselves. It presents this dehumanizing portrait in a spirit of radical generosity: by acknowledging our constitution through, and dependence upon, nonhuman beings and systems, posthumanists suggest that we may finally renounce the speciological chauvinism (and perhaps even the suicidal tendencies) of our self-proclaimed autonomy from nature. Honoring that acknowledgment would necessarily entail a profound rearrangement of current modes of existence at all levels of its ordering. Daunting though this wholesale revolution may be, the hope is that we might yet restructure global biopolitics and neoliberal biocapitalism, reorganize our consumptive and ethical behaviors, and reinvent our cultural and autobiographical narratives to make them, as N. Katherine Hayles puts it, "conducive to the long-range survival of humans and of other life-forms, biological and artificial, with whom we share the planet and ourselves."[4] For posthumanists, the continued flourishing of the human species depends upon embracing its nonhumanity, including the sensitive mechanisms of its organism and the fragile ecosystems of human and nonhuman existence on which human life depends. We must learn to think in terms of collective, planetary survival; indeed, given the porously networked nature of the human organism, there is, posthumanists suggest, no other kind.

But if this effort to dehumanize the human is not intended to be degrading, it is nonetheless still necessary to theorize its relation to the dehumanizing assemblages of racism and sexism that precede it—a task that contemporary posthumanism has yet to rigorously take up. The urgency of specifying this relation is in part a matter of bridge building. Posthumanism's emphasis upon human animality and objecthood understandably sets off alarm bells for those who are or who work on behalf of those struggling to be recognized as fully human and as rights-bearing persons before the law. Christopher Peterson observes that posthumanists therefore "cannot expect racial minorities simply to forget the prolonged history of their dehumanization, as if to say, 'We are all animals, so get over it!'"[5] Insofar as posthumanist critics have begun to address this resistance, there is evidence that they may not yet fully understand its complaint. In the introduction to a recent collection on "the nonhuman turn," for instance—a collection that proposes "to name, characterize, and therefore to consolidate" this emerging posthumanist bent—Richard Grusin suggests that skepticism toward this turn arises from a default suspicion of materiality that is the result of social constructivism's predominance in the past fifty years of critical discourse.[6] "Participants in liberatory scholarly projects," Grusin offers, tend to presume "that any appeal to nature . . . could only operate in service of a defense of the status quo."[7] While Grusin's diagnosis may well be true in many cases, it fails to account for the most compelling concerns raised by scholars of social justice, as I shall attempt to demonstrate below. It also discounts the move away from strict social constructivism that has unfolded across "liberatory" critical discourses, including work in feminist, queer, postcolonial, and critical race theory in recent years—some of which has been vital to posthumanism's emergence.[8] As we shall see in this chapter, then, the concerns that social justice theorists bring to posthumanism do not neatly boil down to an objection to posthumanism's materialism per se but, rather, raise questions about its inattention to human inequality.

This inattention to racism and other forms of discrimination finds expression in posthumanism's rhetorical tendency to invoke the human in the monolithic singular—as if, writes Alexander Weheliye, "we have now entered a stage in human development where all subjects have been granted equal access to western humanity."[9] But of course, as Aimé Césaire memorably observed, Western civilization has as yet never lived "a true humanism—a humanism made to the measure of the world"; instead, as I have discussed in Chapter 1, under biopolitics, Western liberal humanism has sorted biological humans along a racially and sexually coded spectrum from the "fully" human to the "nonhuman."[10] A concern for social justice therefore commits us to attend to the ways in which the human/nonhuman binary not only functions to privilege *Homo sapiens* above other animal species but is simultaneously deployed to differentiate *Homo sapiens* into different categories of legal and social protection. In light of the lethally uneven attribution of "humanity" across *Homo sapiens*, posthumanism's invitation to divest from Western humanism's privileging of humanness can appear to be inequitable itself insofar as it demands a disavowal that is potentially far more costly to those whose life chances are already lowered by their marginalization from the human. Hence Jinthana Haritaworn urges us to ask, "for whom might identifying with the nonhuman be too risky a move?"[11]

On the face of it, this question raises a concern that might easily be countered. After all, it assumes that dehumanized populations have more to lose by identifying with the nonhuman whereas, arguably, divesting from the human promises to be costlier to those populations whose lives have heretofore been systematically protected by this episteme than it is to those who are oppressed and exterminated by it.[12] At the very least, whether biopolitically condemned populations would be better off fighting for recognition under the auspices of Western humanism or, conversely, fighting to overthrow this episteme is a complicated question whose answer cannot be known in advance and whose risks may look very different in the short and the long term. Neither is it clear how the immediate individual perils of living without full liberal recognition can or should be measured against the collective planetary risks of persisting in this epistemic order. What good will a perfected humanism be to a human population facing mass extinction in a climate inimical to human life?

Nonetheless, by flagging the unequal distribution of humanness among *Homo sapiens*, Haritaworn's question crucially interrupts a conflation of the human with *Homo sapiens* that pervades posthumanist critiques of anthropocentrism. The term "anthropocentrism" has been broadly used in both posthumanist and environmentalist circles to indict a myopic selfishness that is, in this critique's strongest formulations, not just ideological but structurally inherent to human consciousness. In recent years, the strong version of this critique has become a central feature of "speculative realism," a distinctive school of posthumanist theory that endeavors to think beyond human "finitude"—beyond, that is, the phenomenologically "centered points of view" endemic to the "organic perception" of all *Homo sapiens* as "sensing and world-oriented beings."[13] This speculative school—which encompasses projects like Claire Colebrook's efforts to envision thought after human extinction, as well as projects that belong to the subfield of object-oriented ontology (OOO)—proposes to think beyond the structural limitations that are physiologically built into the perceptual and cognitive apparatus of *Homo sapiens*. Thus in contrast to the mainstream of posthumanism, which aims to think beyond a particular (Western liberal humanist) episteme of the human, this school of thought attempts to imagine (if that is still the right word) an inorganic perspective divorced from *Homo sapiens*' embodied mind. It seeks to pioneer a perspective that "frees itself from folding the earth's surface around human survival" and from what Quentin Meillassoux terms "correlationism," the philosophical notion that our perception of "reality" is inevitably a representation shaped by (correlated with) the faculties particular to our species.[14] In short, this school of posthumanism explores ways to speculatively move beyond what it views as the "anthropocentric" bias that organically limits the human mind.

The political trouble with this project arises from the way its critique of "anthropocentrism" allows for slippage between a critique of cognitive finitude (an epistemological limitation biologically endemic to *Homo sapiens*) and a critique of environmentally exploitative practices (an ethical failing ideologically endemic to Western civilization).[15] The political fallout of that slippage becomes visible in discussions of the Anthropocene period that blame humanity's anthropocentrism for the environmental degradation of the planet. As Jason Moore points out, whatever its other liabilities, the term "Anthropocene" paradoxically locates the origins of the modern geohistorical shift it names in a distinctly ahistorical force: "Not class. Not capital. Not imperialism. Not even culture. But . . . the *Anthropos*: humanity as an undifferentiated whole."[16] Anthropocenic discourse thus acts as if all *anthros* were equally "anthropocentric"—as if it is *Homo sapiens*, and not a certain (Western) mode of being *Homo sapiens*, that is destroying the Holocene and has been since "we" discovered America, invented the steam engine, exported industrialism to "our" colonies, or exploded the atom bomb (wherever the "golden spike" of the Anthropocene is to be set). By this sleight of hand, Moore objects, the idea of the Anthropocene collectivizes responsibility for climate change without stopping to consider the "inequalities, alienation, and violence inscribed in modernity's strategic relations of power and production" that have ushered in this new geological reality.[17] In this way, critiques of the Anthropocene and of anthropocentrism threaten to naturalize those power relations by treating the extractive economy and social injustice licensed by the West's reigning episteme as if this were the organic expression of *Homo sapiens*' innately limited mind—the inevitable fallout of the ineluctable humanness of human perception. In both its speculative or object-oriented and its environmentalist forms, then, the critique of anthropocentrism frames the present ecological crisis as an outcome determined by a speciological rather than a cultural myopia: the product of epistemological limitations ontologically organic to *Homo sapiens* rather than the contingent results of the hierarchical and extractionist episteme of modern Western civilization.

As advocates for social justice point out, this faulty diagnosis not only ignores the history of human inequality but moreover may intensify that inequality. By suggesting that all humanity (*Homo sapiens*) is accountable for "anthropogenic" climate change, the concept of the Anthropocene justifies charging minority and postcolonial peoples with responsibility for redressing an environmental crisis they have not only not engineered but whose costs they have disproportionately shouldered as the populations most heavily exploited by industrial capitalism and most acutely exposed to its environmental consequences (including poisoned water, landslides, flooding, and climate change–related disasters like Hurricane Katrina). Social justice–minded critics thus point out the inequity implicit in environmentalist policies that, premised on the notion that "we humans" are responsible for engendering a possible sixth mass extinction event, have, for instance, moved to criminalize indigenous hunting practices. Or even more commonly, where such traditional ways of life have been irrevocably interrupted by imperial and economic expansion, indigenous and postcolonial peoples have often come to rely on extractive industries that are now the target of environmental restrictions. As Elizabeth Povinelli observes, despite their devastating effects on the landscape, extractive industries are often among "the few alternatives for landholding groups to sustain their homelands, if in an often severely compromised fashion."[18] Therefore, while the effort to more tightly regulate extractive and polluting industries remains vitally important, advocates of social justice contend that environmentalists must also be attentive to the ways in which even well-intentioned environmental policy may perpetuate historical inequities by further burdening those who have benefitted the least from the ecological despoliations of Western economic "development."

*Expendable Populations: "Nonhuman" ≠ Non–*Homo sapiens

Broadly viewed, then, current theoretical discourse has a tendency to cross its biological and ideological wires. In the instances I have just discussed, anthropocenic discourse confuses ideological and biological critique when it conflates the anthropocentric bias of the modern Western episteme with a critique of the perceptual limitations of *Homo sapiens* as such. If this conflation of "the human" with *Homo sapiens* is problematic, in this section I examine how the corollary conflation—a tendency to treat "the nonhuman" as a category synonymous with non–*Homo sapiens*—likewise makes posthumanism vulnerable to important critiques. Indeed, I submit that, above all, it is posthumanism's tendency to conflate "nonhuman" with non–*Homo sapiens* that lies at the root of its failure to recognize its deep congruencies with the antiracist projects of social justice.

The commonness of this conflation of nonhuman with non–*Homo sapiens* is perplexing given that it is roundly condemned in one of posthumanism's founding texts—Jacques Derrida's collection of essays *The Animal That Therefore I Am*. Here Derrida rebukes the "asinanity" [*bêtise*] of the practice of referring to "the animal" in the monolithic singular, arguing that the definite article elides "a heterogeneous multiplicity of the living, or more precisely . . . of organizations of relations between the living and dead."[19] Derrida thus underscores that, like "the human," "the animal" is also sorted into different biopolitical and necropolitical molds—*e. coli*, cattle, wolves, and French bulldogs enjoy very different life chances and are subject to widely differing regimes of state scrutiny, ranging from legal protection to systematic extermination, exploitation, or lethal neglect. Derrida's point, then, is (as we might expect) antibinaristic: oppositions like human/nonhuman oversimplify our view of extant biological and biopolitical realities, mocking the speciological diversity of planetary life as well as the heterogeneity of ethical relations (all of them contingent, none of them ontologically given) that organize the planetary distribution of living and dying.

In highlighting the myriad relations of similarity and inequality that cut across species lines, Derrida's essay therefore reminds us that the human/nonhuman binary is not, in fact, a speciological distinction but rather an ideological one. Indeed, as Thoreau's transmutationalist critique of Agassiz insists (or as anyone even cursorily familiar with the "trees" of modern evolutionary science knows), species are not originally and immutably different but rather emerge and branch out from each other, fanning into shades of proximate relation organized by differences of degree rather than kind (and featuring, as Derrida insists, differential rather than categorically different capacities for things like language, culture, intelligence, feigning, etc.). The scales of differentiability that speciological evolution creates thus simply do not obey the categorical rules of binaristic logic. Which is to say that *Homo sapiens*, kin as it is to other species, is not the antithesis of the nonhuman; *only* the human is. "Human" and "nonhuman" are ideological designations by which forms of being that are deemed moral and thus worthy of protection are distinguished from forms of being (including object being or "nonlife") that are deemed morally negligible and therefore expendable. As a designation of moral value, the human floats free of the speciological body, trailing a hierarchy of privilege that insinuates divisions *both* within and among species—dividing citizens from slaves and pets from pests, while conversely conflating human chattel with cattle, the poor with the feral, racial others with beasts. The human, in short, is an ideology masquerading as a species.

The force of this point is therefore to suggest that posthumanism is a form of antiracism that does not consistently recognize itself as such. Bracketing for now the speculative branch of posthumanism discussed above— that which understands itself to be attempting to move beyond *Homo sapiens'* perceptual limitations—the vast majority of posthumanists working in this loose-jointed field understand themselves to be engaged in an effort to deconstruct liberal humanism's arbitrary and anti-empirical distinction of human from nonhuman being. Broadly encompassing posthumanist critics working in and after poststructuralism (such as Derrida, Cary Wolfe, Neill Badmington), in science and technology studies (N. Katherine Hayles, Donna Haraway, Bruno Latour), in materialist feminism and new materialism (Jane Bennett, Rosi Braidotti, Elizabeth Grosz, Mel Chen, Stacey Alaimo), and others, this main branch of posthumanist theory seeks, in particular, to depose the drastically reductive materialist philosophy that subtends the transcendental liberal subject, and according to which liberal humanism equates human being with moral freedom and autonomy while condemning all other forms of being to a rigid biological determinism. Against this hierarchical account of the human, posthumanism's revisionary materialism instead highlights the inextricability of human being from the animality and embodied materiality that it derogates and disavows, tracing the imbrications of mind and matter, and natural and cultural agencies within the larger "vital, self-organizing, and yet nonnaturalistic structure of living matter itself."[20]

Posthumanism's effort to deconstruct liberal humanism's hierarchy of the human is therefore nothing less than an effort to dismantle the racializing regime that has functioned to differentiate valorized (human) from devalorized (nonhuman) *Homo sapiens* life. Indeed, as I shall elaborate below, Wynter's work makes this connection particularly explicit by maintaining that, since at least the Middle Ages, the erection of racializing hierarchies (Christian/pagan, and later human/Black) has been the primary function of the Western humanist episteme. As Wynter argues, the task of social justice must therefore be to move beyond the human of this humanist tradition. But although posthumanism's ambition to dismantle the human/nonhuman binary coincides with such antiracist endeavors to deconstruct this same epistemic formation, posthumanism has been slow to recognize the relevance of race to its theoretical undertaking. Indeed, Zakkiyah Jackson observes, "given that appositional and homologous (even co-constitutive) challenges pertaining to animality, objecthood, and thingliness have long been established in thought examining the existential predicament of modern racial Blackness, the resounding silence in the posthumanist . . . literatures with respect to race is remarkable."[21] Despite sharing a common enemy—Western humanism's hierarchical conception of the human—as well as a common critique—of the false empiricism that condemns nonhuman being to embodied essentialism and biological determinism—posthumanism has generally understood itself to be an ontological rather than an antiracist discourse.

In one view, this failure of recognition stems from the problem of posthumanism's theoretical canon. Despite its commitment to moving beyond the episteme of Western liberal humanism, posthumanists have largely gone searching for inspiration in the record of Western philosophy and theory—looking to Derrida and Niklas Luhman, Michel Foucault and Giorgio Agamben, Baruch Spinoza and Gilles Deleuze, Lucretius and Niels Bohr, Charles Darwin and Silvan Tomkins. As Alexander Weheliye observes, posthumanism has thus "rarely considered cultural and political formations outside the world of [Western] Man that might offer alternative versions of humanity." More pointedly, Weheliye notes that posthumanism's neglect of postcolonial and minority criticism means that it has been all the less likely to come across works that could help it to theorize "the tight bonds between humanity and racializing assemblages in the modern era."[22] In this way, the Western bias of its canon may explain posthumanism's tendency to disregard racism's centrality to (perhaps even synonymity with) the epistemic formation that it critiques.

However, posthumanism's failure to recognize antiracist and postcolonial criticism as its precedents may also derive from its persistent conflation of the nonhuman with non–*Homo sapiens* species. That is, despite the critical care they take to identify the object of their critique as a particular episteme of the human, posthumanists nonetheless overwhelmingly tend to treat the nonhuman as if this were a speciological category referring to animals, plants, and objects—to, that is, non–*Homo sapiens* entities—rather than an ideological category referring to forms of being that have been deemed morally negligible. This slippage from the moral category "nonhuman" to the biological category "non–*Homo sapiens*" leads posthumanists to focus on the way Western liberal humanism has systematically devalorized nonhuman species and objects—a form of discrimination they then *compare* to racism and sexism rather than identifying racism and sexism as other names for the structurally discriminatory logic they protest.[23] In other words, this slippage invites posthumanists to imagine that racism and sexism are not what they are talking about when they talk about emancipating the nonhuman.[24] In this way, posthumanism's tendency to treat the nonhuman as a speciological category (designating non–*Homo sapiens*) rather than a moral one (compassing dehumanized *Homo sapiens* as well as non–*Homo sapiens* beings) in turn works to obscure the relevance of antiracist and social justice discourses to the epistemic critique posthumanism frames.[25]

This critique of posthumanism's Western theoretical bias may register as an accusation, but it is even more pressingly an invitation to wider collaboration. By holding more tightly onto the distinction between human and *Homo sapiens*, and between nonhuman and non–*Homo sapiens*, posthumanism opens itself up to a whole new archive of antiracist and social justice thought, and a closer conversation between these theories going forward could produce a powerful new critical matrix. To begin this conversation, my next section turns to the work of Sylvia Wynter, whose sustained critique of Western liberal humanism's constitutive racism affords a particularly productive starting place for thinking conjunctively (although not, as we shall see, seamlessly) across posthumanist and social justice theories. As I shall argue, putting these two discourses in conversation can help each to refine its philosophical commitment—and perhaps, too, the limits of that commitment—to moving beyond the Western episteme of "the human."

Mutual Encounters: Posthumanism as Social Justice

Sylvia Wynter's theory of social justice highlights the structural role that racism plays in the episteme of Western liberal humanism. Her major intervention into the fields of postcolonial, Black, and feminist studies has been to underscore the futility of seeking social justice within this Western episteme of "Man," and to call, therefore, for a posthumanist model of social justice. For Wynter, the story of Western humanism's development cannot be separated from the history of New World colonialism and, in particular, Black slavery. Expanding and sharpening Foucault's genealogical account, Wynter tells the story of Western Man's epistemic development in three grand movements.[26] In the Middle Ages, Western Europe operated with a Christian hierarchy of the human, with the faithful occupying the status of fully moralized beings, and pagans constituting morally negligible beings. In the Renaissance, this Christian hierarchy was partially overwritten by the ostensibly more secular idea of liberal "Man," who is defined not by his relation to God (Christian or pagan) but rather by his relation to the state (citizen or noncitizen, *bios* or *zoe*). In the third movement, which began in the late eighteenth century, the liberal definition of "Man" was further (if again only ostensibly) secularized by the rise of biologism and Darwinian evolutionism. Since this "second variant of *Man*" was understood to originate "in Evolution rather than as before, in Divine Creation," Wynter argues that this "biocentric" turn in Western liberal humanism consolidated racist hierarchy. For whereas in the Renaissance and Middle Ages the human had been understood to have been universally made in God's image (and only subsequently parsed into Christians/pagans, or citizens/noncitizens), now the human was to be represented as an unevenly developed species "in the slow process of evolution from monkey into man."[27] The biologization of Western Man thus introduced the idea of "the *genetic* nonhomogeneity of the human species," distributing *Homo sapiens* along a racialized spectrum from apelike ("the Negroid") to "man" ("the Caucasian").[28]

In Wynter's hands, then, the history of Western liberal humanism is a history of factualizing—of making biologically "scientific"—a hierarchy of human being that has been inscribed in the Western episteme from its earliest days. Of course, this episteme is only one out of a potentially infinite number of stories one could spin about what it means to be human. And yet, as Wynter observes, by posing as an objectively empirical rather than a subjectively political, ethical, philosophical, or religious account of the human, this episteme made it "impossible for [Western thinkers] to conceive of an Other to what they called and continue to call *human*."[29] In the West and its former colonies, the supposed naturalism of this "genre" of human being worked alongside the hegemony of Western power to conceal the contingency of this Western ideology and to occlude the existence of—as well as the possibility of inventing—alternative epistemes of the human.[30]

Wynter's larger aim here is therefore post*humanist* in the sense that her antiracist theory calls upon us to dismantle liberal humanism's hegemonic conception of Man. Indeed, a central premise of her project is that the task of redressing inequity and discrimination ultimately cannot be accomplished by simply redistricting the human within the terms this episteme provides. It is not enough, she suggests, to revalorize marginalized populations and thus, bit by bit, shuffle more beings into the lifeboat of moral privilege that liberal recognition affords. "Such a *moralistic* approach," she writes, "is the logical result of taking our *isms* [racism, sexism] as isolated rather than systemic facts."[31] Instead, she insists, the project of social justice requires us to move beyond the present episteme of the human. For as her genealogy of Western humanism underscores, discrimination is structural to the Western humanistic tradition: this episteme has always operated by constituting "a negative ontological category" (pagan, foreign, Black) to serve as the foil to its representation of the human. Accordingly, Wynter argues that the plight of humanism's dehumanized Others, "like that of the ongoing degradation of the planetary environment, is not even *posable*, not to say *resolvable*, within the conceptual framework of our present order of knowledge."[32] Thus, instead of a more pluralistic liberal politics, Wynter calls for a radical break from the hierarchical and discriminatory episteme that funds liberal politics, pluralistic or otherwise. "In order to call in question this ontologically subordinated function, 'minority discourse' can *not* be merely another voice in the present ongoing conversation," she insists: the challenge is not to expand the conversation but to change it.[33] Linking the dehumanization of racialized, feminized, and impoverished populations to the exploitation of animals and the destruction of the nonhuman environment, Wynter envisions something like a unified minority (or nonhuman) movement that would seek to "bring closure to our present order of discourse" and inaugurate a new one no longer premised upon the derogation of others.[34]

Wynter's conviction that ending racism entails moving beyond (i.e., post-) humanism marks an entry for thinking about the deep congruencies, and perhaps equally entrenched differences, between posthumanist materialism and post*humanist* social justice theory. It is, at least, arguable that posthumanist materialist discourse is where the conceptual work Wynter calls for—this effort to conjure new "genres of the human"—is currently and most actively getting done. Like Wynter, posthumanism attacks the "biocentric" or deterministic logic that arose in the eighteenth and nineteenth centuries, and that holds that human identity is essentially coded in the body, and that bodies can in turn be located along a spectrum of moral evolution "from monkey to man." Against this essentialist, deterministic, and teleological account of embodiment, posthumanism's revisionary materialism insists that acknowledging the imbrication of identity with embodiment does not condemn us to erecting racist, sexist, speciesist, or any other form of moral hierarchy.

Indeed, posthumanism's materialist ontology bears little resemblance to the watchmaker's world of bestial automata and chains of being that subtends the biocentric account of human identity that Wynter decries. Instead, its founding assumption is that acknowledging the force of material embodiment does not condemn us to biological determinism. In this way, posthumanist materialism hopes to displace racial science's taxonomic and hierarchical order of being with a monistic vision of ontological mutuality, or what José Muñoz terms "the potential and actual vastness of *being-with*."[35] As Karen Barad describes this ontology (drawing upon the theory of quantum entanglement), embodied being primordially consists of on-going "relations without preexisting relata."[36] Before we are anything or anyone individually, and thus before any hierarchical system of ordering differentiated entities, we exist more primally as a collective: in other words, the mutuality of being is ontologically prior to any system of order that we might impose on being's dynamically relational field.[37] Before individual subjects and objects, before causes and effects, being is imbricated and unfolding, a complexly conjoint becoming. Posthumanism thus conjures what Roberto Esposito describes as "the flesh": a "vital reality that is extraneous to any kind of unitary organization."[38] As a dynamic material heterogeneity that is as resistant to totalization as it is to individuation and hierarchical ordering, "the flesh" is at once "singular and communal, generic and specific, . . . undifferentiated and different."[39]

The deterministic essentialisms of biological racism, sexism, and speciesism can thus find no purchase in this ontology because the materiality of being-with defies attributions of identity. Indeed (much like we have just seen in Whitman), posthumanism's ontology defies *individuality*. The primordial relationality of being means that any frame we put on being—any attempt to articulate a *particular* being out of being-with (to carve a particular "relatum" out of quantum entanglement or an individual body out of "the flesh")—could only ever be provisional, perspectival, a revisable construction. On this view, far from being grounded *in* being, individual identity can only ever appear as a kind of denial or misrepresentation of being's primordial relationality, a processualism that resists identity. Hence Jasbir Puar describes identity as an attempt "to still and quell the perpetual motion of assemblages, to capture and reduce them, to harness their threatening mobility."[40] This is to say that whether or not we choose to see identitarian regimes as intentionally repressive, posthumanism insists that they are, at least, inherently reductive, premised on the disavowal "of a relation of otherness that is destined to force open the identity presupposed by the body proper."[41] In posthumanism's ontology of "the flesh," bodies, such as they are, are irreducibly open-ended, porous, compound, relational; identities unravel into ongoing processes that are riven with complexity and creative contingency; all nouns melt into verbs. Where racism and sexism imprison identity in the body, posthumanist materialism frees the body of identity, reimagining the "boundary" of the skin as a site of chiasmatic continuity with an alien yet intimate world.[42]

So the question I have been posing is this: Could posthumanism be describing something like the post*humanist* "genre of the human" that Wynter envisions? To what extent might posthumanist materialism and post*humanist* social justice be thought together as two fronts in the same fight against liberal humanism's hegemonic hold on "the human"? The summary of these two theories that I have just offered attempts to highlight their common interests: posthumanist materialism explodes the discriminatory hierarchy of being that Wynter diagnoses as structural to the Western episteme she opposes. But to answer the question of their congruency properly, we would have to know whether posthumanist materialism and post*humanist* social justice oppose the same thing when they set themselves in opposition to liberal humanism. And the answer to this question, which I shall elaborate in my discussions below, will be no, they don't. That is, when we put these theories in conversation it becomes clear that Wynter ultimately endorses humanism's faith that human life is uniquely endowed with freedom and moral import, whereas posthumanist materialism consistently challenges this premise. But if the preservation of human exceptionalism suggests that Wynter's theory does not wholly break with the Western liberal humanism it critiques, posthumanist theory likewise seeks to conserve key aspects of this episteme. As I shall elaborate, despite the anti-individualism of its relational ontology, posthumanism's politics remain deeply indebted to the individualistic institutions of modern liberal democracy. In outlining these two different conservative tendencies below I will be suggesting why it makes sense to view them as theoretical problems for the ostensibly posthumanist and post*humanist* critical traditions in which they respectively arise. Ultimately, however, I will suggest in my Coda why falling short of a radical break from liberal humanism might set desirable or even necessary limits on our posthumanism.

Humanism's Holdovers in Posthumanism

For its part, posthumanism sets itself up in opposition to liberal humanism's transcendental subject; however, this opposition does not extend to a rejection of the liberal political institutions that were organized to honor and accommodate the liberal humanist subject. On the contrary, posthumanists regularly gloss the mutuality of being that their ontology discovers as an invitation to a pluralistic expansion of democratic politics. From Esposito's "affirmative" biopolitics to Latour's "parliament of things" to Levi Bryant's "democracy of objects," posthumanist ontologies routinely double as blueprints for a more pluralistic (a more-than-human) democratic politics whose constituency will finally encompass all beings without exclusion.

On this description, the material connectedness of human and nonhuman being in the primordiality of being-with becomes an argument for extending ethical recognition to nonhuman being on the model of democratic liberalization. As Jane Bennett puts this thought, "If human culture is inextricably enmeshed with vibrant, nonhuman agencies, and if human intentionality can be agentic only if accompanied by a vast entourage of nonhumans, then it seems that the appropriate unit of analysis for democratic theory is neither the individual human nor the human collective but the (ontologically heterogeneous) 'public.' . . . Surely the scope of democratization can be broadened to acknowledge more nonhumans in more ways, in something like the ways in which we have come to hear the political voices of other humans formerly on the outs."[43] The logic, then, of this vision of posthumanist politics imagines that the enmeshed and dependent nature of human being argues for extending respect and recognition to devalued forms of being through which, it turns out, human life and agency move. Between the ontology outlined in the first part of this quote and the pluralism endorsed after the ellipses, we move from a processual materialism that deconstructs individual identity to a politics that is premised upon individual recognition.

Such a comprehensively inclusive politics would seem to constitute a major ethical advancement—how could it not?—and yet it is not immediately clear how posthumanism's ontology supports the pluralistic politics posthumanists invoke. Posthumanism, as we have seen, begins by pointing to the processual nature of being, recasting apparently solid objects as open-ended processes. But this processual ontology creates difficulties for any politics we would construct on its back. The fact of process—what Bennett calls the "public" but what we might more accurately, by Bennett's lights, view as the "publicity" or collectively "enmeshed" nature of all being—is not, after all, a "unit of analysis" but, on the contrary, an account of the ideological contingency (the fictionality) of any unit whatsoever. Nouns like "public" and noun phrases like "a vast entourage of nonhumans" help Bennett manage the contradiction between her processualism and the democratic theory she turns to by precipitating the processual assemblage of being back into a countable array of discrete entities with self-possessed "voices" and political interests. Bennett's vision for a broadened democracy that would "consult nonhumans more closely" and "listen and respond more carefully to their outbreaks, objections, testimonies, and propositions" thus seems like an ethically admirable program that nonetheless sacrifices the central insight of her posthumanist materialism. For her compelling account of agency as a force distributed across human and nonhuman actants—an account that thereby deconstructs differences between human and nonhuman, self and other, vital subjectivity and "vibrant" materiality—suggests, to the contrary, that we exist in a world that is not divisible into speakers and listeners. Indeed, even in Barad's quantum ontology—which does suggest that we might frame *local* "units of analysis" that temporarily resolve "intra-action" into "inter-action"—it is not clear that any entity would have the longevity, let alone the personality, sufficient to support anything we could call an objection, testimony, or proposition.

Versions of this contradiction between posthumanism's processual ontology and its liberal politics recur throughout posthumanist work. It shows up, for instance, in Barad's injunction to "intra-act responsibly," which seems to commit us to an impossibility by enjoining us to act ethically ("make choices, take into account) toward a mode of relation ("intra-action") which Barad defines as belonging to a state of entanglement that is ontologically prior to the differentiation between subjects and objects, or causes and effects. But, of course, in this state of entanglement ethical obligation has nothing or no one to which it might attach.[44] As Matt Taylor argues in his critique of Latour's "parliament of things," ontological theories like these fail to explain how we are meant to adjudicate "between a processual relationality that precedes entities, on the one hand, and a procedural politics or ethics between entities, on the other."[45] There is, in other words, no way to navigate between the ontology of being-with and the unit-based calculus of liberal politics and ethics—at least, there is no way to effect this translation that does not simply betray the mutuality of being that posthumanism champions. Indeed, it seems particularly dubious that an ontology that is, as posthumanists regularly stress, distinctly inimical to the figure of the sovereign and autonomous liberal self could be translated without loss into an expanded liberal politics. Thus while posthumanist plans for incorporating non–*Homo sapiens* into liberal democratic politics seem laudible, they also seem curiously perverse, for invariably they shunt us back into liberal, ethical, and political grammars in which the radical imbrication of being is reduced to interactions between individual beings whose inherent sovereignty, freedom, and autonomy demand to be recognized. In this sense, posthumanism's habit of positioning itself as an emancipatory discourse working in the pluralizing tradition of abolitionism and first-wave feminism arguably undersells the radicalism of its philosophy.

In fact, this is one important area in which a more sustained engagement with social justice theory could help posthumanism to refine its understanding of its own project. Confirming Wynter's sense of the acute limitations of trying to seek social justice within the terms of the Western episteme, recent work in indigenous studies has highlighted the epistemic coerciveness of liberalism's regime of rights and recognition. These studies reveal the steep price of admission exacted from indigenous communities seeking political recognition.[46] As they demonstrate, the very process of establishing claims to rights and sovereignty often subjects indigenous groups to a kind of epistemic neocolonialism, forcing them to abandon or reframe their traditional cultural conceptions of subjectivity, kinship, and community with the nonhuman environment so as to bring them into alignment with liberal accounts of personhood, race, and territory. Indeed, Taiaiake Alfred observes, even multiculturally minded liberal policies tend to resolve any "disconnect between [their] rights-based liberal philosophical orientation and the fundamentals of Indigenous teachings and worldviews" at the latter's expense. In this way, the process of securing tribal rights can end up coercing indigenous peoples to relinquish "traditional notions of belonging . . . and [replace] them with race and gender-based notions of membership designed to reconstitute Indigenous people in ways acceptable to Euroamerican ideologies."[47] Over generations—and, more pointedly, as a result of political policies ostensibly designed to accommodate cultural difference—indigenous peoples can thus come to "hold ideas about identity and their nationhood which reflect colonial attitudes," losing touch with an indigenous "worldview that is illuminated by notions of fluidity [and] flux."[48]

Kim TallBear echoes this critique in her recent study of the popularization of DNA testing in North America as a mechanism for establishing claims to tribal belonging. Although this practice offers seemingly straightforward and objective answers to questions about tribal belonging, TallBear shows how it does so by reducing tribal identity to a genetic fingerprint, drastically simplifying the intricate interplay of both genealogical and cultural inheritances (including what TallBear describes as the "sense of inexplicable inheritance") that has traditionally shaped the logic of tribal belonging. DNA testing therefore proposes to convert a complexly biocultural phenomenon into a set of "particular ideas and vocabularies of race, ethnicity, nation, family, and tribe" that have been codified by the Western liberal-raciological episteme over the past two hundred years. But "for and by whom are such categories defined?" TallBear inquires. "How have continental-level race categories come to matter? And why do they matter more than the 'peoples' that condition indigenous narratives, knowledges, and claims?"[49] Thus, like Alfred, TallBear calls attention to the ways in which the tools for gaining political recognition often subject non-Western peoples and epistemes to a kind of neocolonial disciplining. By underscoring the epistemic price of liberal inclusion—what Elizabeth Povinelli dubs "the cunning of recognition"—indigenous social justice studies like these can serve to alert posthumanists to the ways in which its focus on extending liberal rights and recognition to nonhuman beings may be hostile to the more radical epistemic transformation—the emancipation of being-with—that they ultimately seek.[50]

Indeed, studies of recognition's "cunning" coercions suggest that post-humanism's faith in liberal recognition might not simply sell short its pro-cessualist ontology but, rather, sell it out. By demonstrating how liberal recognition can act as a straightjacket as much as a means to liberation, Alfred, TallBear, and Povinelli help us to see how posthumanism's advocacy for nonhuman recognition and inclusion may in fact be antithetical to the kind of change its ontology tasks us with when it suggests that inclusion is, for better or worse, inescapable—that we are always already onto-logically conjoined whether or not we recognize each other as equals. This is to suggest, as Cary Wolfe also reminds us, that posthumanist materialism in fact has nothing to do with the question of which bodies "matter" (*Homo sapiens*? All primates? All animals? Black lives? All lives?).[51] That is, its key proposition is not to champion the sovereignty (the entitlement to freedom, rights, and recognition) of nonhuman beings but rather to disclose the fictionality of sovereignty as such in a material world in which every being is relationally constituted in and through the being of others.

But if these social justice critiques of liberal politics help us to discern the conservatism of posthumanism's faith in liberal recognition, posthu-manism's critique of human exceptionalism can, conversely, help us to discern the humanism that still haunts even Wynter's ostensibly posthumanist theory of social justice. Although Wynter calls out the discriminatory hi-erarchy that lies at the heart of the Western liberal humanist tradition, the alternative "genre of the human" that she outlines ultimately looks a lot like the liberal humanist subject she proposes to displace. Wynter's ge-nealogy of Western Man pivots on the notion that "the human" is a rep-resentation—an enunciation that passes itself off as a natural fact. Seizing on this demonstration of humanity's capacity for self-narration (which she terms, borrowing from Frantz Fanon, "sociogeny"), Wynter argues that this capacity marks out human being as exceptional to nature. As she ex-plains, sociogeny is an endowment unique to *Homo sapiens*, which affords this species an additional "nonphysical principle of causality"—the power to self-generate cultural codes that prescribe our beliefs and behaviors for

us over and above the promptings of our inherited genetic code.[52] Sociogeny thus liberates human action from material causation: in contrast to the
"purely biological" being of other species (whose identities, she argues, "are
genetically *preprescribed* for them"), we humans "are *simultaneously* story-
telling *and* biological beings."[53] For Wynter, this unique speciological capacity not only affords *Homo sapiens* an intrinsic moral freedom lacking in
all other forms of being, but it simultaneously guarantees the moral equality of all *Homo sapiens* to each other, for if *Homo sapiens* are sociogenic
(self-creating) by definition, this speciological trait means that no member of the species could be genetically "preprescribed" by race or sex. For
Wynters, then, sociogeny not only makes alternative genres of the human
possible (by exposing Western humanism's genre of the human to be a sociogenic rather than an organic fact), but it also (and somewhat paradoxically) provides an ostensibly biological justification for upholding the
exceptional autonomy of all *Homo sapiens* (as the only species endowed with
this special power).

The irony here is thus that Wynter's account of sociogeny reproduces
a version of the same moral hierarchy and "biocentric" reasoning that she
denounces in the Western episteme of Man. Indeed, it's not hard to hear
the echo of racism's biological determinism in her celebration of human
exceptionalism. Scientific racists like Josiah Nott also maintain that human
beings are uniquely free of the biological determinism that rules lesser
forms of being. And although clearly Nott differs from Wynter insofar as
he maintains that this capacity is endemic to only certain races of *Homo
sapiens* and not the whole species, the underlying logic of biological
exceptionalism—the proposition that select organisms are auto-instituting
while all others are physiologically determined—remains the same in both
Nott's and Wynter's accounts of the human. That Nott's racism and Wynter's antiracism are both able to adopt the same criterion to such differing
ends underscores the contingency of the standards by which racial or speciological "autonomy" is defined. That is, whatever we might choose to
count as evidence of a capacity for sociogenic self-making must always itself be an artifact of culture rather than a strictly biological fact. Thus the
definition of what qualifies as "articulate" speech as opposed to animalistic noise, "rational" thought as opposed to brutish self-interest, or "cul-
tured" behavior as opposed to instinctive action may be—and historically
has been—stipulated and gerrymandered as power sees fit.

Indeed, that sociogeny yields its own version of the "cunning of recognition" is a lesson brought home to us by Frederick Douglass, who recognizes in its discrimination of speech from noise a key to the "blood-stained

gate of slavery." At the start of the *Narrative*, Douglass harrowingly recalls witnessing his aunt Hester's torture at the hands of Captain Anthony, during which "no words, no tears, no prayers, from his gory victim, seemed to move his iron heart from its bloody purpose." As numerous critics have pointed out, Douglass's masterful performance of literacy in the prose of this scene, and throughout the *Narrative*, functions as a powerful testament to his humanity, demonstrating his rational intelligence. And yet this primal scene simultaneously labors to expose the brutal capriciousness of language as a test of humanity in the first place. Douglass's depiction of Anthony's indifference to Hester's "words," "prayers," and "heart-rending shrieks" lays bare the ease with which Anthony dismisses her utterances as merely instinctive, animalistic noises (morally indistinguishable from the bellows of the cow whose slaughter would have furnished the "blood-clotted cowskin" at this scene's center).[54]

Douglass's ambivalence in this scene—his implicit appeal to language as expressive of moral being and simultaneous critique of the ease with which language may be dismissed as mere sound—confronts us with what posthumanists describe as the necessarily ideological, rather than empirical, nature of any distinction between human (autonomous, sociogenic) and nonhuman (embodied, "purely biological") life. Thus Derrida argues that correcting the injustice this arbitrary distinction inscribes into being is "not just a matter of giving back to the animal whatever it has been refused" (by, for instance, demonstrating various animals' capacities for "speech, reason, experience of death, mourning, culture" and so forth); instead the challenge is "a matter of questioning oneself concerning the axiom that permits one to accord purely and simply to the human or rational animal that which one holds the just plain animal to be deprived of."[55] It is not enough, in other words, to discover that hitherto excluded beings are capable of "testimony" (to return to Bennett's word). To do this is simply to keep moving the chains down the field of humanism when the task, instead, is to escape the rules of its game. Thus Derrida demands that instead of trying to perfect the axiom by which we distinguish which utterances count as "speech," which events count as "actions," or which beings count as "free," we ought to be asking ourselves whose interests that axiom serves.

But if posthumanism's critique of human exceptionalism thus calls into question Wynter's faith in, and commitment to, *Homo sapiens*'s sociogenic autonomy, its skepticism also arguably forwards Wynter's larger project. Weheliye suggests that Wynter's effort to think "freedom beyond the world of Man" commits us to listening for "language that does not rely on linguistic structures, at least not primarily, to convey meaning . . . transparent to the world of Man."[56] Taking up this invitation (and perhaps taking it farther than Weheliye means it to go), we might conclude that Wynter's desire for a posthumanist genre of the human not only commits us to listening for language among those not already counted as human but also urges us to listen for the nonhumanity of human language. Put differently, instead of imagining that sociogeny (language, culture) is the antithesis of genetic determinism, we can imagine it as a kind of emergent complication within biological order. After all, if the capacity for sociogeny is somehow in *Homo sapiens'* "nature," then the degree of freedom it introduces into human behavior is not a negation of humanity's genetic inheritance but an expression of it. Using this description, then, a capacity for sociogeny does not designate a transcendental freedom but rather introduces a degree of play—of unpredictability or creativity—into speciological behavior. From this perspective, human being still exceeds the embodied determinism which, for Wynter, characterizes racist "biocentrism"; however, that freedom no longer liberates human being from its embodiment, categorically distinguishing *Homo sapiens* from non–*Homo sapiens* being. When we begin to think sociogeny as an embodied trait in this way, it takes on the double movement of Derrida's posthumanist vision, designating a capacity that is something less than the absolute "human" freedom humanism had posited, and therefore identifying something that is potentially more widely shared, to varying degrees, among the diversity of animal life.

Again, my sense is that adopting a more posthumanist view of the human would clarify and strengthen Wynter's project. Exorcising the human exceptionalism from her vision brings it a step closer to realizing her goal of articulating a new episteme that embraces the materiality of "the flesh-and-blood individual subject."[57] Indeed, as Katherine McKittrick demonstrates, Wynter regularly suggests that decolonizing Western Man will mean learning to see how "our flesh and blood and brain matter" work to "unsettle and enmesh the otherwise bifurcated and dichotomized epistemological clusters of science and creativity," or biological and sociogenic production.[58] Moreover, posthumanism's view of the conjugation of freedom with embodiment forwards Wynter's ambition to "move us toward a . . . correlated human species, and eco-systemic ethic."[59] Throughout her work, Wynter calls attention to the ways in which the racism, sexism, and colonialism of the modern era are structurally conjoined with the necropolitics of the sixth extinction event now underway. All of these phenomena, she argues, arise from the same source: liberal humanism's hierarchical division of being. They are, in other words, one problem with several heads: an *integrated* "poverty-hunger-habitat-energy-trade-population-atmosphere-waste-resource problem."[60] Wynter's sense that social injustice and environmental destruction are systemic to the Western genre of "the human" underscores the urgency of decommissioning this episteme's foundational move of disavowing human materiality and thus segregating "human" being from the entangled being-with of planetary life.

By these routes, Wynter's critique of Western Man and posthumanism's materialist ontology begin to coalesce more clearly. The essential intervention of both projects—what constitutes their departure from Western humanism—is their effort to renounce the transcendentally autonomous human subject whose freedom is constituted through the derogation (the racialization/animalization/objectification) of embodied life. Both thus aim to deconstruct this hegemonic episteme—to disassemble, and not simply redistrict, the bounds of the human as we know it. Moreover, when read through one another, each of these projects helps the other to see where their work threatens to collapse back into the hierarchical ontology they wish to revise—where, for instance, posthumanism's liberal politics and Wynter's human exceptionalism betray their primary commitments to reimagining human being as a mode of being-with in which the distinction human/nonhuman no longer holds.

From a certain perspective, this coalescing vision of a thoroughly decolonized posthumanism promises to be radically liberatory. Ultimately pointing beyond the liberal politics of pluralism, these posthumanist projects challenge us to inaugurate a new episteme made to the measure not just of "Man" nor *Homo sapiens* nor even all biological life, but to the heterogeneous and radiantly interanimated ontology of worldly being. Unleashing the revolutionary generosity unwittingly implicit in Césaire's appeal, they urge us to conceive a political ethics truly "made to the measure of the world"—an episteme no longer premised upon the manufacture of a "lesser" class of devalued and exploitable being but, rather, one that embraces all being as one densely conjoined world.

Viewed from another angle, however, it is not clear that liberation is a term that can meaningfully be applied to an ontology of entanglement. Liberation, as we know it, implies disentanglement—an unburdening that restores us to a natural state of freedom, honoring our inherent right, as autonomous selves, to self-sovereignty. But none of these things—freedom, autonomy, sovereignty, the singular "self"—remain readily legible in a world in which being is primordially relational.

In light of this problem, the holdovers of humanism within these posthumanistic discourses may, after all, prove to be strategic inconsistencies. As my readings of Douglass, Thoreau, and Whitman have tried to underscore, the ontology of embodiment has distinctly illiberal tendencies, undermining appeals to human rights, agency, and selfhood as we understand these things. Thus while I began this chapter by suggesting that antislavery materialism may be useful to us today by helping to spotlight the absence of race as a critical term in contemporary posthumanist theory, I'd like to propose now that it also lights up a further aporia in our present discourse. There is an evident tension in these antebellum projects—in the ambivalence with which Douglass embraces animality, aware of the costs of dehumanization; in the fatalism with which Thoreau appeals to evolutionary change despite his desire to believe in the power of conscientious action; and in the manic optimism with which Whitman welcomes the prospect of his own dissolution into an unspooling material cosmos. The unease we find here stems from the incommensurability of these materialist visions with the liberal and romantic ideals these authors also held.

In these ways, these authors' antislavery materialisms confront us with the dreams deferred by a more rigorously materialist account of being. And thus, although critics like Latour and Wynter often frame their work as attempts to construct an empirical episteme that will finally be grounded in material fact rather than in the truths that (human, Western) power invents, we must learn to assess this episteme by a further standard. The question before us is not simply whether a materialist, posthumanist ontology gives us a truer, more empirically accurate account of reality. For whether or not it is truer, the question remains whether the episteme this ontology sponsors is ethically preferable to the humanism it seeks to displace. I turn to this question, via antislavery materialism, in the Coda.

After Romantic Posthumanism

In an important and difficult passage in "Mama's Baby, Papa's Maybe," Hortense Spillers describes an opening of freedom that paradoxically appears amid the horrific confinement of the Middle Passage:

> Those African persons in "Middle Passage" were literally suspended in the "oceanic," if we think of the latter in its Freudian orientation as an analogy for undifferentiated identity: removed from the indigenous land and culture, and not-yet "American" either. . . . They were the culturally "unmade," thrown in the midst of a figurative darkness that "exposed" their destinies to an unknown course. Often enough for the captains of these galleys, navigational science of the day was not sufficient to guarantee the intended destination. We might say that the slave ship, its crew, and its human-as-cargo stand for a wild and unclaimed richness of *possibility* that is not interrupted, not "counted" /"accounted," or differentiated, until its movement gains the land thousands of miles away from the point of departure.[1]

In this brief but provocative moment, Spillers invites us to detect a "richness of possibility" opened up by the sheer unpredictability of physical systems.

As she suggests, the uncertainty of this ship's fate—its vulnerability to volatile Atlantic winds and tides—lays bare the irreducibly speculative and provisional nature of any discursive account of this ship, temporarily suspending cultural authority and unmaking the identities that cultures confer. Until the ship "gains the land" and makes good on the captain's intentions for it, the precise nature of this venture remains undecidable: neither American nor indigenous language speakers can claim to define the "unknown course" they are on, nor can they say for sure if they are "cargo" and "crew" or something else—future mutineers and shark fodder; or everyone the future-drowned. For Spillers it is not only the kidnapped Africans, physically chained and culturally unmoored in the ship's hold, who are exposed to a "wild and unclaimed" unmaking; this whole oceangoing assemblage—"the slave ship, its crew, and its human-as-cargo"—exists as an "undifferentiated identity" suspended in the "darkness" of an uncertain journey.

Although Spillers is not a posthumanist, her account of oceanic suspension could easily come from the pages of recent posthumanist theory. The assemblage of ocean, ship, crew, and human-as-cargo that she conjures highlights the distribution of power across both human and nonhuman agencies in this scene. And in mapping this complex intersection of material and cultural forces (oceanic weather, colonizing and indigenous languages), she insists that neither culture nor matter is finally decisive; each is vulnerable to the other. Spillers thus qualifies the linguistic determinism of social constructivism as well as the physical determinism of biological essentialism by discovering something altogether different in this moment—not determinism but a complexity that produces uncertainty, which she glosses as an unclaimed and unclaimable freedom. In a scene of what otherwise appears to be total domination, Spillers finds bright cracks—interstices of possibility opening up in the unpredictable encounter of myriad forces: the skill of the captain's navigational science intersecting with the power of Atlantic winds, the iron fastness of the chains that hold human cargo countered by the force of that cargo's memory of her name.

But if Spillers's map of human and nonhuman entanglement in this moment is reminiscent of posthumanist accounts of "the flesh," ultimately in this essay she provides an account of "flesh" that is quite different. In the larger essay, the force of nonhuman materiality fades from view and the materiality that concerns Spillers is specifically the flesh of human being, and the power of this human flesh to obdurately persist even after ideology has otherwise denied that being's humanity. Flesh is, as she writes, "that zero-degree of social conceptualization that does not escape concealment under the brush of discourse." What has made her account of the flesh so influential is her counterintuitive suggestion that nonrecognition may also be liberating, that existing at the "zero degree of social conceptual-ization" might in fact enable the inhabitants of the flesh to instantiate an alternative subjectivity not colonized by the dominant social order. Thus Spillers concludes this essay by reclaiming the "monstrosity" of the flesh, recasting the abjection of nonrecognition as an "*insurgent* ground" from which to "rewrite . . . a radically different text" of human being.[2]

A discrepancy exists between the legibly human agency of the flesh that Spillers ultimately champions and the posthumanist vision of material agency that briefly appears in her account of the Middle Passage. For my purposes, this article offers a case study of the difficulty of sustaining a materialist perspective of the actions and events that we call political and that we understand to be charged with ethical significance. Even Spillers, who is deeply committed to thinking about how materiality resists and exceeds ideological inscription, and who is no less deeply committed to changing the terms in which politics is imagined, nevertheless continues to organize her account of political change around the drama of recognition and the struggle between competing constructions of the human. In this sense, her essay may be postrecognition but it is not posthumanist; like the posthumanist and post*humanist* social justice discourses I have exam-ined in Chapter 4, Spillers ultimately suspends her vision of material complexity and entanglement to restore us to a world in which human agency is once again intelligible, and recognition of human sovereignty is once again the endgame.

The question I have promised to ask here is whether this move may be ethically preferable, whether suspending the radically materialist perspec-tive that posthumanist assemblages offer might be necessary in order to construct a political vision we can admire. We might put this even more polemically: the question, at its most extreme, is whether a truly posthu-manist materialism can sustain an ethics or a politics at all. My sense is that it cannot, but more important, in these closing remarks I would like to suggest that one great advantage of studying antislavery materialism today is that these nineteenth-century texts make the apolitics of materialism visible in ways that contemporary posthumanist discourse does not.

Consider, by way of instructive contrast, Frederick Douglass's account of the insurgent slave ship in the climactic scene of *The Heroic Slave*. Even after Madison Washington has seized control of the ship, the white mate, Tom Grant, denies the legitimacy of the coup and Washington proceeds

to lecture to him on the justice of his revolt. But as we have seen, it is not
the ethical force of Washington's words but rather his superior physical
force—and then the even more overwhelming force of a sudden squall—
that ends their showdown.

> The wind howled furiously,—the ocean was white with foam, which,
> on account of the darkness, we could see only by the quick flashes of
> lighting that darted occasionally from the angry sky. All was alarm
> and confusion. . . . For awhile we had dearer interests to look after
> than slave property. A more savage thunder-gust never swept the
> ocean. Our brig rolled and creaked as if every bolt would be started . . . .
> The first words [Madison Washington] uttered after the storm had
> slightly subsided were characteristic of the man. "Mr. mate, you
> cannot write the bloody laws of slavery on those restless billows. The
> ocean, if not the land, is free."[3]

Interrupting the parley between Washington and Grant, Douglass gives
this sublime storm the last word in their dispute. Still refusing to acknowledge that "the principles of 1776" might apply "to one whom I deemed my
inferior," Grant is silenced by the squall that threatens to destroy them all.
But this is also no merely fortuitous vortex of high wind and waves: this
wind howls "furiously"; this sky is "angry." The anthropomorphism of
Douglass's prose turns the squall into an avenging god, an impression con-
firmed by Washington's pronouncement that the storm is a sign of nature's
inherent hostility to "the bloody laws of slavery."

Just as Spillers imagines, ocean weather rises up in *The Heroic Slave* to
exert its own kind of countercultural force, compelling Grant to relinquish
his claim to "slave property." Arguably, however, the only thing that makes
this storm's suspension of slavery *political* is Washington's gloss of it—his
insistence that the storm is not just interruptive but insurgent, that its material force is ethically oppositional. By contrast, when Spillers conjures
the possibility of a slave ship blown off course, she offers this image as an
example of the way in which matter's restless volatility is ultimately hostile
to all fixed laws and systems, slaveholding or otherwise. For Spillers, in
this moment, the ultimately ungovernable dynamism of the ocean-ship-
cargo-crew assemblage means that every ideological system ultimately
rests upon precariously fluid ground. Bruno Latour also insists that the
world's material assemblages are perpetually unsettling to political orders.
As he writes, what the materialist perspective "calls back into question with
such remarkable effectiveness is precisely the possibility of *collecting* the hierarchy of actors and values, according to an order fixed once and for all.

An infinitesimal cause can have vast effects; an insignificant actor becomes central . . . . With political ecology, one is always caught off-guard, struck sometimes by the robustness of systems, sometimes by their fragility."[4] In contrast to Douglass's specifically *antislavery* ocean environment, the post-humanist materialism that Latour and Spillers (in her Middle Passage moment) embrace invites us to recognize the contingency of *all* political and ethical orders. The complexity and unpredictability of material entanglement means that the "bedrock" of empirical reality is, in the long view, oceanic. This fluid materiality is at once the condition of possibility for regimes of human meaning and a force for their continual upheaval. In light of this incalculable restlessness, every future is uncertain; every order is provisional; every life is a life lived at sea.

And herein lies the crux of the problem. However much we may be tempted to conflate this restive unsettling with revolutionary insurgency, or "lines of flight" with liberation, changefulness and open-endedness in and of themselves are neither an ethics nor a politics.[5] Posthumanism's processualist ontology helps us to map the profusion of nonhuman agencies and affectivities at play in human experience and amidst the events and procedures that we call human politics. This mapping shows us, for instance, how lead's mobility and toxicity can re-inflect American racial imaginaries, or how the labor of worms can change national topographies.[6] And by learning to recognize these nonhuman dimensions of political life, we arrive at a new and more comprehensive political realism. But this powerfully expanded map of the entanglements of being and knowing does not tell us what we ought to do with its information. If the dynamic fluidity of posthumanism's assemblage ontology promises openings for change, it cannot tell us what changes to wish for. Its materialist perspective thus helps us to recognize the more-than-human forces that populate politics, but it does not yield a materialist politics.

This is a lesson, I would like to suggest, that antislavery materialism brings home to us particularly vividly by virtue of the providentialism that so explicitly supplements the embodied politics of Douglass, Thoreau, and Whitman. In their late romantic texts, nature itself has an ethics. Thus the physical force of Douglass's "restless billows" *is* political because for Douglass (as we have seen), there is an ethical code inscribed in the material order of nature. Likewise, the force of evolutionary transformation is political in Thoreau's hands because for Thoreau evolution is morally progressive. And if, for Whitman, we are only temporary instantiations in a cascade of material causality (our identities, bodies, desires, and actions arriving on the crest of a wave of antecedent events, and departing in a froth

of proliferating consequences), this "vast clear scheme" of material relationality is nonetheless ethical because for Whitman this fateful system is both
perfect and just.[7] Thus even as these authors confront me with the materiality that therefore I am, the engulfment of my liberal autonomy and the
subsumption of human history into natural history do not register, in these
accounts, as losses. For, these authors assure us, this is an ethical world:
slavery is even now being abolished by the gravitational tug of our animal
instincts; racism is literally being driven from our hearts by evolution; racial equality is already an ontological fact regardless of what auctioneers or
Supreme Court justices say. Thus if there is a kind of fatalism in Douglass's
invocation of "forces in operation which must inevitably work the downfall
of slavery," in Thoreau's really passive resistance, and in Whitman's renunciation of authorial (or political) intent, each of these authors nonetheless
greets our dispossession as a kind of grace because he believes that nature's
changefulness is meliorating.[8] Fate is providential: we are instances of an
unfolding cosmos that is benevolently edging toward greater perfection.

We are, moreover, primed to notice the normativity of the natural system in these accounts because we know these authors as late romantics, and
the beneficence of nature is one of those things we think of as characteristic
of romantic thought. Romanticism's nature is strongly normative: "natural"
is, for the romantics, a synonym for "true" or "good."[9] Thus when, in "Frost
at Midnight" Coleridge sends his son to the countryside so that he might
"see and hear / The lovely shapes and sounds intelligible / Of that eternal
language, which thy God / Utters, who from eternity doth teach / Himself in all," he is speaking of a nature that is above all moral, not simply
material as empiricism frames it for us.[10] Nor is this normative view of
nature limited to the ostensibly unempirical realms of romantic poetry;
through the mid–nineteenth century, scientific writing was similarly convinced of the material order's beneficence, its empirical outlook still con-
tiguous with natural theology. Hence Louis Agassiz understood science
to be "an investigation into the ways of nature, into the ways of the
Creator," and his colleague Arnold Guyot could describe the earth's geological development as "the realization of an intelligent thought . . . of
love to man, who is the end and aim of all creation."[11] Indeed, the ease with
which racial science converted into political doctrine speaks to how widespread the assumption was at midcentury that the material order spells out
natural hierarchies of being and that natural change is progressive, with
humankind at its cutting edge.

In retrospect, the antebellum moment has come to seem like the twi-
light of this mode of thought. The publication of *On the Origin of Species* in

1859 is often, if not wholly accurately, understood to have rung natural theology's death knell and displaced romanticism's normative nature with a vision of materiality that refuses "anything like telos or directionality . . . or a commitment to progressivism."[12] Although it would take several more years to take hold, the indifferently changeful nature that Darwin introduced drained the moralism out of natural systems. Nature could no longer be capitalized, and once no longer credited with a perspective or moral aim, it also could not be credited with a politics. Against this backdrop of romantic science and its eclipse, the renewed political impulse of contemporary materialist discourses swims more clearly into view as an atavism, an impulse to return to the premise that the study of ontology may bear ethical insights. If what the turn to ontology promises is something like a new realism—a return to the obdurate matter that social constructivism seemed to dismiss, and a reaffirmation that this fleshy reality resists "concealment under the brush of discourse"—then what we find within these contemporary materialisms is the stealing back in of suspended norms, the recolonization of a material system with ethical values.

In this Coda and the previous chapter, I have been tracking this subtle yet pervasive reemergence of normativity in contemporary materialist discourse. Thus as we saw in Chapter 4, although posthumanist materialism demonstrates the nonsingularity of being (its entanglement, its constitutive being-with), posthumanist politics tend to revert to the individualizing logic of liberal recognition, as if the proprietary values of freedom and equality were (as Douglass suggests) universally natural demands. By this route, too, the purely material relations this ontology maps start to seem morally laden: in posthumanist discourse, interdependence starts to look like community, entanglement like obligation, mutuality like equality, porosity like love.[13] A version of this naturalization of ethics also occurs in posthumanist social justice theory. Again, as we have seen, although theorists like Wynter and Spillers demonstrate that "the human" is not a natural kind but a status conferred on some bodies and not others for ideological reasons, their politics nonetheless presume that certain material organizations (*Homo sapiens,* monsters of "the flesh") *naturally* bear humanity in them, regardless of whether their humanness goes unrecognized. This is how these *particular* nonhumanized organisms can serve, in Wynters's and Spillers's formulations, as instantiations of alternative genres of the human—because these bodies are understood to always already *be* human, making "the human" once again a natural kind. In these ways, posthumanist and post*humanist* social justice theories reinject systems of value into the ostensibly extra-ideological material reality to which they appeal. At the end of the day, their natures are normative as well.

My reason for highlighting this remnant romanticism is not, however, to call it out. On the contrary, I want to suggest its necessity. Because these discourses do not simply wish to be descriptive—because they have an ethics and a politics to recommend—they cannot be strictly materialist; they must be dual-facing. At the same time, however, I think that there is analytical value in marking the distinction between descriptions of materiality and affirmations of it. We might, then, think of the turn to ontology not as a way to suture the divide between matter and meaning, nor as a surreptitious attempt to disguise policy as nature, but rather as an effort to subject our politics to the persistent skepticism that materiality affords.

Jasbir Puar voices one version of this thought when she suggests that intersectional theories of identity might be productively supplemented by assemblage theory because these theories are "frictional." Assemblage theory's processualist materialism puts pressure on the static identities, representative politics, and recognition that intersectionality strives for. Thus, Puar proposes, "No matter how intersectional our models of subjectivity . . . these formulations may still limit us if they presume the automatic primacy and singularity of the disciplinary subject and its identitarian interpellation."[14] The question therefore becomes how assemblage theory's skepticism of subjectivity and identity might be brought into the political realm. If we embrace nonrepresentationalism, letting go of positionality, identity, and their demands for recognition, what kinds of new politics would we do? "What kinds of political strategies, of 'politics of the open end,' might we unabashedly stumble upon? Rather than rehashing the pros and cons of identity politics, can we think instead of affective politics?"[15] Although Puar does not answer this question, she remains committed to the sense that it has one.

I am offering a slightly different account of the productive frictionality that Puar describes here. I would like to suggest that posthumanist materialism's usefulness to politics is not a matter of grounding (authorizing a new politics of assemblages or affects) but of ungrounding. If politics cannot *but* be a system of allocating finite attention, concern, and resources, what this materiality does is remind us that our systems of ordering are inherently partial, exclusionary, unjust; that no matter how posthumanist our politics, by virtue of being politics they will never be wholly posthumanist. I have suggested above that posthumanism provides a vastly dilated map of the unacknowledged constituents of politics—of the nonhuman agents and material agencies involved and affected—but this metaphor now needs qualification. If this ontological realism is a map, it is a medieval one—pointing to the unknown in all directions, indicating where our knowledge fails on the scale of immeasurable quantum phenomena, on the scale of incomputable cosmic complexity, in what Spillers describes as the "figurative darkness" of the unpredictable future. Instead of being used to ground or authenticate (naturalize) a political ethics, then, posthumanism's unmap of worldly entanglement might better serve to suggest the importance of not settling into our convictions. It suggests that embracing a particular political ethic might in fact not mean committing to a particular arrangement of politics but to constantly readjusting our attentions and revising our sense of who and what counts.

With this view, then, posthumanist materialism becomes a kind of horizon toward which our thought leans, and an abyss that our politics stare into. The reflection it does not return flags the unavoidable mismatch between our political-ideological orderings and the entangled, processual, and finally unpredictable "flesh" of the world. This incommensurability may well give us reason to hope, as Spillers proposes in describing that "richness of possibility" that even slavery could not expunge, or as, for instance, William Connolly suggests in describing the "fragility" of neoliberalism's hegemony to the chaotic dynamics of material and social systems.[16] But the first lesson of this posthumanist materialism is that possibility and fragility yield changes we ultimately cannot foresee or control. Complexity is thus a feature of this ontology that cuts both ways. If it is grounds for hope that we might tip the scales toward change, it is also grounds to believe, as Whitman reminds us, that the changes we make will never be quite (perhaps not even anything *like*) what we meant.

But in what sense is this useful? How is this reminder of the incompleteness of our knowledge and partiality and provisionality of our politics not just a license for resignation? Thoreau offers an image that will do for my answer when he writes of his desire not for knowledge but for "a sudden revelation of the insufficiency of all that we called Knowledge before." It is, he writes, "a lighting up of the mist by the sun."[17] In other words, the value of posthumanism's ontology may be that it ends not in the catharsis of exposure (what D. A. Miller describes as "the 'flash' of increased visibility") but in the brilliance of overexposure: its makes our myopias more radiant.[18] Less mystically, this materialist perspective enjoins us to a form of epistemological modesty. This is different from the ethical modesty that posthumanists endorse when they invite us to check our hubristic "anthropocentrism," to recognize and respect nonhuman being, and to cultivate wonder for this world. I am receptive to all of these ethical recommendations, but as

I have argued, I do not think they are endemic to or entailed by this ontology. More immediately, this ontology invites us to recognize the limits of our practical capacity to project our intentions upon a complexly relational world.

Unlike ethical modesty, then, epistemological modesty does not chiefly seek to check human hubris; if anything, it argues that we ought to be more ambitious in our thinking. For if the unmap of entanglement insists that reality will always exceed our thought of it, and that our policies' effects will always overflow their intentions, by the same token it also reminds us to remain alert to the constitutive uncertainty—the fallibility, the humanness—of our knowledge. Just as a Falling Rocks sign resigns us to disaster but also makes us look up, epistemological modesty can provoke us to try to better anticipate, to the extent that we can, the unintended consequences of our actions. Thus though it may not help us to ground our political ethics, a posthumanist epistemology can help us to assess the actions we take in that ethics' name. For by training our attention on the world's systemic complexity and the externalities this creates, it encourages us to build better, more comprehensive, and dynamic models of material interconnections on spatial and temporal scales we are not used to imagining. While this work of modeling is obviously an empirical endeavor, it is also an imaginative labor, an effort to think the unthought spidering of effects and to conjure the unseen multiplicity of human, nonhuman, embodied, and discursive forces interacting upon any given site of action. This may even be a habit of thought that reading, in particular, can help us to cultivate.[19] By tracing these proliferating externalities, we may find ways to fold them into better calculations of cost and risk, to take a larger view of politics' constituents and a longer view of political action so as to better anticipate what crop our seeds in fact sow. And if, like Whitman, we must be willing to accept that we cannot ultimately control what results from our efforts, we can nonetheless, like Whitman, refuse to view this as a reason to stop working. We are launched upon unknown waters, like always.

ACKNOWLEDGMENTS

Because experience is sprawlingly continuous but narrative likes shape, this project feels like one that has moved with me through several, almost different lives. The present book would not exist without the support of the English Departments at Johns Hopkins University and the University of Mississippi. I have encountered few readers as keenly lucid and generous as Sharon Cameron; the acute energy of her attention has taught me what it looks like to believe that the words on the page matter. The critical sensibilities, advice, and encouragement of Christopher Nealon, Michael Moon, and Frances Ferguson have likewise been invaluable and helped me to develop as a scholar in ways that I am continuing to belatedly realize. Jane Bennett's seminar on Thoreau and Whitman many years ago was formative for my thinking about these authors, but equally important, Jane taught me about mentorship by welcoming me—first as a foundling seminar student from a different department, and later as a neophyte assistant professor—to think alongside her as she worked through an argument. As hallucinatory as it was, the feeling of being a colleague and potential collaborator gave me a much-needed taste of what it might be like to do this work without feeling like a pretender to it. Meanwhile, my friends in graduate school were my oxygen; for their intelligence, humor, barbecue, and zeal for good music and indiscriminate dancing, I might even bury a body for Jennifer Lin, Rob Higney, Hadley Leach, Shlomit Barnea, Daniela Ginsburg, Michael McCarthy, Elisha Cohn, Jason Hoppe, Dewayne Dean, Tony Wexler, Jake Greear, Mabel Wong, Jeremy Arnold, Noora Lori, Suvi Irvine, Adam Culver, Stephanie Fishel, Jairus Grove, Simon Glezos, Bridget Pupillo, Ben Parris, Tara Bynum, Mark Noble, Jason Gladstone, and Dave and Stephanie Hershinow.

At the University of Mississippi, I have been the grateful recipient of summer research grants and a well-timed partial course release that allowed me the time I urgently needed to get this work done. Ivo Kamps may be sick of hearing it at this point but he is an irreplaceable chair whose blend of ambition and pragmatism helped me to navigate substantially reinventing this project without losing my job in the process. I cannot imagine a more congenial group of scholars than the colleagues I now work with, and I'm particularly grateful to my cohort in the department for being such good company during what might easily otherwise have been lonely years of writing: Patrick Alexander, Magalí Armillas-Tiseyra, Monika Bhagat-Kennedy, Lindy Brady, Erin Drew, Ari Friedlander, Derrick Harriell, Melissa Ginsburg, Rachel Johnson, Kate Lechler, Jennie Leitweis-Goff, Chris Offut, Peter Reed, Jason Solinger, Ian Whittington, and Caroline Wigginton. And for making Oxford feel like a place in which I don't just work but live, I'm thankful to Meg and Brad Hayden, Lucky Tucker, Kakki Brown, Arami Harris, John Jordan Proctor, April Harriell, Tom Brady (who's even greater than the one you're thinking of), Tommy Franklin, and Beth Ann Fennelly.

My special gratitude belongs to those who, through sheer generosity or perhaps miscalculation, agreed to read parts of this manuscript and offered invaluable feedback at various stages. For helping me to think and say these things better, my thanks go to Eve Dunbar, Bill Rossi, Caroline Wigginton, and the anonymous readers at Fordham University Press. I'm also grateful to have been so warmly welcomed into the intellectual communities of the MMLA Civil War Caucus (special thanks to Jeffrey Insko for helping me find my way there) and the Thoreau Society (particularly Kristen Case, James Finley, Rochelle Johnson, Bill Rossi, and Laura Dassow Walls).

Finally, as this project moved with me from life to life in Baltimore, Maryland; Antigonish, Nova Scotia; and Oxford, Mississippi (with stops in Berkeley, Philadelphia, Charlemont, Massachusetts, and Syracuse, Indiana), there are those who have been the condition of possibility for my continuance, to whom words like gratitude and debt are too meanly transactional to describe my attachment. To my day ones, Sarah Bennett, Liz Little, Rebecca Onion, Elanor Starmer, and Julia Turner: hi loves. To my family, Cynthia, Peter, Dai, and Tari; to Liz, Sophie, Emily, Tom, and Thor; and to Lora, John, Molly, and Ben: I'll find better ways than an acknowledgments section to express my constantly renewed gladness for you. To my pit bull familiars, Northrop and Tina: thank you sitting on my feet as I worked, and for being patient all those hours I spent writing instead of being awesome. And to Daniel Stout, for sitting on the kitchen counter and talking through these ideas yet again, for running along the trails and talking about anything else, for making me at home in the world from Nova Scotia to Mississippi: I can't wait to keep going just around the next bend with you.

INTRODUCTION. BEYOND RECOGNITION: THE PROBLEM
OF ANTEBELLUM EMBODIMENT

1. Spillers, "Mama's Baby Papa's Maybe," 70.

2. I capitalize "Black" in this study in keeping with what has increasingly become standard usage in American studies and critical race studies scholarship. I make this choice in sympathy with this usage's assertion that, at least in North America, to have black skin is to belong, ascribe, or be assigned to Blackness as an identity, and in support of this usage's instinct to combat, even in this small way, the systematic devaluation of Black life. The decision to capitalize Black is, however, not a simple one, particularly in the context of this book, which will critically examine the historical emergence of modern racialist thought—including the notion that skin color confers identity. Indeed, at issue throughout this study will be a tension between the kinds of idealism needed to posit stable identities (racial or otherwise) and materialisms in which stable identities—indeed, in which all nouns, proper or otherwise—are untenable in light of the porosity, mutuality, and processual changefulness of embodied being. This friction between the reification of identity signaled by the capitalization of "Black" and the dissolution of identity implicit in both antebellum and contemporary posthumanist materialisms will come into particular focus in Chapter 4 and the Coda, which mine the commonalities and conflicts beween posthumanist and social justice theories.

3. In works like *The Order of Things* and *The Birth of Biopolitics*, Foucault dates this transformation in the Western conception of Man to philosophical changes brought about by Enlightenment sciences. However, postcolonial theorists including Sylvia Wynter argue that Western colonialism in the three centuries prior to this moment "prepare[d] the way for changes in the second modernity which are often thought to be the exclusive domain of Enlightenment thought" (Suarez-Krabbe, *Race, Rights, and Rebels*, 7. See also Wynter, "1492.")

4. Foucault, *History of Sexuality*, 142.

5. Foucault, *Order of Things*, 346.

6. Readers interested in tracing the paths of these discourses prior to where this study takes them up might begin with Kramnick's study of embodied accounts of action in eighteenth-century philosophy and literature, in *Actions and Objects*; Richardson's examination of embodied accounts of mind in romantic-era science and literature in *British Romanticism*; and Murison's survey of embodied accounts of mind in nineteenth-century American popular culture and literature in *Politics of Anxiety*.

7. Nott and Gliddon, *Types of Mankind*, 54.

8. As Wynter ("On How We Mistook") describes this, the biologization of man thus effects an "overall devalorization of the human species" by draining "the human" of the moral significance—the unique and universal freedom from material causality—that humanism had accorded it. To unpack this point more fully: whereas humanist "Man" is morally distinct from all other organisms by virtue of his freedom from his body, the biological human is strictly an embodied organism. It may therefore be distinguished from other embodied organisms by differences of degree but not by differences of moral kind: it is endowed with features that character-ize the physical uniqueness of the species *Homo sapiens*, but the materialist idiom to which this figure belongs prevents it from laying claim to features (e.g., soul, moral freedom) that are categorically exceptional to the material order. Thus biological humanity may be *more* sentient or *more* communica-tive or *more* cognitively complex than other species, but in the end these embodied features do not amount to a categorical break such as that posited by the doctrine of humanity's transcendence of its materiality that has traditionally grounded claims for humanity's unique moral value.

9. Russ Castronovo's influential argument in *Necro Citizenship*, for instance, divides this era into two ideological camps, with liberal humanists committed to a disembodied and generic personhood on the one side, and racists, who "sentenced women and slaves to excessive and lethal embodi-ment," on the other (10). Castronovo's thesis—that liberalism can be as hard on the body as racism—is incisive about the limitations of liberal person-hood. However, it also risks flattening the field of antebellum embodied thought. For while it's entirely true that the rising cachet of biological materialism was deployed to underwrite racist and sexist exclusion, racism and sexism were not the only ideologies of embodiment circulating in antebellum America. Thus my readings of antislavery materialism in Frederick Douglass, Henry David Thoreau, and Walt Whitman endeavor to show how these authors navigated between Castronovo's punishing either/ or, threading the needle between the disembodied universalism of abolition-ist humanism and the dehumanizing hierarchies of biological racism.

10. Hartman, *Scenes of Subjection*, 10.

11. For a more thoroughgoing takedown of racial science's empirical inaccuracies, see Gould, *Mismeasure of Man.*

12. Alaimo and Hekman, *Material Feminisms*, 1, 3.

13. I also prefer "posthumanism" to the alternative term currently in circulation—"nonhumanism"—because in the context of my analysis of race and slavery, "nonhumanism's" closer rhetorical connection to animals and animality may invite readers to assume that any argument with humanism is an argument for the *dehumanization* of peoples. It is precisely my purpose here to complicate this sort of assumption. For alternative perspectives on what name this broad theoretical reorientation ought to go by—posthumanism, nonhumanism, inhumanism, and the like—see, for instance, Luciano and Chen, "Has the Queer Ever Been Human?" 195–96. See also Grusin's introduction to *Nonhuman Turn.*

14. Levinson, "Of Being Numerous," 635.

15. Jackson, "Outer Worlds," 216.

16. Weheliye, *Habeas Viscus*, 9–10.

17. Thomas Taylor, *Rights of Brutes*, iii, 103.

18. Ibid., v–vi.

19. See Kramnick, *Actions and Objects*, for an investigation of this line of reasoning in eighteenth-century philosophy and literature.

20. Thomas Taylor, *Rights of Brutes*, 11.

21. Ibid., 103.

22. American fugitive slave James W. C. Pennington attests to this logic when he writes, "The being of slavery, its soul and its body, lives in the chattel principle, the property principle, the bill of sale principle. . . . You cannot constitute slavery without the chattel principle" (quoted in David Brion Davis, *Inhuman Bondage*, 193).

23. Foucault, *Birth of Biopolitics*, 271. See also Wynter, "On How We Mistook," 122–26. Note that this biologization of "Man" is sometimes sold as part of a story about the secularization of modernity, but it is nothing so simple as that. As J. Kameron Carter notes, "the discourse of theology aided and abetted the processes by which 'man' came to be viewed as a modern, racial being," while at the same time theology itself underwent a "subtle, inner transformation . . . in giving itself over to the discursive enterprise of helping to racially constitute the modern word as we have come to know it" (*Race*, 3). Here I depart from Wynter's suggestion that biologized Man is a "purely secular" figure ("On How We Mistook," 123).

24. Foucault, *Society Must Be Defended*, 245.

25. Ibid., 245. See also Foucault, *Birth of Biopolitics.*

26. Brown, *Undoing the Demos*, 83.

27. Hartman, *Scenes of Subjection*, 10.

28. Foucault, *Society Must Be Defended*, 258. Although Foucault here notes racism's enabling relation to biopower, he nonetheless arguably underestimates the centrality of racism to the biopolitical order. In defining racism's role in biopower in *Society Must Be Defended*, Foucault ambivalently represents racism as endemic to biopolitics or, alternatively, as supplementary to biopolitics (as he writes, "racism intervenes" in the biopolitical state's commitment to cultivating populational life in order to introduce a rationale for making or letting some of that population die [254]). For a trenchant revisionary account of biopolitics as a racializing assemblage, see Weheliye, *Habeas Viscus*.

29. Foucault, *Society Must Be Defended*, 255.

30. Esposito, *Immunitas*. For an incisive account of how descriptions of biopolitics, such as the one I have just broadly sketched, systematically overlook how biopolitics also reinvented the state's relation to animal life, see Shukin, *Animal Capital*.

31. Wynter, "1492," 28–50.

32. Hayles, *How We Became Posthuman*, 5.

33. Thrift, *Non-Representational Theory*, 5.

34. McGurl, "New Cultural Geology," 388.

35. "Transcorporeal" is Stacy Alaimo's term, riffing on Donna Haraway's suggestion that the human body does not "end at the skin." See Alaimo, *Bodily Natures*. "Intra-active" is Karen Barad's term; see *Meeting the Universe Halfway*. Esposito defines "the flesh" as the continuum of living matter that "precedes the body," constituting "a being that is both singular and communal, generic and specific . . . undifferentiated and different" (Esposito, *Bios*, 167).

36. Puar, "'Rather Be a Cyborg,'" 57.

37. Bennett, *Vibrant Matter*; Mel Chen, *Animacies*. See also Latour, *Politics of Nature*. Because it envisions life as an entangled continuum or network of being, posthumanism is sometimes described as framing a nongenocidal or "affirmative biopolitics" (Esposito, *Bios*)—a politics that refuses to inscribe lethal "caesuras" or value distinctions within life but instead embraces what Foucault (*Society Must Be Defended*) terms "life itself" as a field unstratified by hierarchies of racial, sexual, or speciological difference. Along these lines, Giorgio Agamben calls for "a politics in which bare life is no longer separated and excepted"—in which the material plenum of being is no longer artificially segregated into selected ("fully" human) and dysselected ("bare" or nonhuman) forms (Agamben, *Homo Sacer*, 9).

38. For instance, several new works in medieval studies spotlight proto-posthumanisms in medieval texts. See Mitchell, *Becoming Human*;

Joy and Dionne, "When Did We Become Post/Human?"; Cohen, *Medieval Identity Machines*. Or again, although these studies do not mention posthumanism by name, Justin E. H. Smith's investigation of Leibniz's proto-biological empiricism and Jonathan Kramnick's exploration of the philosophy of action and mental causation in the eighteenth-century novel are examples of scholarship that points the way to a prehistory of contemporary posthumanism in early modern and Enlightenment thought. See Justin E. H. Smith, *Divine Machines;* and Kramnick, *Actions and Objects*.

39. McGurl, "New Cultural Geology," 381.

40. Frederick Douglass, "West India Emancipation," speech delivered at Canandaiga, N.Y., August 3, 1857, in *Selected Speeches and Writings*, 368.

41. Thoreau "Last Days of John Brown," 148.

42. Ibid., 147.

43. Castiglia, *Interior States*; Coviello, *Intimacy in America*, 4.

44. Bruno Latour lays out his proposal for a "parliament of things" in *Politics of Nature;* Levi Bryant describes "a democracy of objects" in *Democracy of Objects*; the longer quote is from Bennett, *Vibrant Matter*, 109.

45. Bennett, "Systems and Things," 224.

46. Emerson, Journals and Miscellaneous Notebooks, 3:70.

47. Murison, *Politics of Anxiety*; Thrailkill, *Affecting Fictions*.

48. Tompkins, *Racial Indigestion*; Boggs, *Animalia Americana*.

49. Matt Taylor, *Universes without Us*; Mark Noble, *American Poetic Materialism*.

1. DOUGLASS'S ANIMALS: RACIAL SCIENCE AND THE PROBLEM OF HUMAN EQUALITY

1. The framers of the Constitution deferred the question of suffrage to the states, most of whose laws of suffrage remained largely unchanged from the pre–Revolutionary War era. While the rules of suffrage in most states were modeled on British law, there were variations in property, race, and sex requirements from state to state.

2. Adams cited in Keyssar, *Right to Vote*, 1. As Keyssar notes, although the irrationalism of the poor was the most commonly cited rationale for not enfranchising them, this argument "that the poor should not vote because they had 'no will of their own' coexisted with an altogether contradictory argument, often expressed by the same people: that the poor or propertyless should not vote because they would threaten the interests of property—that is, they would have too much will of their own. If men without property could vote, reflected the judicious conservative John Adams, 'an immediate revolution would ensue'" (Keyssar, *Right to Vote*, 9).

3. Ibid., 35. The proposition Keyssar is quoting, "that every full-grown, featherless biped, who wears a hat instead of a bonnet, has a *natural* right to vote," is G. S. Hillard (writing as "Silas Standfast"), contributor to *Discussions on the Constitution Proposed to the People of Massachusetts by the Convention of 1853*, 117.

4. *Proceedings and Debates of the Virginia State Convention of 1829–30* (Richmond: Samuel Shepherd, 1830), 27.

5. Standfast (Hillard), *Discussions on the Constitution*, 118.

6. Walker, "Walker's Appeal."

7. Garrison, "To the Public," 1.

8. Bay, *White Image*, 13.

9. Nott and Gliddon, *Types of Mankind*, 50.

10. Douglass, "The Claims of the Negro Ethnologically Considered" (pamphlet, Rochester N.Y., 1854), in *Selected Speeches and Writings*, 287.

11. Douglass, "West India Emancipation," speech delivered at Canandaiga, N.Y., August 3, 1857, in *Selected Speeches and Writings*, 368.

12. As Kyla Schuller argues, racial scientists often explicitly positioned their empiricism (which is based upon sensory experience) as offering a usefully restrained antidote to antislavery sentimentalism. As she writes, in this discourse "the Anglo-Saxon female absorbs the instability of impressibility and its tendency to excess, leaving her male counterpart to enjoy the benefits of *sentiment* while relieving him of the liabilities of *sentimentality*" ("Taxonomies of Feeling," 278). Dana D. Nelson examines the role of sentiment in polygenist science in "'No Cold or Empty Heart.'"

13. Nott and Gliddon, *Types of Mankind*, 457.

14. Linnaeus cited in Agamben, *Open*, 24.

15. Jordan cited in Bay, *White Image*, 19.

16. Tucker, *Moment of Racial Sight*, 61.

17. Thus, for instance, Nancy Stepan wonders "why it was that, just as the battle against slavery was being won by abolitionists, the war against racism in European thought was being lost," and Susan Buck-Morss lambastes the "glaring discrepancy between thought and practice" in the era of liberalism and slavery. Stepan, *Idea of Race in Science*, 1; Buck-Morss, "Hegel and Haiti," 821.

18. As Tucker argues, racialism is the direct product of "two not entirely compatible principles of the [Enlightenment] era: a commitment to universal equality and a commitment to the truth of evidence drawn from empirical observation" (*Moment of Racial Sight*, 25).

19. Samuel Stanhope Smith, *Essay*, 204.

20. "Are not the blacks of Guinea, the dwarfs of Siberia, degenerate races compared with the inhabitants of France, or England, of Turkey, or Persia?," Smith rhetorically asks (ibid., 311).

21. Thus Smith assures us that even the "degenerate" Guinean and Siberian "are found to improve in their appearance and form, by being removed from their own climate," even as "the European, on his removal to Africa or Lapland," comes to bear "a nearer resemblance to the natives of those countries" (ibid., 311). Already, he observes, "The American negro is visibly losing the most uncouth peculiarities of the African person" (252).

22. Frederickson, *Black Image*, 97.

23. Catlin, *Letters and Notes*, 61; Conway quoted in Lemire, *"Miscegenation,"* 129.

24. Frederickson, *Black Image*, 101.

25. Samuel George Morton, *Crania Americana*, 3.

26. Gossett, *Race*, 65; Dain, *Hideous Monster of the Mind*, 225.

27. M. Jacquinot cited in Nott and Gliddon, *Types of Mankind*, 56; Agassiz, "Sketch of the Natural Provinces," lxxiv.

28. For instance Agassiz, a steadfast creationist, defended his polygenist views by arguing that the "greatness, prescience, omniscience, [and] providence" manifest in the orderly distribution of life on earth could only be the handiwork of God, proving that species have not haphazardly migrated across the earth and evolved, "but have made their successive appearance upon earth by the immediate intervention of the Creator" (Agassiz, *Contributions*, 135). Elsewhere, Samuel Cartwright defended the scriptural bona fides of polygenism with a complicated biblical hermeneutics, arguing that in the original Greek, Genesis 1:24 refers to the separate creation of Black and Native American races among the "living creatures" and "beasts of the earth" that God creates before Adam. "If the 24th verse of the 1st chapter were literally and fully translated, it would save the necessity of torturing Scripture and scientific truth to procure a white father and mother for the Missouri negroes and the Missouri Indians," he concludes (Cartwright, "Unity of the Human Race," 132). For a full account of the polygenist reading of Genesis, see Frederickson, *Black Image*, 86–89. For a broader and trenchant discussion of the anachronism of trying to distinguish "scientific" from "theological" argument in midcentury racial science, see Hickman, "Douglass Unbound," 323–62.

29. Douglass, "Claims," 287.

30. For instance, see Cartwright's reading of Genesis 1:24 discussed above.

31. Fitzhugh, *Sociology for the South*, 258; Fitzhugh, *Cannibals All!*, xi.

32. Bachman, *Doctrine of the Unity*, 8.

33. Nott and Gliddon, *Types of Mankind*, liii. Thus, as Thomas Cobb concludes in his 1858 *Inquiry into the Law of Negro Slavery in the United States*

of America, the difference between polygenism and monogenism is "much-mooted": "Whether the negro was originally a different species, or is a degeneration of the same, is a matter indifferent in the inquiry as to his proper status in his present condition" (Cobb, *Inquiry*, 27).

34. Nott and Gliddon, *Types of Mankind*, 54.
35. Garrison, "No Compromise," 55.
36. Mays, "Divine Legation," 529.
37. Nott and Gliddon, *Types of Mankind*, 50, 59.
38. Frederickson, *Black Image*, 126–27.
39. Diamond, "Difficulty of Reality," 57.
40. Nelson, "No Cold or Empty Heart"; Schuller, "Taxonomies of Feeling."
41. Nott and Gliddon, *Types of Mankind*, 50.
42. I sense a version of this reluctance to embrace Douglass's post-Garrisonian politics in the tendency of several readers to stress the continuity between Douglass's pre- and post-Garrisonian biographies. Thus, for instance, Elizabeth Barnes and Colleen Glenney Boggs suggest that in *My Bondage and My Freedom* (1855) Douglass does not distance himself from the rhetoric of sympathy and moral suasion but rather deploys it in modified form. See Barnes, "Manhood"; Boggs, *Animalia Americana*.
43. Chesnutt, *Frederick Douglass*, 69.
44. Douglass, *My Bondage and My Freedom* (1855), in *Autobiographies*, 374.
45. Noble, "Sympathetic Listening," 58.
46. Douglass, "Claims," 287.
47. Dain, *Hideous Monster of the Mind*, 249.
48. Douglass, "Claims," 282.
49. Bay (*White Image*) begins her study of this tradition with John Russworm's 1827 essay, "The Mutability of Human Affairs." Russert also documents this rich tradition in "Science of Freedom."
50. Bay, *White Image*, 37.
51. Russwurm quoted in ibid., 30.
52. Easton, *Treatise*, 43.
53. Ibid., 26.
54. Garnet, *Past and Present Condition*, 7.
55. Easton, *Treatise*, 20.
56. Garnet, *Past and Present Condition*, 25.
57. Easton, *Treatise*, 18, 20.
58. Bay, *White Image*, 71.
59. Ibid., 36.
60. Delaney, "Political Destiny," 247.
61. Ibid., 252.
62. Douglass, "Claims," 295.

63. Ibid., 283.

64. Ibid.

65. Ibid., 284.

66. Ibid., 284, 287, 289, 287. The truth of Douglass's statement specifically as a critique of polygenist science has been demonstrated by Stephen Jay Gould's failed efforts to replicate Morton's craniological measurements (narrated in *The Mismeasure of Man*).

67. Ibid., 285.

68. Ibid., 286–87.

69. Hickman, "Douglass Unbound," 333.

70. Douglass, "Claims," 296.

71. Ibid., 296.

72. Foucault, *Birth of Biopolitics*, 274; Douglass, "Claims," 296.

73. Douglass, "Claims," 297.

74. Ibid.

75. Douglass, *My Bondage and My Freedom*, 263.

76. Douglass, *The Narrative of the Life of Frederick Douglass* (1845), in Douglass, *Autobiographies*, 46.

77. Douglass, "The Heroic Slave" (1853), in *Selected Speeches and Writings*, 221.

78. Wilson, *Specters of Democracy*, 33.

79. Douglass, "Freedom's Battle at Christiana," *Frederick Douglass' Paper*, September 25, 1851, in *Selected Speeches and Writings*, 182.

80. Indeed, in an 1873 speech, Douglass condemns the abuse of farm animals in terms that expressly invoke his analysis of the slave's proper duty to an oppressive government. There he advises, "All loud and boisterous commands, all brutal flogging should be banished from the field, and only words of cheer and encouragement should be tolerated. A horse is in many respects like a man. He has the five senses, and has memory, affection and reason to a limited degree. . . . Convince him that he is a creature of law as well as of freedom by a judicious and kindly application of your superior power, and he will conform his conduct to that law, far better than your most law-abiding citizen" (Douglass, *Address*). I'm grateful to my graduate student Savannah DiGregorio for bringing this passage to my attention.

81. Sundquist, *To Wake the Nations*; Castronovo, *Fathering the Nation*.

82. Castronovo, *Fathering the Nation*, 190.

83. Douglass, "Is It Right and Wise to Kill a Kidnapper?," *Frederick Douglass' Paper*, June 2, 1854, in *Selected Speeches and Writings*, 277–80.

84. I further develop this idea that freedom is endemic to nature in Douglass's 1850 writings in my article, "Amoral Abolitionism," which identifies this as a key theme of *My Bondage and My Freedom*.

85. Douglass, "Peaceful Annihilation of Slavery Is Hopeless," *Frederick Douglass' Paper*, November 28, 1856, in *Selected Speeches and Writings*, 344.

86. Levine, *Martin Delany*, 101.

87. Douglass, "West India Emancipation," speech delivered at Canandaigua, N.Y., August 3, 1857, in *Selected Speeches and Writings*, 368 (emphasis added).

88. Douglass, "The Present Conditions and Future Prospects of the Negro People," address to the American and Foreign Antislavery Society, May 11, 1854, in *Selected Speeches and Writings*, 259 (emphasis added). The point here is not that Douglass has lost faith in moral truth—that is, I would not go quite so far as to propose, with Paul Giles, that Douglass has arrived at a rather nihilistic "view of society as a cycle of conflict, riven by power struggles" for domination. However, I do suggest that he has begun to understand slavery's moral dimension as unnecessary—though by no means irrelevant—to the argument for abolition (Giles, "Narrative Reversals and Power Exchanges," 803).

89. Douglass, "Heroic Slave," 223.

90. Noble, "Sympathetic Listening"; Foreman, "Sentimental Abolition"; DeLombard, "Eye-Witness to the Cruelty."

91. Douglass, *My Bondage and My Freedom*, 184.

92. For discussions of Douglass's transnationalism in the 1850s, see Marrs, "Frederick Douglass in 1848"; Giles, *Virtual Americas*; Tamarkin, *Anglophilia*.

93. Douglass, "The Revolution of 1848," speech at West India Emancipation Celebration, Rochester, N.Y., August 1, 1848, in *Selected Speeches and Writings*, 105. I am indebted to Cody Marrs for bringing this passage to my attention; see Marrs, "Frederick Douglass in 1848."

94. Boggs, *Animalia Americana*, 86.

95. Ibid., 106–7.

96. Fielder, "Animal Humanism," 488, 510.

97. Pratt, "Douglass and Recognition after 1845," 265.

98. Douglass, *My Bondage and My Freedom*, 179; Douglass, "The Meaning of July Fourth for the Negro," address to the Rochester Ladies' Antislavery Association, July 5, 1852, in *Selected Speeches and Writings*, 205.

99. Douglass, "Meaning of the Fourth of July," 205.

100. Ibid., 195.

101. Hyde, "Climates of Liberty," 489.

102. Latour, *Politics of Nature*, 53.

103. Chen, *Animacies*.

104. Ellis, "Amoral Abolitionism."

105. Douglass, "The Heroic Slave," 242–43.

106. Ibid., 243–44.
107. Ibid., 244.
108. Ibid., 245.
109. Ibid., 245–46.
110. Hyde, "Climates of Liberty," 481–84.
111. Ibid., 490, 494.

2. THOREAU'S SEEDS: EVOLUTION AND THE PROBLEM OF HUMAN AGENCY

1. Emerson quoted in Davis, *Bits of Gossip*, 44.
2. Nott and Gliddon, *Types of Mankind*, 50.
3. Cameron, *Writing Nature*; Buell, *Environmental Imagination*; Walls, *Seeing New Worlds*.
4. Mid-twentieth-century critics tended to portray Thoreau as a somewhat tragic figure, an aspiring Transcendentalist who finally retreated into the privacy of nature in the late 1850s out of frustration with his failure in the literary marketplace, or because age had sapped his youthful capacity for poetic inspiration. See Miller, *Consciousness in Concord*; and Paul, *Shores of America*. Versions of these theses also appear in Van Doren, *Henry David Thoreau*; and Hodder, *Thoreau's Ecstatic Witness*. By contrast, in the wake of Cameron's pathbreaking study of Thoreau's *Journal* (*Writing Nature*), Buell's monumental *Environmental Imagination*, and Walls's landmark *Seeing New Worlds*, the prevailing narrative has been that Thoreau's empiricism or "ecocentrism" displaced his interest in natural symbols, thus yielding a discourse on nature that was less and less prone to moral reflection and parable making. Of these three foundational studies, Walls's stands out for resisting the hypostasized distinction between human and natural history that, as I argue above, funds the conclusion that Thoreau's naturalistic studies are premised upon a relinquishment of concern for the social world.
5. Buell, *Environmental Imagination*, 138, 135.
6. Buell thus concludes that "the hypothesis of Thoreau as 'deep ecologist'" helps us "to overcome the traditional opposition between the 'naturist' and the 'social protester'" (*Environmental Imagination*, 369). That the politics we associate with Thoreau's late naturalism are more or less strictly environmentalist is suggested by the fact that none of these three important studies of Thoreau's late works mentions the antislavery essays he wrote for John Brown at the height of his "ecocentric" phase.
7. Schneider, "Thoreau's Human Ecology."
8. Chakrabarty, "Climate of History," 201.
9. Cameron, *Writing Nature*, 24; Robinson, *Natural Life*, 7.
10. Latour, *Politics of Nature*, chap. 1.
11. Lurie, *Louis Agassiz*, 125; Irmscher, *Louis Agassiz*, 107.

12. Lurie, *Louis Agassiz*, 135.

13. Abbot Lawrence in a letter to Harvard Treasurer Samuel Atkins Eliot, June 7, 1847, cited in Lurie, *Louis Agassiz*, 137.

14. Lurie, *Louis Agassiz*, 135; James, "Louis Agassiz," also cited in Walls, "Agassiz,"

15. In giving this account of Agassiz's preeminence in midcentury U.S. scientific circles, I am arguably falling into what Branka Arsić describes, in her dazzling reading of Thoreau's vitalism, as a misguided tendency to assign Agassiz "the central place in our understanding of natural science at Harvard in the 1840s" (134–35). The problem with this, Arsić argues, is that the overrepresentation of Agassiz and his theory of sequential special creation has functioned to eclipse attention to the strong and countervailing tradition of vitalist science at Harvard that crystallized in the 1820s and 1830s. I am grateful to her study for highlighting this vitalist tradition as one source of Thoreau's own anti-Agassizian science, and although her book was not yet available when I wrote this chapter, I now find that my own reading of Thoreau's materialism often resonates strongly with hers (as I shall note below). On this particular point, though, I would nonetheless maintain that in the decade upon which I am focusing (the 1850s), Agassiz's recent arrival and unprecedented visibility at the helm of Harvard's new school of science did, in fact, put Harvard's remaining vitalists in the shade. Although science at Harvard remained theoretically diverse (as demonstrated by Asa Gray's public debates with Agassiz over Darwinian evolution), in the 1850s Agassiz's outsized reputation meant that it was his theory of creation and his methodologies that Thoreau felt compelled to contend with. For more on vitalism at Harvard, see Arsić, *Bird Relics*.

16. Agassiz, "An Essay on Classification," in *Contributions*, 61. Robert Sattelmeyer reports that Thoreau read this essay in 1857 or 1858 (*Thoreau's Reading*, 118).

17. Agassiz, *Lake Superior*, 142, 145.

18. Agassiz and Gould, *Principles of Zoology*, 2.

19. Agassiz, "Essay on Classification," 7.

20. Henry David Thoreau letter to Horatio R. Storer, February 15, 1847, in Harding and Bode, *Correspondence of Henry David Thoreau*, 175.

21. Humboldt cited in Walls, *Seeing New Worlds*, 84.

22. Walls, *Seeing New Worlds*, 11.

23. Agassiz, "Diversity of Origin," 35–36.

24. Thoreau, *Walden*, in *Walden and Civil Disobedience*, 214.

25. Rossi, "Following Thoreau's Instincts"; Thoreau, *Walden*, 220.

26. Thoreau, *Walden*, 220.

27. Thoreau, "Walking," in *Excursions*, 200.

28. Walls, *Seeing New Worlds*, 122.

29. Cameron, *Writing Nature*, 60–61.

30. Ibid., 140.

31. Ibid., 149.

32. Thoreau, *Journal*, 6:592–94 (July 21, 1851). The scholarly edition of Thoreau's journal is still a work in progress; the Princeton edition currently runs to September 1854. The editors of the edition have made transcripts of the remaining unedited journal material available online, and I will refer to these transcripts when citing journal material from after 1854. Those transcripts are available at http://thoreau.library.ucsb.edu/writings _journals.html.

33. Ibid., 6:84–85 (January 30, 1854).

34. Ibid., 8:242 (October 27, 1851).

35. Ibid., 3:341 (March 9, 1852).

36. Ibid., 5:11 (March 8, 1853).

37. Arsić, *Bird Relics*, 254.

38. See Arsić, *Bird Relics*, for an illuminating account of how this "quintessentially materialist" epistemology generates, in Thoreau, a style and theory of communication committed to what she terms "literalization," a process that involves "turning the word into some sort of thing, capable of affecting bodies; and bringing words closer to objects, recovering the presence of objects in names" (8).

39. Walls, "Textbooks and Texts," 3.

40. Thoreau, *Journal*, 3:155–56 (December 25, 1851).

41. Ibid., 6:236–38 (May 6, 1853).

42. Thoreau, *Journal* (transcript), November 5, 1857. Reflecting on this passage, Robert Richardson argues that "it is highly likely that the problematic scientist challenged in the passage is Louis Agassiz, and much of Thoreau's longstanding ambivalence about science—though not about natural history or botany or zoology—can be understood in the context of his long association with and eventual rejection of the views of Louis Agassiz" (Richardson, *Henry Thoreau*, 363).

43. Thoreau, *Journal* (transcript), October 13, 1860.

44. Thoreau, *Journal* (transcript), October 18, 1860.

45. Along these lines, Darwin outlines his theory of the social construction of speciological difference in *On the Origin of Species*, concluding that "varieties cannot be distinguished from species," and that all currently acknowledged species "once existed as varieties, and thus originated" via speciation (47–48). In "Taxonomies of Feeling," Kyla Schuller profiles a fascinating riposte to Darwinian evolution formulated in the 1870s by the "American School of Evolution," which sought to reconcile the fluidity of

species with racist hierarchy. Led by Alexander Cope, this alternative school of evolution held that insensibility to influence is a defining feature of inferior races, whereas superior races are correspondingly more impressionable and susceptible to change. Intriguingly, if one can bring oneself to bracket its racist agenda, this theory's insistence that sensibility rather than sexual selection is the mechanism of human development bears certain affinities with Thoreau's sensuous empiricism.

46. Dean, "Thoreau and Greeley Exchange Letters," 630. Alfred Tauber also observes that "Thoreau actually first noted seeming anomalies concerning the growth of trees and the possible role of animals and wind in dispersing seeds in 1850" (*Moral Agency of Knowing*, 147). Walter Harding gives an account of Thoreau's early interest in succession, and the pivotal day on April 28, 1856, when George Hubbard brought to his attention the phenomenon that a pine wood once cut often comes back all oak. See Harding, *Days of Henry Thoreau*, 438–39.

47. Agassiz, "Sketch of the Natural Provinces," lxxv.

48. Thoreau, *Journal*, 5:4–5 (March 5, 1853).

49. Richardson, *Henry Thoreau*, 368.

50. Thoreau, *Journal* (transcript), March 5, 1858.

51. Thoreau, *Journal* (transcript), June 3, 1858. To put Thoreau's sense of scientific superiority in perspective, however, his own guess is that "they fell from the clouds in the form of spawn or tadpoles—or young frogs. I think it more likely that they fell down than that they hopped up."

52. Thoreau, *Journal* (transcript), August 23, 1858. See also journal entries for November 26, 27, 30, 1858, where Thoreau reflects at length on evidence of speciological migration and interconnection.

53. Richardson, *Henry Thoreau*, 369.

54. Agassiz, *Contributions*, vii.

55. Thoreau, *Wild Fruits*, 3.

56. Ibid., 4–5.

57. Ibid., 83.

58. Robinson, *Natural Life*, 196; Thoreau, *Wild Fruits*, 82.

59. A word search on "racy" reveals no occurrences in *A Week on the Concord and Merrimack Rivers, Walden, Maine Woods, Cape Cod*, or *The Dispersion of Seeds*. Two instances appear in Princeton's digitized (post-1854) transcripts of the *Journal*—both referring to the wild apple.

60. See Lurie, *Louis Agassiz*, chap. 7; Irmscher, *Louis Agassiz*, chap. 5. It is possible that Thoreau attended one or more of Gray's lectures: Thoreau was in Boston on December 10, 1858, when Gray delivered his first paper in support of Darwin's theory at the Cambridge Scientific Society, and he was again in Boston January 11, 1859, when Gray presented crucial evidence that

he had been supplying to Darwin about the similarity between Japanese and North American plants.

61. Gray, "Darwin on Origin of Species."

62. Darwin, *Origin of Species*, 354.

63. Ibid., 340; also quoted in Berger, *Thoreau's Late Career*, 50–51.

64. Berger, *Thoreau's Late Career*, 50.

65. Thoreau, "The Succession of Forest Trees," in *Wild Apples*, 95.

66. Ibid., 96.

67. Harding, *Days of Henry Thoreau*, 439–40.

68. Thoreau, "Succession of Forest Trees," 93.

69. The quoted phrases are Laura Dassow Walls's description of modern readers' reactions (*Seeing New Worlds*, 200). Harding affirms this impression by noting that both the Middlesex Agricultural Society and the Massachusetts Board of Agriculture excised these "humorous" opening remarks when they published the lecture (*Days of Henry Thoreau*, 439).

70. Walls, *Seeing New Worlds*, 204.

71. I am grateful to Bill Rossi for pointing out to me Thoreau's horticultural pun on "bizarre."

72. Fleck, *Indians of Thoreau*, 7. It is unclear whether Thoreau planned to write a book on "the history and qualities of the North American Indian" (as his friend Franklin Sanborn once attested), or whether, as Robert Sayre argues, this research was merely source material for other projects. Either way, Thoreau was committed to this work, adding an average of twenty-four pages of notes per month to his "Indian Books" every year from 1850 through 1861. See Sayre, *Thoreau and the American Indians*; I have compiled Thoreau's page average from Sayre's table (110), absenting notebook 2, whose dates are unknown. The standard deviation is eleven pages.

73. Between 1856 and 1861, Thoreau read several works of racial science as well as others that included scientific speculations about Native American racial origins. Indeed, Joshua Bellin suggests that the late notebooks "palpably gain in excitement (as measured by authorial commentary) whenever talk of origins enters their orbit" (Bellin, "In the Company of Savagists," 10). The polygenist texts Thoreau read include Morton's *Crania Americana* (Thoreau had also visited Morton's skull collection in Philadelphia in 1854), Charles Pickering's *The Races of Man*, and Nott and Gliddon's two collections, *Types of Mankind* and *Indigenous Races of the Earth* (although not listed in Sattelmeyer's indispensable index, *Thoreau's Reading*, Thoreau's notes on *Indigenous Races* appear in "Indian Notebooks," 12). Both of the latter two volumes prominently feature contributions by Agassiz. However, Thoreau read a greater number of texts sympathetic to some version of monogenism. In 1856 he took fifty-eight pages of notes on James Adair's

History of the American Indians, a book offering "observations, and arguments, in proof of the American Indians being descended from the Jews,"
and which refers to its subjects as "the copper colour American Hebrews"
(96). Thoreau also perused a strange little book by George Burder titled *The
Welch Indians*, which speculates about "a people whose ancestors emigrated
from Wales to America, in the year 1170, with prince Modoc" and who "are
now said to inhabit a beautiful country on the west side of the Mississippi"
(Burder, *Welch Indians*). In addition, in 1851 he read Arnold Guyot's *Earth
and Man*, and in 1856 he read Benjamin Smith Barton's *New Views on the
Origin of the Tribes and Nations of America*.

74. Of course, it is impossible to know with certainty what Thoreau
thought of the statements he copied out from his readings, since the "Indian
Notebooks" chiefly contain transcriptions with very little personal commentary. Nonetheless, there is a subtly subversive logic to Thoreau's transcriptions from the polygenist works he read, which suggestively corroborates the
developmentalist outlook of his *Journal*. For one thing, his engagements
with polygenist texts tend to be rather perfunctory: on Nott and Gliddon's
650-page tome, *Indigenous Races of the Earth*, Thoreau took a comparatively
scant seven pages of notes. Moreover, in these few pages he seems to be
seizing on moments in which the argument for polygenism is particularly
wobbly. Thus, for instance, from Joseph Leidy's prefatory letter to the
volume, Thoreau excerpts the author's admission that "neither upon nor
beneath the surface of the earth" are "the bones of the generations of
red-men, of herds of bison, and of other animals which have lived and died
in past ages" to be found. As Thoreau dutifully records, Leidy speculatively
attributes this absence of a fossil record to the work of "devouring succes-
sors, and the combined influence of air and moisture, [which] have completely extinguished their traces." From here, however, Thoreau's notes skip
two pages ahead in Leidy's account to his conclusion that "it is quite as
probable that the [American Indian] had his origin on this continent, as that
men originated elsewhere," Leidy insists. Thoreau's selective transcriptions
thus highlight how Leidy inexplicably converts the total lack of physical
evidence for the ancient tenure of human beings in the Americas into proof
of the Native American's perpetual residence therein.

Leidy is not the only victim of Thoreau's silently critical reading practice.
Later in his notes on *Indigenous Races*, Thoreau juxtaposes two passages from
J. Aitken Meigs's contribution to the volume (an essay on "The Cranial
Characteristics of the Races of Men, with eighty-seven woodcuts"). First he
transcribes Meigs's citation of Morton's raciological distinction between
Appalachian peoples and peoples living west of the Alleghenies on the
grounds that the latter, as Morton observes, have distinctly elongated skulls.

Without a break in his page, Thoreau next copies a passage from three pages later in this essay, in which Meigs acknowledges evidence that "the Huns used artificial means for giving Mongolian physiognomy to their children . . . in an effort to approach a [flattened and elongated] form, which, among the Huns, was held in greater regard." Read sequentially, as Thoreau's selective transcription offers them, these two moments show how the craniometrical method Morton and Meigs use to construct their racial typographies may be unreliable, given the susceptibility of skulls to cultural practices of artificial shaping. (J. Meigs, "The Cranial Characteristics of the Races of Men," in Nott and Gliddon, *Indigenous Races*, 332, 335; cited in Thoreau, "Indian Notebook," 12). In the *Journal*, Thoreau makes similar use of Charles Pickering's *Races of Man* in 1853, from which he transcribes a passage noting that Aesop's fables migrated eastward to Madagascar and Malaysia. "A fame on its way round eastward with the Malay race to this western continent!," Thoreau crows, at the end of his citation: "P. gives California to the Malay race!" (*Journal* 7:30 [September 1, 1853]). Or again, after reading Morton's *Crania Americana* in 1852, Thoreau takes particular note of an anecdote Morton relates about how Chinese porcelain vessels had been found in the catacombs of Thebes in Egypt. While Thoreau's comments on this story focus on the Chinese inscription (which celebrates the coming of lilies in spring), he was no doubt pleased with this evidence of intercontinental intercourse "as old as the Pharaonic period" (*Journal* 5:204 [July 9, 1852]). Indeed, that Thoreau understood this anecdote to be relevant to the question of racial unity is supported by the fact that sentences from this journal entry end up in the concluding discussion of "Slavery in Massachusetts."

75. Barton, *New Views*, v. Thoreau's notes on Barton appear in "Indian Notebook," 10. Thoreau, *Journal* (transcript), September 27, 1857. Thoreau's journal entry suggests that by 1857 he had rejected Guyot's theory that Native Americans migrated to North America from the west, a theory that (as Schneider points out) had inspired Thoreau's musings on humankind's westering instinct in "Walking," first drafted in 1851.

76. Thoreau, *Journal* (transcript), February 3, 1859.

77. See Schneider, "Thoreau's Human Ecology"; Bellin, "In the Company of Savagists"; and an excellent piece by Neill Matheson, "Thoreau's Inner Animal."

78. Myers, *Converging Stories*, chap. 3; Sayre, *Thoreau and the American Indians*; Fleck, *Henry Thoreau and John Muir*.

79. I have compiled the following timeline of Thoreau's drafting, lecturing, and publishing activities from Bradley Dean's "Thoreau Chronology," in *Wild Fruits*, 273–75, and from Raymond Borst's chronology in *Thoreau Log*, 542–73.

80. Richardson argues that after the memorial service for Brown on December 2, 1859, "Thoreau's absorption in John Brown ceased almost as suddenly as it began. By December 8, 1859, Thoreau had picked up his natural history pursuits again and was absorbed in another rediscovery, this time of Aristotle on animals, and the writings of the roman naturalist Pliny. Within a month a copy of Darwin's *Origin of Species* would arrive in Concord and Thoreau's own vast natural history projects would take one last turn" (*Life of the Mind*, 372–73). Sherman Paul characterizes Thoreau's late political essays as moments of weakness in which he proves "insufficiently the hermit," proposing that Thoreau meant to "flee society" in the 1850s but found it "increasingly distracting him" until it "infected him" with the "need to champion principle" (*Shores of America*, 269–70). Sattelmeyer more dispassionately describes this period as one of bifurcation in Thoreau's output, characterizing his mature "development . . . [as] clearly in the direction of increasing interest in the study and writing about nature on the one hand, and on the other the expression of increasingly sharp and out-spoken views on sensitive social and political issues of the day" (*Thoreau's Reading*, 78).

81. Henry David Thoreau, "A Plea for Captain John Brown," in *Reform Papers*, 119.

82. Thoreau, *Wild Fruits*, 80.

83. Ibid., 83.

84. Henry David Thoreau, "Resistance to Civil Government," in *Reform Papers*, 81.

85. Thoreau, *Wild Fruits*, 83.

86. I am reasonably confident that Thoreau would have had this Latin origin in mind because—besides his well-known predilection for etymology—the eulogy he composed for Brown closes with a translation of Tacitus on Agricola's death, commending the transmission of Agricola's spirit and virtues to his immediate posterity ("Martyrdom of John Brown," in *Reform Papers*, 139–44).

87. Thoreau, "A Plea," 133, 125, 126, 121–22, 121.

88. Henry David Thoreau, "The Last Days of John Brown," in *Reform Papers*, 148.

89. For a description of this trope in racial scientific discourse, see Frederickson, *Black Image*, 57–58. See also Briggs, "Race of Hysteria."

90. Agassiz, "Diversity of Origin," 36.

91. Thoreau, "Slavery in Massachusetts," in *Reform Papers*, 103.

92. Thoreau, "A Plea," 135.

93. Ibid., 136.

94. Thoreau, "Last Days," 153, 147.

95. Thoreau, "A Plea," 138.

96. Dimock, *Through Other Continents*, 14.

97. Ibid., 16. For a related revisionary account of political action, defending the efficacy of Thoreau's political speeches, see Turner, "Performing Conscience," 497. Susan Lucas makes a similar argument about the catalytic political force of Thoreau's public address in "Counter-Frictions."

98. Dimock, *Through Other Continents*, 13, 20.

99. Thoreau, *Dispersion of Seeds*, 101.

100. Thoreau, "Last Days," 153.

101. Thoreau, *Journal*, 3:155–56 (December 25, 1851).

102. Thoreau, *Dispersion of Seeds*, 102.

103. Connolly, *Fragility of Things*, 75, 10.

104. Massumi, *Parables for the Virtual*, and Protevi, *Political Affect*.

105. McGurl, "New Cultural Geology," 388–89.

3. WHITMAN'S COSMIC BODY: BIOELECTRICITY AND THE PROBLEM OF HUMAN MEANING

1. Whitman, "Song of Myself," in *Leaves of Grass* (1855), 679 (l. 487).

2. Gray, "Darwin on the Origin of Species."

3. Indeed, even in its machinic applications—for instance, as the operative mechanism of the telegraph—electricity retained a distinct connection to the occult, producing what critics like Jeffrey Sconce, Richard Menke, and Paul Gilmore have described as the spiritualizing tendencies of mid-century media discourse. For further discussion of the curiously immaterial materiality of nineteenth-century electrical media, see Sconce, *Haunted Media*; Menke, *Telegraphic Realism*; and Gilmore, *Aesthetic Materialism*.

4. John Kucich and Erik Seeman point out that, beyond mesmerism and phrenology, the American Spiritualist movement was also importantly related to a range of earlier traditions of spiritual communication, including Native American spiritualist practices, African conjure and vodun practices, and Western European evangelical practices. See Kucich, *Ghostly Communion*; and Seeman, "Native Spirits, Shaker Visions." Similarly, Ann Braude (*Radical Spirits*) also links Spiritualism to mystical traditions within Christianity. R. Laurence Moore, however, cautions that "in noting these important and obvious connections" between Spiritualism and other traditions of religious mysticism, "we risk losing sight of spiritualism's connections with the dominant cultural values in the nineteenth century. Any interpretation of spiritualism's impact must begin with what has appeared to many as an anomaly. Spiritualism became a self-conscious movement precisely at the time it disassociated itself from occult traditions of secrecy. It appealed not

to the inward illumination of mystic experience, but to the observable and verifiable objects of empirical science. There was little new in the spirit manifestations of the 1850s except this militant stance, which proved to be exactly the right position to gain the attention of an age that wanted to believe that its universe operated like an orderly machine" (R. Laurence Moore, *In Search of White Crows*, 7).

5. *American Phrenological Journal* (1846) quoted in Mackey, "Phrenological Whitman."

6. Dods, *Philosophy of Electro-Biology*, 103.

7. Ibid., 102.

8. Andrew Jackson Davis, *Philosophy of Spiritual Intercourse*, 18.

9. Andrew Jackson Davis, *Morning Lectures*, 283.

10. Phelps, *Gates Ajar*, 41.

11. Ibid., 46.

12. Ibid., 66.

13. Ibid., 79.

14. Ibid., 69, 43.

15. Ibid., 79.

16. For analyses of Spiritualism's connection to bourgeois Victorian materialism, see for instance Helen Sootin Smith, introduction to *Gates Ajar*; Douglas, *Feminization of American Culture*.

17. Davis, *Philosophy of Spiritual Intercourse*, 18. Phelps's novel partly echoes this sentiment in its suggestion that those who embrace Spiritualist doctrine are (or become) physiologically more refined and advanced than those who do not. The novel's most outspoken skeptic of Spiritualism is Deacon Quirk, a working-class white character who is described in phrenological terms that mark him as racially inferior. Thus in the midst of a theological argument with Aunt Forceythe, Quirk is described as sporting a "narrow forehead braided tight" as well as an "obstinate face with . . . stupid, good eyes and animal mouth." By contrast, Aunt Forceythe is described in this scene as "the white, finely cut woman, with . . . serene smile and rapt, saintly eyes,—every inch of her, body and soul, refined not only by birth and training, but by the long nearness of her heart to Christ" (Phelps, *Gates Ajar*, 86–88).

18. Andrew Jackson Davis, *Present Age and Inner Life*, 277; Cox, *Body and Soul*, 195.

19. Davis, *Philosophy of Spiritual Intercourse*, 26.

20. McGarry, *Ghosts of Futures Past*, 159.

21. Braude, *Radical Spirits*, 58.

22. Modern, *Secularism in Antebellum America*, 178–79.

23. LeMenager, "Not Human, Again," 407.

24. Andrew Jackson Davis, *Death and the Afterlife*, 4, 9–12.

25. See Charles Taylor, *A Secular Age*.

26. Cox, *Body and Soul*, 3.

27. Spiritualism, and the broader currents of what I refer to as bioelectrical bohemia, made its way through Whitman's New York via traveling demonstrations, lectures, séances, and a steady stream of publications, many of them issued by the Manhattan-based phrenological firm, Fowler and Wells. It was through the Fowlers that Whitman was first introduced to phrenology, a related discourse of nervous embodiment, which he defended as belonging "among the sciences" after attending a lecture in 1846 (Whitman, *Brooklyn Daily Eagle*, 2). By 1855, when Fowler and Wells became one of only two known retailers to carry Whitman's self-published first edition of *Leaves of Grass*, and 1856, when it brought out Whitman's second edition on the Fowler and Wells imprint, the firm was an established publishing hub for a variety of progressive movements including mesmerism and Spiritualism. Moving in the Fowler and Wells circle, Whitman therefore would have encountered a community of thinkers for whom bioelectricity was understood to inaugurate a whole new metaphysics of the self. Indeed, with its proclamations of the divinity of the body and of the nonfinality of death, *Leaves of Grass* invokes topoi that would have been readily familiar to readers of Fowler and Wells's other authors, including Andrew Jackson Davis and "electro-biologist" Reverend John Bovee Dods. For a more comprehensive introduction to Whitman's exposure to Spiritualist, mesmeric, and phrenological ideas, see Reynolds, *Walt Whitman's America* and *Beneath the American Renaissance*.

28. Whitman, "Poem Incarnating the Mind," *Notebooks and Unpublished Writings*, 1:106.

29. Darwin letter to Asa Gray (February 1860) in *Life and Letters of Charles Darwin*, 2:273.

30. Whitman, preface to *Leaves of Grass* (1855), 621.

31. Maslan, *Whitman Possessed*, 52.

32. Readers may recall here Nott and Gliddon's pronouncement, likewise borne from their embodied theory of personhood, that "the intellectual man is inseparable from the physical man; and the nature of the one cannot be altered without a corresponding change in the other" (Nott and Gliddon, *Types of Mankind*, 50).

33. Whitman, "Song for Occupations," in *Leaves* (1855), 714 (l. 101).

34. Whitman, "Song of Myself," in *Leaves* (1855), 704 (ll. 1163–66).

35. Ibid., 710 (ll. 1328–30).

36. Warner, "Whitman Drunk," 40.

37. Whitman, preface to *Leaves* (1855), 618–19.

38. Douglass and Thoreau would recognize the environmentalist theory of race invoked in Whitman's suggestion here that "the hereditary countenance" that comes down to this poet is itself a product not just of race or bloodline but also of local natural historical and cultural conditions. Moreover, they would recognize that this environmentalism furnishes the logic behind Whitman's conclusion that the sheer diversity of America's landscapes and peoples promises to make its inhabitants "the race of races": a kind of racial compendium, born of diversity. But whereas the environmentalist theory of race imagines this process of physiological adaptation and incorporation to span generations, Whitman's poet, like a medium in trance, absorbs impressions from his surrounding world and is at once transformed into a channel for those forces' expression. The quasi-messianic status Whitman ascribes to the poet thus stems from his sense of the poet's peculiar temporality, his untimeliness. More so than his peers, this poet has a talent for reception that allows him to embody the culmination "of old and new"; he is "himself the age transfigured," a prophetic specimen, as Thoreau might call him, who stands "where the future becomes the present" and "glows a moment on the extremest verge" (Whitman, preface to *Leaves* (1855), 633 (l. 710); 623–24 (ll. 311–15).

39. Emerson, "The Poet," in *Essays and Lectures*, 458; Shelley, "A Defence of Poetry," in *Romantic Poetry and Prose*, 750.

40. Whitman, preface to *Leaves of Grass* (1855), 622 (ll. 249–55).

41. Both Tenney Nathanson and Mark Bauerlein find Whitman's embodied poetry guilty of magical thinking, and as such of both obfuscating mysticism and anti-intellectualism (Nathanson, *Whitman's Presence*; Bauerlein, *Whitman and the American Idiom*). Ecocritical readers, by contrast, have tended to commend Whitman's "mysticism" as a laudably ecopoetical effort to communicate the "unsaid and unsayable" essence of nonhuman being while resisting the anthropocentrism of human language. Outka, "(De)Composing Whitman," 52. See also Killingsworth, *Walt Whitman and the Earth*; and Warren, "Whitman Land."

42. Anonymous, "Editor's Table," 699.

43. In *How We Became Posthuman*, N. Katherine Hayles develops her account of the difference between the conception of information as having a body (as being indissociable from the material specificity of its medium), and the notion that information is distinct from the medium in which it is stored. Hayles tracks these alternatives through the development of cybernetics information theory in the twentieth century, but, as Richard Menke points out, the nineteenth-century discourse of electrical communication also raised this question decades earlier (Menke, *Telegraphic Realism*, 75–77).

44. This Whitmanian gloss has found new life in some neuroscientific circles. On the assumption that brain states may be taken to be expressive of mental states, neuroscientists are currently developing technology that proposes to allow us to "read" the thoughts and intentions electrically "expressed" in fMRI scans of the brain. See for instance, Kerri Smith, "Brain Decoding."

45. Whitman, "Song for Occupations," in *Leaves of Grass* (1855), 710 (ll. 1–6).

46. Nathanson, *Whitman's Presence*, 2. Like Tenney Nathanson, Mark Bauerlein also finds Whitman's embodied poetry guilty of magical thinking and hence, Bauerlein argues, of anti-intellectualism (Bauerlein, *Whitman and the American Idiom*).

47. Outka, "(De)Composing Whitman," 52. See also Killingsworth, *Walt Whitman and the Earth*; and Warren, "Whitman Land."

48. Coviello, *Tomorrow's Parties*, 49, 64. Coviello's analysis leans on two major earlier queer theoretical readings of Whitman's conflation of poems and bodies: Michael Warner's argument that Whitman seeks, thereby, "to make sex public," and Michael Moon's suggestion that this is a deliberate fiction designed to light up the discursiveness of bodily and sexual identity more generally, producing a "heightened . . . sense of the constructedness and hence the dense politicality of all bodily experience." See Warner, "Whitman Drunk," 42; and Moon, *Disseminating Whitman*, 4.

49. Breitweiser, *National Melancholy*, 137; Moon, *Disseminating Whitman*, 5.

50. Vendler, *Invisible Listeners*, 36.

51. Coviello, *Intimacy in America*, 155.

52. Coviello, *Tomorrow's Parties*, 60–61.

53. In suggesting that sensuality may be a more accurate term than sexuality for the generative economy of embodied affinities that Whitman describes, I do not mean to suggest that sensuality and sexuality are mutually exclusive terms. Rather, I suggest that the discourse on sexuality is too narrow a lens for understanding the physics of embodied attachment, indiscriminate affiliation, and self-loss that distinguish the Whitmanian body. To be sure, since Foucault, analyses of sexuality have been careful not to limit our understanding of sexuality to only those behaviors and affective economies explicitly linked to genital sex. But even in its expanded senses, the rubric of sexuality tends to filter back to the problem of sexual reproduction by focusing on economies of feeling (as opposed to sensation generally), interpersonal relations (as opposed to both human and human-nonhuman relations), object selection (at the exclusion of involuntary and indiscriminate attachments), questions of identity and typology (as opposed to trans-corporeal contiguity and self-loss), and so forth. As I argue in my discussion

of "is this then a touch?," perhaps the most crucial insight to be gained
by reading Whitman's bioelectrical body in light of not just sexuality but
sensuality more broadly is that doing so allows us to recognize his sustained
refutation of autonomous identity. In this sense, my reading of *Leaves* argues
more generally for an expanded approach to Whitman's treatment of
embodied affinities. Before Darwin made sexual selection the prime mover
of evolution, and before the field of sexology made sexuality as a defining
feature of personal identity, the sensuously impressionable body also
appeared—in Spiritualist discourse and environmentalist racial theory
alike—to be world-making, diffusing sympathetic attachments including but
not limited to those forms of attachment we deem sexual.

54. Whitman, "Song of Myself" in *Leaves* (1855), 663 (ll. 23–24).

55. Whitman, "Whoever you are holding me now in hand" (originally
tentatively titled, "These leaves conning, you con at peril"), in *Leaves of Grass*
(1860), 100 (ll. 27–33).

56. Whitman, "Song of Myself," in *Leaves of Grass* (1855), 698–701 (ll.
990–1081).

57. Warner, "Whitman Drunk," 40.

58. Michaels, *Shape of the Signifier*, 123.

59. As Michaels puts this, "Reports of what something makes us feel are
not beliefs about what it means." This is to say, in other words, "that there is
a logical difference between the effects any work of art actually produces
and the effects it was intended to produce and that the interpretation of a
work of art has everything to do with the effects it was intended to produce
and nothing whatsoever to do with the effects it in fact produces" (Michaels,
"Intention at the College").

60. Wimsatt and Beardsley, "Affective Fallacy," 44.

61. Michaels, *Shape of the Signifier*, 117.

62. Michael Fried makes a version of this point in his discussion of the
function of the frame in modern art in "Art and Objecthood."

63. Whitman, "Song of Occupations," in *Leaves of Grass* (1855), 712 (ll.
49–50).

64. Whitman, preface to *Leaves of Grass* (1855), 624. Whitman repeats a
version of this claim in "Song of Myself": "Do you guess I have some
intricate purpose? / Well I have . . . . for the April rain has, and the mica on
the side of a rock has" ("Song of Myself" in *Leaves* (1855), 676 (ll. 381–82)).

65. Pinsky, *Situation of Poetry*, 3.

66. MacLeish letter to Norman Holes Pearson (1937), cited in Donaldson, *Archibald MacLeish*, 150.

67. Paul Gilmore observes that Whitman persistently "returns to the
idea that his poetry is necessarily incomplete, that it requires an historically

situated reader to produce any sort of meaning, a meaning that is never completely stable" (Gilmore, *Aesthetic Materialism*, 156). While I share Gilmore's sense that poetry is, for Whitman, essentially social, I think it is important to stress the paradox implicit in Gilmore's suggestion that Whitman both urgently wants his poems read and is happy for them "to produce any sort of meaning." Gilmore thus puts his finger on the unorthodoxy of Whitman's sense of poetry, which at once insists on an audience and yet denies responsibility or even concern for the outcome of that encounter.

68. Whitman, preface to *Leaves of Grass* (1855), 634.

69. James, "Address at the Centenary," 1124.

70. Lee Edelman cited in Tiffany, *Infidel Poetics*, 13.

71. Ibid., 4.

72. Ibid., 12.

73. Ibid., 8.

74. Indeed, if we follow Vincent Bertolini's suggestion that Whitman "convey[s] messages that are enveloped even from his own understanding," we might well conclude that Whitman's disavowals of meaning uncannily anticipate Tiffany's theory of lyric obscurity (Bertolini, "'Hinting' and 'Reminding,'" 1050, 1053).

75. Whitman, "Song of Myself," in *Leaves* (1855), 682 (l. 547).

76. Bennett, "Whitman's Sympathies," 608.

77. Hartman, *Scenes of Subjection*, 18–19.

78. Bennett, "Whitman's Sympathies," 616.

79. For richer accounts of Whitman's shifting attitude toward slavery and his affinity for white nationalist discourse, see Klammer, *Whitman, Slavery, and the Emergence of Leaves of Grass*, and Coviello, *Intimacy in America*. Although my reading of the auction in "I Sing the Body Electric" will highlight its antiracist egalitarianism, I do not mean to suggest that Whitman was therefore a committed advocate of antiracism. Instead, my focus on the processual logic from which Whitman's antiracism derives should indicate that he was a committed advocate of an embodied ontology whose entailments for racial politics he occasionally attempted to specify. Whitman's pronouncements on racial politics remained variable and somewhat opportunistic in the 1850s; however, his views on the materiality of the body were clear and consistent.

80. Whitman, "I Sing the Body Electric," in *Leaves* (1855), 735 (ll. 74–79).

81. Klammer, *Whitman, Slavery*, 141–42.

82. Erkkila, *Whitman the Political Poet*, 126; Killingsworth, *Whitman's Poetry of the Body*, 142. See also Sánchez-Eppler, *Touching Liberty*. Sánchez-Eppler highlights a tension inherent in the poem's desire to assert the sacredness of the body by reducing it to a "common" blood, whereas

Killingsworth is satisfied that the body constitutes a "common denominator among all classes, races, divided groups" (Killingsworth, *Whitman's Poetry of the Body*, 143).

83. Whitman, "I Sing the Body Electric," in *Leaves* (1855), 735–36 (ll. 85–103).

84. My discussion here draws from my argument in "Numb Networks."

85. Lawrence, "Whitman" (1923), in *Studies in Classic American Literature*.

86. Sánchez-Eppler, *Touching Liberty*, 56.

87. The imagery of inhaled perfumes and atmospheres in the ensuing lines invite us to imagine atoms recirculating in and out of the speaker's body; moreover, as Mark Noble argues, the recombinatory nature of matter is central to the materialist imaginary of the early *Leaves*. As a defense of democratic equality, however, I submit that this empirical claim does not do the work that Whitman asks of it. See Noble, *American Poetic Materialism*.

88. My reading here is partially in agreement with Dimock's argument in "Whitman, Syntax, and Political Theory." There, Dimock argues that the radical egalitarianism of Whitmanian syntax makes no concessions to the distinctly non-egalitarian logic of affection, which privileges "selective attachment" over "the democratic need for substitutability and interchangeability" (72). She concludes, "If nothing else, Whitman makes us long for what he does not and cannot offer: an ethics of preference, one that, in giving voice to what is not exhausted by a language of formal universals . . . might suggest some way of reconciling the democratic and the affective, some way of rescuing 'love' from being the lost soul of political theory" (78). Like Dimock, I find that Whitman's leveling vision precludes us from making distinctions between entities. On Dimock's reading, this is a problem with the way democracy takes no account of special preference (love—or sexual attraction, for that matter). On my reading, however, the undifferentiability Whitman conjures is a problem *for* democracy: Whitmanian egalitarianism—an artifact not just of his syntax but of his metaphysical commitments—does not allow us to ontologically distinguish one entity from another, and therefore is not, properly speaking, an egalitarianism at all, since it blurs the individual units in which democratic equality trades. For what it's worth, I do not share Dimock's sense that love is "the lost soul" of democratic politics; on the contrary, my sense is that love's "ethics of preference" is precisely what democratic and legal formalisms are designed to offset. Justice and democratic equality ask us to look beyond the biases of our affective ties (whether these be ties of kinship, tribe, or race—or ties of ideological consensus) in order to recognize the claims of even those whom we do not know or love.

89. Whitman, "Song of Myself," in *Leaves* (1855), 679 (l.487).

90. Whitman, preface to *Leaves* (1855), 626.

91. Castronovo, *Necro Citizenship*, 8–10.

4. POSTHUMANISM AND THE PROBLEM OF SOCIAL JUSTICE: RACE AND
MATERIALITY IN THE TWENTY-FIRST CENTURY

1. Jackson, "Outer Worlds," 216.

2. Ibid.; Weheliye, *Habeas Viscus*, 8.

3. Latour, *Pandora's Hope*, 297.

4. Hayles, *How We Became Posthuman*, 291.

5. Peterson, *Bestial Traces*, 7.

6. Grusin, *Nonhuman Turn*, vii.

7. Ibid., xviii.

8. Materialist feminism and queer theory, for instance, are liberatory scholarly fields that have been engines of posthumanist theorizing. These fields have also held important conversations about the tension between their political and posthumanist commitments (see, for instance, Luciano and Chen, "Has the Queer Ever Been?"). There has also been a broader shift back to the body in recent theorizing about race, and important new works reopen the nineteenth-century question of race's material ontology. See, for instance, Puar, "'Rather Be a Cyborg'"; Saldanha, "Bastard and Mixed-Blood"; Hames-Garcia, "How Real Is Race?"; Wright, *Physics of Blackness*. Sarah Ahmed also highlights the risk of oversimplifying poststructuralist feminism's relation to materiality in "Imaginary Prohibitions." This list suggests that the resistance to posthumanist theory has other sources than a distrust of materiality per se.

9. Weheliye, *Habeas Viscus*, 10.

10. Césaire, *Discourse on Colonialism*, 73.

11. Haritaworn, "Decolonizing the Non/Human," 212.

12. Sylvia Wynter, as we will see, argues that social justice depends upon reinventing this current genre of "the human."

13. Colebrook, *Death of the Posthuman*, 23. Like Colebrook, posthumanist scholars associated with speculative realism and object-oriented ontology prescribe an ontological turn that does not turn *to* the ontology of human being (for instance, by emphasizing the materiality of the self and embodied nature of knowledge), but that seeks instead to constitute a form of knowledge independent of the mediating function of human sensation, perception, and cognition.

14. Bogost, *Alien Phenomenology*, 4. See also Meillassoux, *After Finitude*, and works by those directly affiliated with object-oriented ontology: Harman, *Guerrilla Metaphysics*, and *Prince of Networks*; Bryant, *Democracy of Objects*; Morton, *Hyperobjects*.

15. This slippage is, for instance, particularly notable in the work of Graham Harman, the architect of OOO. Harman objects to post-Kantian philosophy's acceptance of human finitude not because he faults its logic—not, that is, because he thinks humans *do* have unmediated perceptual access to reality—but because he faults its ethics. Harman understands Kant's circumscription of philosophical knowledge to things "as they appear for us" to constitute an ethical violence: he describes post-Kantian philosophy as a "Hiroshima of metaphysics" that sets up a "global apartheid" against speculation into reality as nonhumans experience it (*Prince of Networks*, 102–3). With this description, then, ontological finitude starts to look like an ethical choice.

16. Moore, "Capitalocene," 2.

17. Ibid.

18. Povinelli, *Geontologies*, 32.

19. Derrida, *Animal That Therefore I Am*, 86.

20. Braidotti, *Posthuman*, 2.

21. Jackson, "Outer Worlds," 216.

22. Weheliye, *Habeas Viscus*, 9–10. See also Weheliye's critique of biopolitics discourse in *Habeas Viscus*, and Julia Suarez-Krabbe's account of the "colonial death project" in *Race, Rights, and Rebels*.

23. A word on comparisons of racism and speciesism: the divergence between posthumanism's focus on nonhuman animal life and posthumanist social justice's focus on dehumanized human life is sometimes expressed as a competition over whether racism or speciesism is the primordial instance of the epistemic discrimination that both seek to contest. Thus, for instance, Christopher Peterson suggests that "negative stereotypes about nonhuman animals are the condition of possibility for negative stereotypes about social and political minorities," while Jackson contends that "blackness conditions and constitutes the . . . nonhuman" (Peterson, *Bestial Traces*, 9; Jackson, "Outer Worlds," 216). The point is that Peterson and Jackson are both right. That is, when we hold onto the recognition that the moral statuses "human" and "nonhuman" are not synonyms for "*Homo sapiens*" and "non–*Homo sapiens*," it becomes clearer that racism and speciesism are two names for the same ideological operation: the disaggregation of communal being into a typological hierarchy of beings that do, and beings that do not merit moral regard. When I suggest that racism and speciesism are two names for the same ideological operation, I am not arguing that we ought to begin to treat speciesism as a problem that is as ethically urgent as racism. More perplexingly, I am suggesting that part of the challenge of thinking beyond the humanist episteme is learning to see antiracism and antispeciesism as structurally conjoined rather than analogous or even competitive social projects.

24. As Weheliye observes, this in turn leads posthumanists to write of the human as if "we have now entered a stage in human development where all subjects have been granted equal access to western humanity" (*Habeas Viscus*, 10).

25. To suggest that posthumanism's Eurocentric bias is methodologically unsound is not to suggest that identity and episteme have any natural or necessary connection. It is not therefore to presume that indigenous, postcolonial, or queer of color perspectives necessarily instantiate exemplary posthumanist epistemologies by virtue of their eccentric vantage from the margins of the hegemonic regime of the human. Thus Weheliye warns that the voices of marginalized peoples "should not be construed as fountains of suffering authenticity" (*Habeas Viscus*, 82). Nor should these voices be construed as univocal: as Kim TallBear writes of indigenous scholars, "We are diverse thinkers" ("Indigenous Perspective," 230). Conversely, to suggest that posthumanists would benefit from consulting more nonwhite and non-Western thinkers is not to presume that the work of Western-born thinkers is therefore epistemically "Western": that Deleuze is a white Frenchman does not mean that his ontology must necessarily be complicit with Western humanism. But it is neither reductive nor essentializing to observe that the project of conceptualizing modes of being outside or orthogonal to the discriminatory modern Western praxis of "Man" has been carried forward in minority scholarly studies for decades, and in non-Western cultural traditions for even longer. As TallBear notes, "indigenous peoples have never forgotten that nonhumans are agential beings engaged in social relations that profoundly shape human lives" (234). And therefore, however committed posthumanism is, in theory, to thinking beyond Western "Man," that commitment will continue to seem gestural and incomplete so long as these extra- and counterhegemonic cultural and scholarly traditions remain peripheral to posthumanist work.

26. Wynter gives several accounts of this genealogy, each of which differs slightly. Here I am most closely following the history she gives in "On How We Mistook," and in Wynter and McKittrick, "Unparalleled Catastrophe." See also Wynter, "1492."

27. Wynter, "On How We Mistook," 118, 127.

28. Wynter, "1492," 40.

29. Wynter, "On How We Mistook," 123.

30. Wynter suggests that alternative epistemes in the postcolonial world may be rare, and offers the Masai people of Kenya as one possible locus of thinking outside of the Western episteme. See Wynter, "Unparalleled Catastrophe."

31. Wynter, "On How We Mistook," 237.

32. Wynter, "No Humans Involved," 59.

33. Wynter, "On How We Mistook," 233.

34. Wynter, "Disenchanting Discourse," 208.

35. Muñoz, "Sense of Brownness," 210.

36. Barad, *Meeting the Universe Halfway,* 139.

37. Ibid.

38. Esposito, *Bios,* 164. Esposito borrows this term from Merleau-Ponty, not Hortense Spillers. I will discuss this divergence in the Coda.

39. Ibid., 167.

40. Puar, *Terrorist Assemblages,* 213.

41. Esposito, *Bios,* 167, 160.

42. The iconic line here is Donna Haraway's, who asks, "Why should our bodies end at the skin?" (*Simians, Cyborgs and Women,* 178).

43. Bennett, *Vibrant Matter,* 108–9.

44. Barad, *Meeting the Universe Halfway,* 396.

45. Matt Taylor, *Universes without Us,* 176.

46. In addition to the writings of Alfred, TallBear, and Povinelli cited below, see also, for instance, Suarez-Krabbe, *Race, Rights and Rebels*; Coulthard, *Red Skin, White Masks.* For a consideration of how recolonization occurs in literary representations, see Rifkin, *Beyond Settler Time.*

47. Alfred, "First Nations Perspectives," 10.

48. Ibid., 5.

49. TallBear, *Native American DNA,* 6–8.

50. Povinelli, *The Cunning of Recognition.*

51. Wolfe, "'Animal Studies,' Disciplinarity, and the (Post)Humanities," in *What Is Posthumanism?*

52. Wynter and McKittrick, "Unparalleled Catastrophe," 34. The phrase "nonphysical principle of causality" is a citation from Christian theologian Keith Ward. The modulation of Wynter's project I am about to suggest would not apply if she were to follow Ward in believing that human being is uniquely ensouled. If sociogeny, for Wynter, is not in fact a speciological trait (i.e., arising from the nature of the body) but rather a trait wholly unrelated to human embodiment—if, in short, sociogeny refers to a form of transcendent freedom that stems from humanity's possession of an immaterial soul—then Wynter's project is dualistic and cannot be combined with posthumanist materialism. However, despite Wynter's invocation of Ward and of sociogeny's independence from matter, her project seems otherwise distinctly nondualist. As I shall discuss, she shows a recurring interest in the material substrates of sociogeny.

53. Wynter and McKittrick, "Unparalleled Catastrophe," 34, 29.

54. I am indebted here to Colleen Glenney Boggs's astute reading of this scene, which differs from my own but which first signaled to me the importance of animality to this scene's critical register. See Boggs, *Animalia Americana*, 89–98.

55. Derrida, *Animal That Therefore I Am*, 95, 135.

56. Weheliye, *Habeas Viscus*, 126. Indeed, Weheliye argues that Wynter's work has been overlooked in contemporary biopolitical and posthumanist theory precisely because lingering racism in the academy has meant that "minority discourses seemingly cannot inhabit the space of proper theoretical reflection" (6). Ultimately, however—and counterintuitively, given the argument I cite here—Weheliye follows Wynter in insisting upon the exceptional freedom of human being.

57. Wynter, "1492," 47.

58. McKittrick, "Axis Bold as Love," 144.

59. Wynter, "No Humans Involved," 69.

60. Wynter citing Barney in "On How We Mistook," 132.

CODA: AFTER ROMANTIC POSTHUMANISM

1. Spillers, "Mama's Baby, Papa's Maybe," 72.

2. Ibid., 67, 80. For a far more in-depth analysis of the distinction between Spillers's "flesh" and posthumanism's "flesh" (more specifically, Agamben's notion *zoe* or bare life), see Weheliye, *Habeas Viscus*.

3. Douglass, "Heroic Slave," 246.

4. Latour, *Politics of Nature*, 25.

5. Dana Luciano and Mel Chen offer an incisive and illuminating discussion of this tension in "Has the Queer Ever Been Human?"

6. These examples of posthumanism's wonderful reorganization of political physics are drawn from Chen, *Animacies*, and Bennett, *Vibrant Matter*. Luciano and Chen also suggest that posthumanism might be "a new mode of critical realism," and I find myself deeply sympathetic to the account that they give ("Has the Queer Ever Been," 191). It is not my sense, however, that this realism amounts to a historical "recognition that the nature of 'reality' itself is changing as power moves away from the individual" under the conditions of biopolitical "control society." The material realism I find in posthumanism does tend to dwarf the agency of the individual by contextualizing it within the myriad vectors of human and nonhuman power, but this situation—the comparative smallness of individual agency vis-à-vis systemic power—is, on my reading of posthumanism, not an artifact of political history but of human embodiment, the materiality of being as such.

7. In the "vast clear scheme" of the world, Whitman insists, "every motion and every spear of grass and the frames and spirits of men and women and all that concerns them are unspeakably perfect miracles all referring to all and each distinct and in its place." Whitman, preface to *Leaves of Grass* (1855), 626 (l. 422). Indeed, Whitman assures us, the perfection of this processual universe is both beautiful, just, and good. "The fruition of beauty is no chance hit or miss . . . it is inevitable as life. . . . it is as exact and plumb as gravitation" (Whitman, preface to *Leaves* (1855), 623 (ll. 280–81). The good deeds we do in "the direct lifetime" accrue "onward afterward through the indirect lifetime . . . . The interest will come around" (Whitman, preface to *Leaves* (1855), 631–33 (ll. 625–86). "Whither I walk I cannot define, but I know it is good,/The whole universe indicates that it is good. . . . What is called good is perfect, and what is called sin is just as perfect,/ The vegetables and minerals are all perfect . . . and the imponderable fluids are perfect;/Slowly and surely they have passed on to this, and slowly and surely they will yet pass on" (Whitman, "To Think of Time," in *Leaves* (1855), 723 (ll.116–24).

8. Douglass, "Fourth of July," in *Selected Speeches and Writings*, 204.

9. There are, of course, important exceptions to this tendency within romantic thought, particularly prevalent in certain treatments of the sublime as indicative of the natural world's amoralism and indifference to man. See, for instance, Shelley's "Mont Blanc" and Thoreau's "Ktaadn."

10. Timothy Morton elaborates this reading of romanticism's normative nature in *Ecology without Nature*.

11. Agassiz, "Diversity of Origin," 3; Guyot, *Earth and Man*, 309.

12. Grosz, *Nick of Time*, 90.

13. Some examples: Karen Barad converts quantum entanglement into a call to responsibility—material relation becomes ethical obligation. Jane Bennett closes *Vibrant Matter* with a "Nicene Creed" to entangled complexity, turning a material condition into an article of not just empirical but moral faith. Or Michelle Wright, embracing a fluid ontology of identity, concludes that if "we are not fixed quantities but ever-shifting qualities," then "equality . . . is a matter of qualitative connection rather than quantitative sameness": mutual involvement here becomes equivalent to mutual respect (*Physics of Blackness*, 34).

14. Puar, *Terrorist Assemblages*, 206.

15. Ibid., 215.

16. Connolly, *Fragility of Things*, 10.

17. Thoreau, "Walking," in *Excursions*, 128.

18. Although this is a citation from D. A. Miller's *The Novel and the Police*, the discussion I am thinking of here is Eve Kosofsky Sedgwick's analysis of

the hermeneutics of suspicion (where she quotes this line from Miller) in
Touching Feeling, 139.

19. Caroline Levine raises this possibility in her analysis of the "affordances of form" in literary fiction. In her argument for "broadening our definition of form to include social arrangements," Levine shows how formalist analysis can "be as valuable to understanding sociopolitical institutions as it is to reading literature." Posthumanist materialism can itself be understood as chiefly a shift in form—an attempt to reimagine the world from the perspective of processes and assemblages rather than individuals and identities. In this respect, we can think of posthumanism as a mode of formal analysis, and literature as a particularly rich and rewarding site for developing our attentiveness to the morphology of connectivity (Levine, *Forms*, 2).

Adair, James. *The History of the American Indians*. London: Edward and Charles Dilley, 1775.

Agamben, Giorgio. *Homo Sacer: Sovereign Power and Bare Life*. Stanford, Calif.: Stanford University Press, 1998.

———. *The Open: Man and Animal*. Stanford, Calif.: Stanford University Press, 2003.

Agassiz, Louis. *Contributions to the Natural History of the United States of America*. Vol. 1. Boston: Little, Brown, 1857.

———. "The Diversity of Origin of the Human Races." *Christian Examiner* (July 1850): 1–36.

———. *Lake Superior: Its Physical Character Vegetation and Animals Compared with Those of Other and Similar Regions*. Boston: Gould, Kendall and Lincoln, 1850.

———. "Sketch of the Natural Provinces of the Animal World and their Relation to the Different Types of Man." In *Types of Mankind*, 2nd ed., edited by Josiah Nott and George Gliddon, lviii–lxxvi. Philadelphia: Lippincott Grambo, 1854.

Agassiz, Louis, and Augustus Gould. *Principles of Zoology*. Boston: Gould, Kendall, and Lincoln, 1848.

Ahmed, Sarah. "Imaginary Prohibitions: Some Remarks on the Founding Gestures of the 'New Materialism.'" *European Journal of Women's Studies* 15:1 (2008): 23–39.

Alaimo, Stacy. *Bodily Natures: Science, Environment, and the Material Self.* Bloomington: Indiana University Press, 2010.

Alaimo, Stacy, and Susan Hekman, eds. *Material Feminisms*. Bloomington: Indiana University Press, 2008.

Alfred, G. Taiaiake. "First Nations Perspectives on Political Identity." *First Nations Citizenship Research and Policy Series: Building Towards Change*. Ottawa: Assembly of First Nations, 2009.

Anonymous. "Editor's Table." *Harper's New Monthly Magazine* 4:23 (April 1852): 699–702.

Arsić, Branka. *Bird Relics: Grief and Vitalism in Thoreau*. Cambridge, Mass.: Harvard University Press, 2016.

Bachman, Rev. John. *The Doctrine of the Unity of the Human Race*. Charleston, S.C.: C. Canning, 1850.

Barad, Karen. *Meeting the Universe Halfway: Quantum Physics and the Entanglement of Matter and Meaning*. Durham, N.C.: Duke University Press, 2007.

Barnes, Elizabeth. "Manhood and the Limits of Sympathy in Douglass and Melville." In *Frederick Douglass and Herman Melville: Essays in Relation*, edited by Robert Levine and Samuel Otter, 233–57. Chapel Hill: University of North Carolina Press, 2008.

Barton, Benjamin Smith. *New Views on the Origin of the Tribes and Nations of America*. Philadelphia: Printed for the author by John Bioren, 1797.

Bauerlein, Mark. *Whitman and the American Idiom*. Baton Rouge: Louisiana State University Press, 1991.

Bay, Mia. *The White Image in the Black Mind: African-American Ideas about White People, 1830–1920*. Oxford: Oxford University Press, 2000.

Bellin, Joshua. "In the Company of Savagists." *Concord Saunterer* 16 (2008): 1–32.

Bennett, Jane. "Systems and Things: On Vital Materialism and Object-Oriented Philosophy." In *The Nonhuman Turn*, edited by Richard Grusin, 223–39. Minneapolis: University of Minnesota Press, 2015.

———. *Vibrant Matter: A Political Ecology of Things*. Durham, N.C.: Duke University Press, 2010.

———. "Whitman's Sympathies." *Political Research Quarterly* 69:3 (September 2016): 607–20.

Berger, Michael. *Thoreau's Late Career and the Dispersion of Seeds*. Rochester, N.Y.: Camden House, 2000.

Bertolini, Vincent. "'Hinting' and 'Reminding': The Rhetoric of Performative Embodiment in *Leaves of Grass*." *ELH* 69 (2002): 1047–82.

Boggs, Colleen Glenney. *Animalia Americana: Animal Representations and Biopolitical Subjectivity*. New York: Columbia University Press, 2013.

Bogost, Ian. *Alien Phenomenology, or What It's Like to Be a Thing*. Minneapolis: University of Minnesota Press, 2012.

Borst, Raymond. *The Thoreau Log: A Documentary Life of Henry David Thoreau, 1817–1862*. New York: G. K. Hall, 1992.

Braidotti, Rosi. *The Posthuman*. Cambridge: Polity Press, 2013.

Braude, Ann. *Radical Spirits: Spiritualism and Women's Rights in Nineteenth-Century America*. Boston: Beacon Press, 1989.

Breitweiser, Mitchell. *National Melancholy: Mourning and Opportunity in Classic American Literature.* Stanford, Calif.: Stanford University Press, 2007.

Briggs, Laura. "The Race of Hysteria: 'Overcivilization' and the 'Savage' Woman in Late Nineteenth-Century Obstetrics and Gynecology." *American Quarterly* 52:2 (2000): 246–73.

Brown, Wendy. *Undoing the Demos: Neoliberalism's Stealth Revolution.* New York: Zone Books, 2015.

Bryant, Levi. *The Democracy of Objects.* London: Open Humanities Press, 2011.

Buck-Morss, Susan. "Hegel and Haiti." *Critical Inquiry* 26:4 (Summer 2000): 821–65.

Buell, Lawrence. *The Environmental Imagination: Thoreau Nature Writing and the Formation of American Culture.* Cambridge, Mass.: Harvard University Press, 1995.

Burder, George. *The Welch Indians; or, A Collection of papers respecting a people whose ancestors emigrated from Wales to America in the year 1170, with prince Modoc . . . and are now said to inhabit a beautiful country on the west side of the Mississippi.* London, 1787.

Cameron, Sharon. *Writing Nature: Henry Thoreau's Journal.* Chicago: University of Chicago Press, 1989.

Carter, J. Kameron. *Race: A Theological Account.* Oxford: Oxford University Press, 2008.

Cartwright, Samuel. "Unity of the Human Race Disproved by the Hebrew Bible." *DeBow's Review* 29:2 (August 1860): 129–36.

Castiglia, Christopher. *Interior States: Institutional Consciousness and the Inner Life of Democracy in the Antebellum United States.* Durham, N.C.: Duke University Press, 2008.

Castronovo, Russ. *Fathering the Nation: American Genealogies of Slavery and Freedom.* Berkeley: University of California Press, 1995.

———. *Necro Citizenship: Death, Eroticism, and the Public Sphere in the Nineteenth-Century United States.* Durham, N.C.: Duke University Press, 2001.

Catlin, George. *Letters and Notes on the Manners, Customs, and Condition of the North American Indians.* Vol. 1. London: Published by the author, 1841.

Césaire, Aimé. *Discourse on Colonialism.* Translated by Joan Pinkham. New York: Monthly Review Press, 2000.

Chakrabarty, Dipesh. "The Climate of History: Four Theses." *Critical Inquiry* 35 (2009): 197–222.

Chen, Mel Y. *Animacies: Biopolitics Racial Mattering and Queer Affect.* Durham, N.C.: Duke University Press, 2012.

Chesnutt, Charles. *Frederick Douglass.* Boston: Small Maynard, 1899.

Cobb, Thomas. *Inquiry into the Law of Negro Slavery in the United States of America.* 1858. Athens: University of Georgia Press, 1999.

Cohen, Jeffrey Jerome. *Medieval Identity Machines.* Minneapolis: University of Minnesota Press, 2003.

Colbert, Charles. *Haunted Visions: Spiritualism in American Art.* Philadelphia: University of Pennsylvania Press, 2011.

Colebrook, Claire. *Death of the Posthuman.* Vol. 1. London: Open Humanities Press, 2014.

Connolly, William. *The Fragility of Things: Self-Organizing Processes, Neoliberal Fantasies, and Democratic Activism.* Durham, N.C.: Duke University Press, 2013.

———. "Species Evolution and Cultural Freedom." *Political Research Quarterly* 67:2 (June 2014): 441–52.

Coulthard, Glen. *Red Skin, White Masks: Rejecting the Colonial Politics of Recognition.* Minneapolis: University of Minnesota Press, 2014.

Coviello, Peter. *Intimacy in America: Dreams of Affiliation in Antebellum America.* Minneapolis: University of Minnesota Press, 2005.

———. *Tomorrow's Parties: Sex and the Untimely in Nineteenth-Century America.* New York: New York University Press, 2013.

Cox, Robert. *Body and Soul: A Sympathetic History of American Spiritualism.* Charlottesville: University of Virginia Press, 2003.

Dain, Bruce. *A Hideous Monster of the Mind: American Race Theory in the Early Republic.* Cambridge, Mass.: Harvard University Press, 1996.

Darwin, Charles. *Life and Letters of Charles Darwin.* 3 vols. Edited by Francis Darwin. London: John Murray, 1888.

———. *On the Origin of Species.* Oxford: Oxford University Press, 2008.

Davis, David Brion. *Inhuman Bondage: The Rise and Fall of Slavery in the New World.* Oxford: Oxford University Press, 2006.

Davis, Rebecca Harding. *Bits of Gossip.* Boston: Houghton Mifflin, 1904.

Davis, Andrew Jackson. *Death and the Afterlife: Eight Evening Lectures on the Summer-Land.* Rochester, N.Y.: Austin Publishing, 1911.

———. *Morning Lectures: Twenty Discourses Delivered before the Friends of Progress in the City of New York in the Winter and Spring of 1863.* New York: C. M. Plumb, 1865.

———. *The Philosophy of Spiritual Intercourse.* New York: Fowler and Wells, 1851.

———. *The Present Age and Inner Life.* New York: Partridge and Britton, 1855.

————. *A Stellar Key to the Summer Land*. Part 1. Boston: William White, 1867.

Dean, Bradley. "Henry D. Thoreau and Horace Greeley Exchange Letters on the Spontaneous Generation of Plants." *New England Quarterly* 66:4 (December 1993): 630–38.

Delany, Martin. "The Political Destiny of the Colored Race on the American Continent." In *Martin Delany: A Documentary Reader*, edited by Robert S. Levine, 245–79. Chapel Hill: University of North Carolina Press, 2003.

DeLombard, Jeannine. "'Eye-Witness to the Cruelty': Southern Violence and Northern Testimony in Frederick Douglass's 1845 Narrative." *American Literature* 73:2 (2001): 245–75.

Derrida, Jacques. *The Animal That Therefore I Am*. New York: Fordham University Press, 2008.

Diamond, Cora. "The Difficulty of Reality and the Difficulty of Philosophy." In *Philosophy and Animal Rights*, edited by Cary Wolfe, 43–90. New York: Columbia University Press, 2008.

Dimock, Wai Chee. *Through Other Continents: American Literature across Deep Time*. Princeton, N.J.: Princeton University Press, 2006.

————. "Whitman, Syntax, and Political Theory." In *Breaking Bounds: Whitman and American Cultural Studies*, edited by Betsy Erkkila and Jay Grossman, 30–43. New York: Oxford University Press, 1996.

Discussions on the Constitution Proposed to the People of Massachusetts by the Convention of 1853. Boston: Little, Brown, 1854.

Dods, Rev. John Bovee. *The Philosophy of Electro-Biology*. New York: Fowler and Wells, 1851.

Donaldson, Scott. *Archibald MacLeish: An American Life*. Boston: Houghton Mifflin, 1992.

Douglas, Ann. *The Feminization of American Culture*. New York: Avon, 1977.

Douglass, Frederick. *Address Delivered by Hon. Frederick Douglass, at the Third Annual Nashville Fair of the Tennessee Colored Agricultural and Mechanical Association*. Washington, D.C.: Library of Congress. http://hdl.loc.gov/loc.mss/mfd.22023. Accessed May 19, 2017.

————. *Frederick Douglass: Autobiographies*. Edited by Henry Louis Gates. New York: Library of America, 1994.

————. *Frederick Douglass: Selected Speeches and Writings*. Edited by Philip Foner and Yuval Taylor. Chicago: Lawrence Hill Books, 1999.

Easton, Hosea. *Treatise on the Intellectual Character and Civil and Political Condition of the Colored People of the United States and the Prejudice Exercised toward Them*. Boston: I. Knapp, 1837.

Ellis, Cristin. "Amoral Abolitionism: Frederick Douglass and the Environmental Case Against Slavery." *American Literature* 86:2 (Summer 2014):
275–303.

———. "Numb Networks: Race, Identity, and the Politics of Impersonal
Sympathies." *Political Research Quarterly* 69:3 (September 2016): 626–32.

Emerson, Ralph Waldo. *Emerson: Essays and Lectures.* Edited by Joel Porte.
New York: Library of America, 1983.

———. *Journals and Miscellaneous Notebooks.* 16 vols. Edited by William H.
Gilman, Ralph H. Orth et al. Cambridge, Mass.: Harvard University
Press, 1960–82.

Erkkila, Betsy. *Whitman the Political Poet.* Oxford: Oxford University Press,
1989.

Esposito, Roberto. *Immunitas: The Protection and Negation of Life.* Cambridge:
Polity Press, 2011.

———. *Bios: Biopolitics and Philosophy.* Minneapolis: University of Minnesota
Press, 2008.

Fielder, Brigitte. "Animal Humanism: Race, Species, and Affective Kinship
in Nineteenth-Century Abolitionism." *American Quarterly* 65:3 (September 2013): 487–514.

Fitzhugh, George. *Cannibals All! Or, Slaves without Masters.* Edited by C.
Vann Woodward. Cambridge, Mass.: Belknap Press, 1988.

———. *Sociology for the South; or, The Failure of Free Society.* Richmond, Va.:
A. Morris, 1854.

Fleck, Richard. *Henry Thoreau and John Muir among the Indians.* Hamden,
Conn.: Archon Books, 1985.

Fleck, Richard, ed. *The Indians of Thoreau: Selections from the Indian Notebooks
of Henry David Thoreau.* Albuquerque, N.M.: Hummingbird Press, 1974.

Foreman, F. Gabrielle. "Sentimental Abolition in Douglass's Decade:
Revision, Erotic Conversion, and the Politics of Witnessing in 'The
Heroic Slave' and *My Bondage and My Freedom.*" In *Criticism and the Color
Line: Desegregating American Literary Studies,* edited by Henry B. Won-
ham, 191–204. New Brunswick, N.J.: Rutgers University Press, 1996.

Foucault, Michel. *The Birth of Biopolitics: Lectures at the Collège de France,
1978–79.* Translated by Graham Burchell. Edited by Michel Senellart.
New York: Palgrave MacMillan, 2008.

———. *The History of Sexuality,* Vol. 1. Translated by Robert Hurley. New
York: Vintage Books, 1978.

———. *The Order of Things: An Archaeology of the Human Sciences.* New York:
Routledge Classics, 2002.

———. *Society Must Be Defended: Lectures at the Collège de France, 1975–1976.*
London: Picador, 2003.

Frederickson, George. *The Black Image in the White Mind: The Debate on Afro-American Character and Destiny, 1917–1914*. Middletown, Conn.: Wesleyan University Press, 1987.

Fried, Michael. "Art and Objecthood." 1967. In *Art and Objecthood: Essays and Reviews*, 148–72. Chicago: University of Chicago Press, 1998.

Garnet, Henry Highland. *The Past and the Present Condition and the Destiny of the Colored Race*. Troy, N.Y.: J. C. Kneeland, 1848.

Garrison, William Lloyd. "No Compromise with the Evil of Slavery." 1854. In *Ripples of Hope: Great American Civil Rights Speeches*, edited by Josh Gottheimer, 55–58. New York: Basic Civitas Books, 2003.

———. "To the Public." *The Liberator* 1 (January 1831): 1.

Giles, Paul. "Narrative Reversals and Power Exchanges: Frederick Douglass and British Culture." *American Literature* 73:4 (2001): 779–810.

———. *Virtual Americas: Transnational Fictions and Transatlantic Imaginary*. Durham, N.C.: Duke University Press, 2002.

Gilmore, Paul. *Aesthetic Materialism: Electricity and American Romanticism*. Stanford, Calif.: Stanford University Press, 2009.

Gossett, Thomas. *Race: The History of an Idea in America*. Oxford: Oxford University Press, 1997.

Gould, Stephen Jay. *The Mismeasure of Man*. 1981. Reprint, New York: W. W. Norton, 1996.

Gray, Asa. "Darwin on the Origin of Species." *Atlantic Monthly* (July 1860): 229–38. http://www.theatlantic.com/magazine/archive/1860/07/darwin-on-the-origin-of-species/304152. Accessed September 25, 2016.

Grimes, J. Stanley. *Phreno-Geology: The Progressive Creation of Man Indicated by Natural History*. Boston: James Monroe, 1851.

Grosz, Elizabeth. *The Nick of Time: Politics, Evolution, and the Untimely*. Durham, N.C.: Duke University Press, 2004.

Grusin, Richard, ed. *The Nonhuman Turn*. Minneapolis: University of Minnesota Press, 2015.

Guyot, Arnold. *The Earth and Man: Lectures on Comparative Physical Geography in Its Relation to the History of Mankind*. Translated by C. C. Felton. Boston: Gould, Kendall, and Lincoln, 1849.

Hames-Garcia, Michael. "How Real Is Race?" In *Material Feminisms*, edited by Stacy Alaimo and Susan Hekman, 308–30. Bloomington: Indiana University Press, 2008.

Haraway, Donna. *Simians, Cyborgs and Women: The Reinvention of Nature*. New York: Routledge, 1991.

Harding, Walter, and Carl Bode, eds. *The Correspondence of Henry David Thoreau*. Washington Square: New York University Press, 1958.

Harding, Walter. *The Days of Henry Thoreau.* 1962. Reprint, New York: Dover, 1982.

Haritaworn, Jinthana. "Decolonizing the Non/Human." *GLQ* 21:2–3 (June 2015): 210–13.

Harman, Graham. *Guerrilla Metaphysics: Phenomenology and the Carpentry of Things.* Chicago: Open Court, 2005.

———. *Prince of Networks: Bruno Latour and Metaphysics.* Melbourne: re:press, 2009.

Hartman, Saidiya. *Scenes of Subjection: Terror, Slavery, and Self-Making in Nineteenth-Century America.* Oxford: Oxford University Press, 1997.

Hayles, N. Katherine. *How We Became Posthuman: Virtual Bodies in Cybernetics, Literature, and Informatics.* Chicago: University of Chicago Press, 1999.

Hickman, Jared. "Douglass Unbound." *Nineteenth-Century Literature* 68:3 (December 2013): 323–62.

Hodder, Alan. *Thoreau's Ecstatic Witness.* New Haven, Conn.: Yale University Press, 2001.

Hyde, Carrie. "The Climates of Liberty: Natural Rights in the Creole Case and 'The Heroic Slave.'" *American Literature* 85:3 (September 2013): 475–504.

Irmscher, Christopher. *Louis Agassiz: Creator of American Science.* New York: Houghton Mifflin Harcourt, 2013.

Jackson, Zakiyyah. "Outer Worlds: The Persistence of Race in Movement 'Beyond the Human.'" *GLQ* 21:2–3 (June 2015): 215–18.

James, William. "Address at the Centenary of Ralph Waldo Emerson, May 25, 1903." In *William James: Writings 1902–1910,* edited by Bruce Kuklick, 1119–25. New York: Literary Classics of the United States, 1987.

———. "Louis Agassiz: Words Spoken by Professor William James at the Reception of the American Society of Naturalists by the President and Fellows of Harvard College at Cambridge." December 30, 1896. Cambridge: Printed for the university, 1897.

Joy, Eileen, and Craig Dionne, eds. "When Did We Become Post/Human?" *postmedieval* 1:1–2 (Spring/Summer 2010).

Keyssar, Alexander. *The Right to Vote: The Contested History of Democracy in the United States.* Rev. ed. New York: Basic Books, 2000.

Killingsworth, M. Jimmie. *Walt Whitman and the Earth.* Iowa City: University of Iowa Press, 2004.

———. *Whitman's Poetry of the Body: Sexuality, Politics, and the Text.* Chapel Hill: University of North Carolina Press, 1989.

Klammer, Martin. *Whitman, Slavery, and the Emergence of Leaves of Grass.* University Park: Pennsylvania State University Press, 1995.

Kramnick, Jonathan. *Actions and Objects from Hobbes to Richardson*. Stanford, Calif.: Stanford University Press, 2010.

Kucich, John. *Ghostly Communion: Cross-Cultural Spiritualism in Nineteenth-Century American Literature*. Hanover, N.H.: Dartmouth University Press, 2004.

Latour, Bruno. *Pandora's Hope: Essays on the Reality of Science Studies*. Cambridge, Mass.: Harvard University Press, 1999.

———. *Politics of Nature: How to Bring the Sciences into Democracy*. Translated by Catherine Porter. Cambridge, Mass.: Harvard University Press, 2004.

Lawrence, D. H. "Whitman." In *Studies in Classic American Literature*, edited by Ezra Greenspan, Lindeth Vesey, and John Worthen, 148–61. 1923. Reprint, Cambridge: Cambridge University Press, 2014.

LeMenager, Stephanie. "Not Human, Again." *J19: The Journal of Nineteenth-Century Americanists* 1:2 (Fall 2013): 401–10.

Lemire, Elise Virginia. *"Miscegenation": Making Race in America*. Philadelphia: University of Pennsylvania Press, 2009.

Levine, Robert. *Martin Delany, Frederick Douglass, and the Politics of Representative Identity*. Chapel Hill: University of North Carolina Press, 1997.

Levine, Caroline. *Forms: Whole, Rhythm, Hierarchy, Network*. Princeton, N.J.: Princeton University Press, 2015.

Levinson, Marjorie. "Of Being Numerous." *Studies in Romanticism* 49:4 (Winter 2010): 633–57.

Lucas, Susan. "Counter-Frictions: Writing and Activism in the Work of Abbey and Thoreau." In *Thoreau's Sense of Place: Essays in American Environmental Writing*, edited by Richard Schneider, 266–79. Iowa City: Iowa University Press, 2000.

Luciano, Dana, and Mel Chen. "Has the Queer Ever Been Human?" *GLQ* 21:2–3 (June 2015): 183–207.

Lurie, Edward. *Louis Agassiz: A Life in Science*. Chicago: University of Chicago Press, 1960.

Mackey, Nathaniel. "Phrenological Whitman." *Conjunctions* 29 (Fall 1997). http://www.conjunctions.com/archives/c29-nm.htm. Accessed February 21, 2014.

Marrs, Cody. "Frederick Douglass in 1848." *American Literature* 85:3 (September 2013): 447–73.

Maslan, Mark. *Whitman Possessed: Poetry, Sexuality, and Popular Authority*. Baltimore: Johns Hopkins University Press, 2001.

Massumi, Brian. *Parables for the Virtual: Movement, Affect, Sensation*. Durham, N.C.: Duke University Press, 2002.

Matheson, Neill. "Thoreau's Inner Animal." *Arizona Quarterly* 67:4 (Winter 2001): 1–26.

Mays, R. B. "The Divine Legation of Thomas Jefferson—Are All Men Created Free!—Are All Men Created White." *DeBow's Review* 30 (May–June 1861): 521–32.

McGarry, Molly. *Ghosts of Futures Past: Spiritualism and the Cultural Politics of Nineteenth-Century America*. Berkeley: University of California Press, 2012.

McGurl, Mark. "The New Cultural Geology." *Twentieth-Century Literature* 57:3 and 57:4 (Fall/Winter 2011): 380–90.

McKittrick, Katherine. "Axis Bold as Love: On Sylvia Wynter, Jimi Hendrix, and the Promise of Science." In *Sylvia Wynter: On Being Human as Praxis*, edited by Katherine McKittrick, 142–63. Durham, N.C.: Duke University Press, 2015.

Meillassoux, Quentin. *After Finitude: An Essay on the Necessity of Contingency*. London: Continuum, 2008.

Menke, Richard. *Telegraphic Realism: Victorian Fiction and Other Information Systems*. Stanford, Calif.: Stanford University Press, 2007.

Michaels, Walter Benn. "Intention at the College Art Association." *Nonsite* 6 (July 1, 2012). http://nonsite.org/article/intention-at-the-college-art -association-2010. Accessed October 28, 2013.

———. *The Shape of the Signifier*. Princeton, N.J.: Princeton University Press, 2004.

Miller, Perry. *Consciousness in Concord*. Boston: Houghton Mifflin, 1958.

Mitchell, J. Allen. *Becoming Human: The Matter of the Medieval Child*. Minneapolis: Minnesota University Press, 2014.

Modern, John Lardas. *Secularism in Antebellum America*. Chicago: University of Chicago Press, 2011.

Moon, Michael. *Disseminating Whitman: Revision and Corporeality in Leaves of Grass*. Cambridge, Mass.: Harvard University Press, 1993.

Moore, Jason. "The Capitalocene, Part I: On the Nature and Origins of Our Ecological Crisis." 2014. http://www.jasonwmoore.com/uploads/The _Capitalocene__Part_I__June_2014.pdf. Accessed June 28, 2016.

Moore, R. Laurence. *In Search of White Crows: Spiritualism, Parapsychology, and American Culture*. New York: Oxford University Press, 1977.

Morton, Samuel George. *Crania Americana; or, A Comparative View of the Skulls of Various Aboriginal Nations*. Philadelphia: J. Dobson, 1839.

Morton, Timothy. *Ecology without Nature: Rethinking Environmental Ethics*. Cambridge, Mass.: Harvard University Press, 2007.

———. *Hyperobjects: Philosophy and Ecology after the End of the World*. Minneapolis: University of Minnesota Press, 2013.

Muñoz, José Esteban. "The Sense of Brownness." *GLQ* 21:2–3 (June 2015): 209–10.

Murison, Justine. *The Politics of Anxiety in Nineteenth-Century America.* Cambridge: Cambridge University Press, 2011.

Myers, Jeffrey. *Converging Stories: Race, Ecology, and Environmental Justice in American Literature.* Atlanta: University of Georgia Press, 2005.

Nathanson, Tenney. *Whitman's Presence: Body, Voice, and Writing in "Leaves of Grass."* New York: New York University Press, 1992.

Nelson, Dana. "'No Cold or Empty Heart': Polygenesis, Scientific Professionalization, and the Unfinished Business of Male Sentimentalism." *differences* 11:5 (1999–2000): 29–56.

Noble, Mark. *American Poetic Materialism from Whitman to Stevens.* Cambridge: Cambridge University Press, 2014.

Noble, Marianne. "Sympathetic Listening in Frederick Douglass's 'The Heroic Slave' and *My Bondage and My Freedom.*" *Studies in American Fiction* (Spring 2006): 56–76.

Nott, Josiah, and George Gliddon. *Indigenous Races of the Earth.* Philadelphia: J. B. Lippincott, 1857.

———. *Types of Mankind.* 2nd ed. Philadelphia: Lippincott, Grambo, 1854.

Outka, Paul. "(De)Composing Whitman." *ISLE* 12:1 (2005): 41–60.

Owen, Alex. *The Darkened Room: Women, Power, and Spiritualism in Late Victorian England.* Philadelphia: University of Pennsylvania Press, 1990.

Paul, Sherman. *Shores of America.* Urbana: University of Illinois Press, 1958.

Peterson, Christopher. *Bestial Traces: Race, Sexuality, Animality.* New York: Fordham University Press, 2012.

Phelps, Elizabeth Stuart. *Gates Ajar in Three Spiritualist Novels.* Chicago: University of Illinois Press, 2000.

Pinsky, Robert. *The Situation of Poetry: Contemporary Poetry and Its Tradition.* Princeton, N.J.: Princeton University Press, 1976.

Povinelli, Elizabeth. *The Cunning of Recognition.* Durham, N.C.: Duke University Press, 2002.

———. *Geontologies: A Requiem to Late Liberalism.* Durham, N.C.: Duke University Press, 2016.

Pratt, Lloyd. "Douglass and Recognition after 1845." *American Literature* 85:2 (2013): 247–72.

"Procedings and Debates of the Virginia State Convention of 1829–30." Richmond: Samuel Shepherd & Co., 1830.

Protevi, John. *Political Affect: Connecting the Social and the Somatic.* Minneapolis: University of Minnesota Press, 2009.

Puar, Jasbir. "'I Would Rather Be a Cyborg than a Goddess': Becoming-Intersectional in Assemblage Theory." *philoSOPHIA* 2:1 (2012): 49–66.

———. *Terrorist Assemblages: Homonationalism in Queer Times.* Durham, N.C.: Duke University Press, 2007.

Reynolds, David. *Beneath the American Renaissance.* New York: Knopf, 1988.

———. *Walt Whitman's America: A Cultural Biography.* New York: Vintage Books, 1996.

Richardson, Alan. *British Romanticism and the Science of the Mind.* Cambridge: Cambridge University Press, 2004.

Richardson Jr., Robert. *Henry Thoreau: A Life of the Mind.* Berkeley: University of California Press, 1986.

Rifkin, Mark. *Beyond Settler Time: Temporal Sovereignty and Indigenous Self-Determination.* Durham, N.C.: Duke University Press, 2017.

Robinson, David. *Natural Life: Thoreau's Worldly Transcendentalism.* Ithaca, N.Y.: Cornell University Press, 2004.

Rossi, William. "Following Thoreau's Instincts." In *More Day to Dawn: Thoreau's Walden for the Twenty-First Century,* edited by Sandra Petrulionis and Laura Dassow Walls, 82–99. Amherst: University of Massachusetts Press, 2007.

Russert, Britt. "The Science of Freedom: Counter-Archives of Racial Science on the Antebellum Stage." *African American Review* 45:3 (Fall 2012): 291–308.

Saldanha, Arun. "Bastard and Mixed-Blood Are the True Names of Race." In *Deleuze and Race,* edited by Arun Saldanha and Jason Michael Adams, 6–34. Edinburgh: Edinburgh University Press, 2013.

Sánchez-Eppler, Karen. *Touching Liberty: Abolition, Feminism, and the Politics of the Body.* Berkeley: University of California Press, 1993.

Sattelmeyer, Robert. *Thoreau's Reading.* Princeton, N.J.: Princeton University Press, 1988.

Sayre, Robert. *Thoreau and the American Indians.* Princeton, N.J.: Princeton University Press, 1977.

Schneider, Richard. "Thoreau's Human Ecology." *Nineteenth-Century Prose* 35:2 (Fall 2008): 1–74.

Schuller, Kyla. "Taxonomies of Feeling: The Epistemology of Sentimentalism in Late-Nineteenth-Century Racial and Sexual Science." *American Quarterly* 64:2 (June 2012): 277–99.

Sconce, Jeffrey. *Haunted Media: Electronic Presence from Telegraphy to Television.* Durham, N.C.: Duke University Press, 2000.

Sedgwick, Eve Kosofsky. *Touching Feeling: Affect, Pedagogy, Performativity.* Durham, N.C.: Duke University Press, 2003.

Seeman, Erik. "Native Spirits, Shaker Visions: Speaking with the Dead in the Early Republic." *Journal of the Early Republic* 35:3 (Fall 2015): 347–53.

Shelley, Percy Bysshe. "A Defence of Poetry." In *Romantic Poetry and Prose,* edited by Harold Bloom and Lionel Trilling, 746–62. Oxford: Oxford University Press, 1973.

Shukin, Nicole. *Animal Capital: Rendering Life in Biopolitical Times*. Minneapolis: University of Minnesota Press, 2009.

Smith, Helen Sootin. Introduction to *The Gates Ajar*, by Elizabeth Stuart Phelps. Cambridge, Mass.: Belknap-Harvard University Press, 1964.

Smith, Justin E. H. *Divine Machines: Leibniz and the Sciences of Life*. Princeton, N.J.: Princeton University Press, 2011.

Smith, Kerri. "Brain Decoding: Reading Minds." *Nature*, October 23, 2013. http://www.nature.com/news/brain-decoding-reading-minds-1.13989. Accessed May 12, 2014.

Smith, Samuel Stanhope. *An Essay on the Causes of the Variety of the Complexion and Figure in the Human Species*. 2nd ed. New Brunswick, N.J.: J. Simpson, 1810.

Spillers, Hortense. "Mama's Baby Papa's Maybe: An American Grammar Book." *Diacritics* 17:2 (1987): 64–81.

Stepan, Nancy Leys. *The Idea of Race in Science: Great Britain 1800–1960*. New Haven, Conn.: Macmillan Press, 1982.

Suarez-Krabbe, Julia. *Race, Rights, and Rebels: Alternatives to Human Rights and Development from the Global South*. New York: Rowman and Littlefield, 2016.

Sundquist, Eric. *To Wake the Nations: Race in the Making of American Literature*. Cambridge, Mass.: Belknap Press, 1993.

TallBear, Kim. "An Indigenous Perspective on Working beyond the Human/Not Human." *GLQ* 21:2–3 (June 2015): 230–36.

———. *Native American DNA: Tribal Belonging and the False Promise of Genetic Science*. Minneapolis: University of Minnesota Press, 2013.

Tamarkin, Elisa. *Anglophilia: Deference, Devotion, and Antebellum America*. Chicago: University of Chicago Press, 2008.

Tauber, Alfred. *Henry David Thoreau and the Moral Agency of Knowing*. Berkeley: University of California Press, 2003.

Taylor, Thomas. *A Vindication of the Rights of Brutes*. 1792. Gainesville, Fla.: Scholars' Facsimiles and Imprints, 1966.

Taylor, Matt. *Universes without Us: Posthuman Cosmologies in American Literature*. Minneapolis: University of Minnesota Press, 2013.

Taylor, Charles. *A Secular Age*. Cambridge, Mass.: Harvard University Press, 2007.

Thoreau, Henry David. *The Dispersion of Seeds*. In *Faith in a Seed: The Dispersion of Seeds and Other Late Natural History Writings*, edited by Bradley Dean, 23–210. Washington, D.C.: Island Press, 1993.

———. *Excursions*. Edited by Joseph J. Moldenhauer. Princeton, N.J.: Princeton University Press, 1975.

———. *The Higher Law: Thoreau on Civil Disobedience and Reform*. Edited by Wendell Glick, 145–54. Princeton, N.J.: Princeton University Press, 2004.

———. "Indian Notebook." MA 596-606, Pierpont Morgan Library, Department of Literary and Historical Manuscripts, New York.

———. *The Journal of Henry D. Thoreau*. 7 vols. Edited by John C. Broderick, Robert Sattelmeyer, Elizabeth Hall Witherell et al. Princeton, N.J.: Princeton University Press, 1972.

———. *Reform Papers*. Edited by Wendell Glick. Princeton, N.J.: Princeton University Press, 1973.

———. *Walden and Civil Disobedience*. Edited by Owen Thomas. New York: W. W. Norton, 1966.

———. *"Wild Apples" and Other Natural History Essays*. Edited by William Ross. Athens: University of Georgia Press, 2002.

———. *Wild Fruits*. Edited by Bradley Dean. New York: W. W. Norton, 2000.

Thrailkill, Jane. *Affecting Fictions: Mind, Body, and Emotion in American Literary Realism*. Cambridge, Mass.: Harvard University Press, 2007.

Thrift, Nigel. *Non-Representational Theory: Space, Politics, Affect*. New York: Routledge, 2007.

Tiffany, Daniel. *Infidel Poetics: Riddles, Nightlife, Substance*. Chicago: University of Chicago Press, 2009.

Tompkins, Kyla. *Racial Indigestion: Eating Bodies in the Nineteenth Century*. New York: New York University Press, 2012.

Tucker, Irene. *The Moment of Racial Sight*. Chicago: University of Chicago Press, 2012.

Turner, Jack. "Performing Conscience: Thoreau, Political Action, and the Plea for John Brown." *Political Theory* 33:4 (August 2005): 448–71.

Van Doren, Mark. *Henry David Thoreau: A Critical Study*. Boston: Houghton Mifflin, 1916.

Vendler, Helen. *Invisible Listeners: Lyric Intimacy in Herbert, Whitman, and Ashbery*. Princeton, N.J.: Princeton University Press, 2005.

Walker, David. "Walker's Appeal, in Four Articles; Together with a Preamble, to the Coloured Citizens of the World, but in Particular, and Very Expressly, to Those of the United States of America, Written in Boston, State of Massachusetts, September 28, 1829." Boston: Revised and published by David Walker, 1830. http://docsouth.unc.edu/nc/walker/walker.html. Accessed November 17, 2015.

Walls, Laura Dassow. "Agassiz." In *The American Renaissance in New England: Third Series*, edited by Wesley Mott, 3–13. Detroit: Gale Group, 2001.

————. *Seeing New Worlds: Henry David Thoreau and Nineteenth-Century Natural Science*. Madison: University of Wisconsin Press, 1995.

————. "Textbooks and Texts from the Brooks: Inventing Scientific Authority in America." *American Quarterly* 49:1 (March 1997): 1–25.

Warner, Michael. "Whitman Drunk." In *Breaking Bounds: Whitman and American Cultural Studies*, edited by Betsey Erkkila and Jay Grossman, 30–43. New York: Oxford University Press, 1996.

Warren, Jim. "Whitman Land: John Burroughs's Pastoral Criticism." *ISLE* 8:1 (Winter 2001): 83–96.

Weheliye, Alexander. *Habeas Viscus: Racializing Assemblages, Biopolitics, and Black Feminist Theories of the Human*. Durham, N.C.: Duke University Press, 2014.

Whitman, Walt. Editorial. *Brooklyn Daily Eagle*, November 16, 1846.

————. *Leaves of Grass and Other Writings*. Edited by Michael Moon. New York: W. W. Norton, 2002.

————. *Notebooks and Unpublished Writings*. 6 vols. Edited by Edward Grier. New York: New York University Press, 2007.

Wilson, Ivy. *Specters of Democracy: Blackness and the Aesthetics of Politics in the Antebellum U.S.* Oxford: Oxford University Press, 2011.

Wimsatt, William K., and Monroe C. Beardsley. "The Affective Fallacy." *Sewanee Review* 57:1 (1949): 31–55.

Wolfe, Cary. *What Is Posthumanism?* Minneapolis: University of Minnesota Press, 2010.

Wordsworth, William. *The Prose Works of William Wordsworth*. 3 vols. Edited by W. J. B. Owen and Jane Worthington Smyser. Oxford: Clarendon Press, 1974.

Wright, Michelle. *Physics of Blackness: Beyond the Middle Passage Epistemology*. Minneapolis: University of Minnesota Press, 2015.

Wynter, Sylvia. "1492: A New World View." In *Race, Discourse, and the Origin of the Americas*, edited by Vera L. Hyatt and Rex Nettleford, 5–57. Washington, D.C.: Smithsonian Institution Press, 1995.

————. "Disenchanting Discourse: 'Minority' Literary Criticism and Beyond." *Cultural Critique* 7 (Fall 1987): 207–44.

————. "No Humans Involved: An Open Letter to My Colleagues." *Forum N.H.I.: Knowledge for the Twenty-First Century* 1:1 (1994): 42–73.

————. "On How We Mistook the Map for the Territory and Re-Imprisoned Ourselves in Our Unbearable Wrongness of Being, Desêtre: Black Studies Toward the Human Project." In *Not Only the Master's Tools: African-American Studies in Theory and Practice*, edited by Lewis Gordon and Jane Gordon, 107–69. New York: Routledge, 2005.

Wynter, Sylvia and Katherine McKittrick. "Unparalleled Catastrophe for
    Our Species? Or to Give Humanness a Different Future: Conversations."
    In *Sylvia Wynter: On Being Human as Praxis*, edited by Katherine
    McKittrick, 9–89. Durham, N.C.: Duke University Press, 2014.